Also by Craig Pittman

Paving Paradise
Manatee Insanity
The Scent of Scandal
Oh, Florida!

CAT TALE

THE WILD, WEIRD BATTLE
TO SAVE THE FLORIDA PANTHER

CRAIG PITTMAN

HANOVER
SQUARE
PRESS

HANOVER
SQUARE
PRESS™

Recycling programs
for this product may
not exist in your area.

ISBN-13: 978-1-335-93880-0

Cat Tale

This edition published by arrangement with Harlequin Books S.A.

Hanover Square Press
22 Adelaide St. West, 40th Floor
Toronto, Ontario M5H 4E3, Canada
HanoverSqPress.com
BookClubbish.com

Printed in U.S.A.

For my dad,
who introduced me to the pleasures of wandering
in the Florida woods

Table of Contents

CAT UNDER GLASS

The panther ran as fast as it could.

The dogs gave chase, plowing through the underbrush, howling with delight. This was what they were bred to do, to sniff out and chase down big cats like this one. Their master, the tall man in the cowboy hat, would be pleased.

The female panther they pursued was a scrawny thing, seriously underweight. It wasn't strong enough to keep the chase going long. Finally it leaped onto a tree trunk and clawed its way up onto a branch, then stopped to look down.

The dogs circled the trunk, panting, their eyes trained on their quarry up above. Then the cat heard more noises approaching— a group of humans, all but one of them men.

One of the men climbed partway up the tree with a gun, then

raised it, and fired. The cat flinched. A dart hit it in the leg and everything went dark.

Then the cat was falling.

When it hit the ground, it didn't move again. One of the men, and then the lone woman, bent over it. They put their lips on the panther's hairy mouth, blowing their breath into its lungs, trying to revive it with mouth-to-mouth resuscitation.

They were too late.

You can find the most important Florida panther that ever lived in a glass case in the R.A. Gray Building in downtown Tallahassee. It's just a couple of floors up from a towering mastodon skeleton named Herman that's on display in the Museum of Florida History.

Tallahassee is not the place you'd ever expect to see a panther. It's too far north, for one thing. For another it's home to two colleges and their football teams whose fans pack the place on the weekends. Panthers prefer solitude. Sometimes they don't even like to see other panthers.

Plus it's Florida's state capital, its seat of government. That means that instead of cypress trees and wild palms and thick stands of palmetto, you've got lots of marble office buildings and sidewalks and pavement and parking garages. The Gray Building looks pretty much like its name, sitting two blocks down from Florida's remarkably phallic Capitol Building, just past the far more dignified Florida Supreme Court.

The museum is low-key but impressive, what with the mastodon skeleton and other displays about Florida history. But all that's downstairs. To see the panther, you've got to ride the elevator up to the State Archives, where it stands alone outside the entrance.

The first time I saw it, I thought it was a statue. Not a very good statue, mind you. It looked like one made by an enthusiastic but unskilled amateur working with inferior materials. I figured that was why it was sitting up there away from all the other, more professional-looking exhibits.

Not until later did I realize that this had been an actual panther, a seventy-pound female that once prowled South Florida's swamps and forests, its shoulders rolling like the waves on the ocean, its tail twitching restlessly, its topaz eyes opened wide to detect any movement in the surrounding darkness.

Now it was stuffed and mounted, its limbs stiff, its eyes glass.

In different places in the Western Hemisphere, this animal goes by different names. It's all one species—puma—but it's been called a cougar, a mountain lion, a catamount, even a tiger. It has adapted itself to live in a staggering variety of habitats, from desert scrub to tropical rainforest to the Hollywood sign looming high above Los Angeles.

Because this one is in Florida, it's known as a panther. A Florida panther.

This cat under glass isn't just some random ratty bit of taxidermy. It's actually Florida's official state animal.

And for a time, it looked like this one would be among the last.

Two centuries ago, panthers like this one ranged across the whole American South, from the red clay hills of Georgia to the dusty plains of Texas. They were feared by the early settlers, who knew they were intruders in the panthers' habitat, and knew that their own hold on the wilderness was a tenuous one.

These cats were part of a family of pumas that roamed all across the North American continent, and down into South America as well. You could find them as far north as Canada and as far south as Argentina and from the Pacific to the Atlantic. They weren't exactly the same cat everywhere, but they were similar to each other—as recognizable as a set of cousins, all of them silent hunters, swift assassins, tenacious fighters.

When panthers are born, they're fluffy little balls of spotted fur. But once they're grown, everything about these animals screams "predator." Every part of a panther's body is attuned to enhancing its hunting ability. It has a light but strong skeleton that's attached to heavy muscles. The rear legs are longer than the legs of other cats, allowing the pumas to make vertical leaps of up to fifteen feet and horizontal leaps of up to forty-five feet. That allows them to surprise their prey by flying in from above, seemingly out of nowhere. Their long tail lets them keep their balance during such long leaps. If the hunted animal tries to run, the puma's front legs are built to provide good traction for turns, a definite advantage during a pursuit. When they're ready to kill, their retracted claws pop out to grab onto whatever they've caught, and they chomp down hard with their powerful jaws, with sixteen teeth on the top and fourteen on the bottom. In the wild, they can keep doing this, hunting by night, sleeping by day, for around a dozen years.

By being such fierce predators, panthers, pumas, cougars and mountain lions play a crucial role in the health of any ecosystem where they live. For one thing, they keep in check the population of their prey—deer, hogs and so forth. Usually they do not gobble up all of their prey at once but eat their fill and hide the rest for later. Their leftovers become ready-made meals for more than two hundred species of birds and mammals. Then the insects move in, some spending their whole lives in those left-behind carcasses. They break down what remains and release its nutrients into the soil.

As fierce as the pumas are, the continents once thundered with the roars of even more fearsome cats: the lion-like *Panthera atrox*, the cheetah-esque *Miracinonyx trumani*, the saber-toothed *Smilodon* and *Homotherium*. But at the end of the Pleistocene, some twelve thousand years ago, all those big carnivores faded away, nobody knows why, leaving behind nothing but their bones. Yet the pumas somehow survived.

The modern descendants of those fearsome prehistoric felines, the house cats, are so ubiquitous these days that it's easy to miss what's going on with their wild counterparts. All around the world, big cats—tigers, lions, jaguars and leopards—are in danger of going extinct. They have already been extirpated from vast swaths of their habitat: lions have gone extinct in twenty-six countries, cheetahs have disappeared from 76 percent of their historic range. Tiger populations in the wild have plummeted so low that there are now more tigers in captivity in the United States (5,000) than roaming the jungle (3,200).

The big cats of North America haven't fared any better. Pumas, mountain lions, cougars—no matter what you call the various subspecies, they have been going, going, gone. The last confirmed sighting of a cougar in Vermont was in 1881. The cats vanished from Tennessee in 1930. A hunter killed the last known specimen in New Brunswick, Canada, in 1932, and another hunter killed the last one seen in Maine in 1938.

In 2019, two environmental groups petitioned California to add its native mountain lions to the endangered list, citing the risks of being run over by cars and inbreeding that produces genetic defects—the same woes that have afflicted Florida panthers.

West of the Mississippi, the pumas still survive, but in only sixteen states. East of the Mississippi, they remain in only one—Florida—and a 1992 study predicted the Florida panthers would disappear by 2016.

Yet they hung on.

How did Florida panthers manage to persist when the other big cats did not? Especially when the panthers have so few places to live these days? Modern panthers, like the one in the glass case, live in a world where humans have steadily wiped out places where panthers can survive.

Throughout the panther's one-time habitat, the marshes have been filled in to make way for suburbs and strip shopping centers. The clumps of palmettos that provide a panther with shelter have been ripped out to make room for lawns and golf courses and college campuses and airport runways and mines. The trees that offer a high vantage spot have been felled, first for lumber, then to make way for highways packed with cars and trucks. All around them, there's so much noise from the humming air conditioners and rumbling vehicles that a panther can't even hear itself purr, whistle, mew, chirp, hiss or growl. Only one of its blood-curdling night screams might cut through the din—but that would spoil its preference to pass unseen and undetected.

None of this—the noise, the development, the speeding vehicles—is what killed the cat in the glass case. This one was killed by science. You could even say it was the one cat killed by someone else's curiosity.

You won't see it on the label, but the panther in the glass case has a name: FP3.

That means it was the third Florida panther that biologists fitted with a radio collar so they could track its movements. They started putting the collars on the cats in the early 1980s, and they're still doing it today. Those radio-collar readings have helped them map out where panthers live, and how they live.

FP3 was supposed to keep running, keep jumping, keep on being a panther so the biologists could follow it from afar. Instead, because of a terrible accident, it fell dead at their feet, blood dripping from its nose.

Two of the biologists on the capture team tried to save it with mouth-to-mouth resuscitation. Can you imagine doing that? Putting your mouth on a dying panther, a wild thing with sharp teeth for biting through a deer's windpipe? Trying to breathe life back into this enormous cat, the way you might do a drowning child? They didn't hesitate, either.

But they failed to revive it. Their leader, a stoic man not prone to showing emotion, lifted the lifeless carcass onto his shoulders and carried it out of the woods. It was a heavy load, but the guilt he felt over what happened was even heavier, and it grew with every step. He was sure that the death of FP3 foretold the doom of all panthers. Depression overtook his life. His career went into a tailspin. His marriage nearly came apart.

He was wrong. The death of FP3 changed everything, but for the better. The tragedy led to the discovery of a way to save the panthers' future.

You won't find that out by looking at the stuffed panther in the case, though. The label on the case offers only generic panther lore. It doesn't tell the story of FP3. The panther itself, of course, says nothing. The folks at the State Archives, whose job is to maintain Florida's institutional memory, didn't even know its story, not until I told them.

As a reporter for the *Tampa Bay Times*, the South's largest newspaper, I've been writing about Florida panthers for more than twenty years. The first one I ever saw was dead, run down by a speeding vehicle on Interstate 4, closer to Walt Disney World than to the place where panthers normally are found.

The second one was alive, but it was locked up in an ancient roadside menagerie that was called Everglades Wonder Gardens. As I watched this gorgeous animal, it kept pacing back and forth like a prison inmate plotting an escape. It stared at me briefly, then its gaze flicked away, its attention returning to the search for an exit.

The third, of course, was the cat in the glass case.

That's three more panthers than most Floridians have ever seen.

Despite its status as the state animal, Florida's twenty-one million residents have seen more Florida Panther hockey games, Florida panther school mascots, and Florida panther license plates than actual, live panthers skulking through the forest.

It's easier to find one now than it used to be. There was a time in the mid-1990s when Florida's panther population fell to about twenty animals. Some scientists think the number was even smaller—just six of the big cats, and only one of them a female.

At that rate, the only panther anyone would ever see would be FP3, on display like a tree in Joni Mitchell's tree museum.

As panthers hurtled toward oblivion, scientists and bureaucrats cast about for a way to bring them back. But the standard methods for rescuing a vanishing animal would not work. In desperation, state officials launched an unprecedented experiment—one that worked, but which, as a side effect, exposed new problems for places trying to preserve at least a bit of wilderness for their own endangered species.

This is the story of the panther's rapid decline, the effort to rescue it from the brink of extinction, and all that resulted from this effort, both good and bad. It's the story of more than just the struggle over saving a charismatic cat. It's also a tale of raw courage, of scientific skulduggery and political shenanigans, of big-money interests versus what's best for everyone.

I have read that some people claim that the return of wolves to Yellowstone National Park is the greatest conservation victory in US history. Compared with what it took to reel panthers back from oblivion, though, I don't think so.

This being Florida, there's going to be a little weirdness sprinkled into this tale. Florida's version of Bigfoot, the fabled and fragrant Skunk Ape, makes an appearance. So does a former alligator wrestler who killed a panther and ate its heart. Also a bumbling bow hunter nicknamed Scuttlebutt. And don't get me started about what sometimes goes on at the headquarters of the Florida Panther National Wildlife Refuge.

Over the years, the more I learned about panthers, the more fascinated I became by the people who have been working so hard at saving them, the fighters in this cat fight: the hunter who once stalked and killed big cats, then decided he liked them better than the livestock he'd been hired to protect. The whistleblower who was willing to risk his career exposing phony science. Those biologists giving FP3 mouth-to-mouth resuscitation. There are heroes and villains in this story, and one in particular switches sides to become the other.

My goal with this book is to use the story of what happened to the Florida panther to show you how all these humans have behaved in dealing with what one federal official told me was "the greatest conservation challenge in America."

This is also a scientific cautionary tale. As our Earth warms up and we continue laying waste to more of it, lots of species teeter on the brink of extinction the way panthers once did. (The way things are going, we might soon be one of them.) At a time when the term "mass extinction" frequently shows up in headlines, this is a guide to what extraordinary efforts it takes to bring back just one subspecies—one that's particularly popular— and what unexpected costs such a decision brings.

The story begins with a fussy archaeologist, a tiny wooden carving and a wealthy playboy with a ninety-foot houseboat.

CHAPTER ONE

THE CAT OF GOD

The hired man pushed the shovel blade deep into the Marco Island muck. Sweat poured off him, soaking through his clothes. This was hot work, digging up peat for his boss's vegetable garden. Of course, all work was hot work in Florida in 1895. Air conditioning and insecticide hadn't yet tamed the two great enemies to Florida's development.

Then the shovel hit something solid—something that had been hiding in the earth for a long, long time. The hired man dug it out and brought his discovery to the boss, who took it to someone else, someone who made sure it found its way to experts in Philadelphia. Soon one of those experts, a pale and sickly man named Frank Hamilton Cushing, came hurrying southward as fast as a train and a sailboat could carry him.

Cushing was a classic nineteenth-century figure: a pioneer-

ing anthropologist with few if any academic credentials but a
tremendous amount of intensely personal experience. While
enrolled at Cornell University, he spent more time arranging
a museum exhibit of Native American artifacts than he did in
class. He eventually dropped out, yet was named curator of the
exhibit. At nineteen, he became curator of the ethnological
department of the National Museum in Washington, DC. He
spent years in New Mexico living with the Zuni Pueblo tribe,
studying their rituals and society. At one point Zunis who didn't
appreciate his sketching of their ceremonies confronted him,
to which he responded by brandishing a knife. Tribal members
gave him much freer access after he stood up for himself. His
bosses in Washington eventually summoned him home, in part
because of how much taxpayer money he was spending. That's
why he was able to respond so quickly to the news from Marco
Island—and why he was inclined to hurry down and see these
treasures for himself. He was tired of being stuck in the office.

When Cushing arrived in Southwest Florida, he concluded
that what the hired man had dug up were ancient artifacts from
Florida's original inhabitants, a vanished tribe known as the
Calusa, who lived in that area around AD 300 to AD 1500.
They dined largely on seafood they caught in the estuary and
then turned what was left, the fish bones and shells, into tools
and weapons. They also dabbed the tips of their arrow points
with the poisonous sap of the manchineel tree, which grew
there. That's how they killed Juan Ponce de León when he tried
to land there in 1521, just seven years after he gave Florida its
name. The Spanish got the Calusa back by giving them germs
that eventually wiped them out.

By the time the hired man had uncovered their artifacts,
the Calusa had been gone for more than three hundred years.
Their culture was a complete mystery to Florida's inhabitants
of the 1890s.

Under Cushing's supervision, a work crew unearthed ceremonial masks, tools and other reminders that Florida's past looked nothing like its Victorian present. Fortunately, Cushing brought with him a talented illustrator who made sketches of everything the team uncovered. Unfortunately, many of the wooden items, well preserved in the muck, crumbled to dust after being exposed to the air, so all we have left are the sketches.

One notable exception was a remarkable carving of a figure just six inches high. Uncovered in March 1896, the figure is made of wood, highly polished. The shape of the bottom half is human and vaguely female. It consists of a torso and legs, kneeling, with hands resting on the knees. The top of the figure, though, is clearly a large cat, its eyes wide and staring.

Cushing, in his journal, recounted digging up the figure he called "The Mountain Lion God," which he said was "equal in all ways to any from Egypt or Assyria."

The Key Marco Cat, as it became known, is a symbol of the respect that the Calusa felt for the sleek feline predators that stalked through the underbrush outside their village at night. They regarded the panther as a spiritual guide. They respected its stealth and its silence, its ability to find its way through the darkest night. Other long-ago Florida tribes—the Tequesta and the Apalachee, to name two—apparently felt the same, judging by the artifacts they left behind.

In the 1700s, Creek Indians fleeing persecution in other Southern states sought refuge in Florida's swamps. They became known as the Seminoles, and they, too, regarded the panther as a spiritual being. They saw it as a favorite of the Creator, the first creature to walk upon the earth. The animal had the power to heal, they thought. That's why all Seminole medicine men were said to be descendants of the panther clan.

Native American tribes all over the South viewed the panther with awe. The Cherokees called the panther *klandagi,* which means "lord of the forest," and to the Chickasaw it was *ko-icto,* the "cat of God." (According to Kevin Hansen's book *Cougar:*

The American Lion, there are more than 80 names for pumas in North and South America, more than any other animal.)

But the white men saw them differently. The hotel on Marco Island where Cushing stayed during the dig catered to plenty of tourists. They weren't there to venerate the panthers. They wanted to shoot them.

Despite what happened to Ponce de León, the Spaniards kept coming to Florida. Hernando de Soto and his army of three hundred landed in 1539, looking for gold and finding only hostile natives, misery and, eventually, death. An account of the expedition said they saw "many lions" along with bears, wolves, deer and jackals. They had seen nothing like the panther before— Europe once had its own puma species, but it vanished after the Pleistocene era.

Soto's greatest contribution to the panther was an accident. The expedition had brought along hundreds of pigs for the troops to eat. The pigs got loose and their descendants remain a scourge on the South today, feral hogs that use their sharp tusks to tear up everything they see. Panthers find them particularly tasty.

As Soto and his tin-hatted army forged on northward to areas that saw cold temperatures in the winter, they found tribes where the people wrapped themselves in furs that were "long and shaggy, made of the skins of panthers, bucks, bears, beavers, and otters." Thus veneration lost out to warmth.

You can't necessarily trust everything these early explorers wrote, of course. The sixteenth-century slave trader John Hawkins, who in 1565 visited the ill-fated French forts built on Florida's Atlantic coast, wrote that the land teemed with such wildlife as "lions and tygres as well as unicorns." He also claimed there was a "serpent with three heads and foure feet." It's clear Hawkins either had bad eyesight or a good imagination.

No matter what their name, the cats were plentiful. In the

1770s, pioneering naturalist William Bartram reported that Florida's "tygers" were "very large, strong, and fierce, and are too numerous, and are very mischievous." (This made me picture them pulling pranks on the pioneers, like tying their bootlaces together or leaving a flaming bag of panther poo on a doorstep.)

The white and black settlers who began populating Florida in the eighteenth and nineteenth centuries did not see the big cats as merely mischievous. They were flat-out scared of them.

Bear in mind, now, that these pioneers were not exactly shrinking violets. On the swampy frontier, many lived in thatched-roof homes that were so hot day and night that they generally did all their cooking outdoors. They kept mosquitoes and other bugs at bay by burning smudge pots that filled up their homes with smoke. What I'm trying to say is that they were tough and smelly and generally unafraid of anything.

But the sight of a panther filled these hardy folks with fear. They called the panthers "lions," "tigers" or "catamounts." According to one 1870s visitor, they were "spoken of with dread by the crackers." An ornithologist visiting in 1883 noted that "old hunters warned me against passing through the thick woods in the early morning or late in the evening as they said the Tigers were usually on the alert at such times and might be tempted to spring upon one if he were alone."

When you think about it, their fear makes a kind of sense. The panthers' stealth, the way they would scream in the night, the stunning ferocity of their attack—all those factors combined to make them what one writer called "the most dreaded beast in early American folklore."

So after seeing what the panthers could do, the pioneers' general reaction to spotting a panther was to shoot it. They viewed the cats as a threat to the settlers' mangy cattle and their families as well. Although the documentation tends to be iffy, stories about Florida's settlers are rife with tales of men and women who were maimed or even killed by a marauding panther. Reading through these stories always reminded me of seeing an antique chair in a friend's house: while its luster has been rubbed to a high gloss by the years, I'm hesitant to sit in it for fear it won't hold up.

My favorite one of these hand-me-down tiger tales is somewhat less violent than the others. It concerns a couple who had settled near the Ocklawaha River in the center of the state. The husband went out hunting for some food. The wife, who was pregnant, walked over to visit nearby relatives.

As she walked back home through the woods, she heard a scream behind her. She knew that sound was a panther, and she skedaddled toward home as fast as she could. She knew she wouldn't make it unless she found a way to distract the cat. So this resourceful pioneer woman started pulling off her clothes piece by piece, tossing them aside. Each piece of clothing she tossed down caught the panther's attention, and she could hear it tearing apart first her hat, then her blouse, then her dress. She ran out of clothes just as she made it through the door, latching it behind her.

At least, that was the story she told her husband when he got home and found his wife naked. Curiously, he found no sign of a panther anywhere around the cabin.

Panther panics made big headlines for the Florida papers of the day, and helped other businesses as well. An 1895 edition of the *Florida Times-Union* in Jacksonville led off with the large-type header "PANTHER STILL PROWLS" followed by a series of subheads such as "Over A Hundred Hunters After Him Yesterday," and concluding with, "Gun Stores Are Doing a Land-Office Business—Buckshot Go Up."

A few of these crazed-cat-goes-after-human stories made the out-of-state papers. In 1897, the *New York Times* passed along the thinly sourced stories of three panther attacks in the Sunshine State. In the most dramatic one, a couple driving a buggy near Tarpon Springs noticed "two baby catamounts by the roadside" that they stopped to pick up—at which point "the mother catamount sprang on the buggy" and attacked them. The man clubbed the cat, the cat clawed back, the man pulled a knife, the wife began wielding the club, and the three-sided battle raged on as the horse kept racing along the road. Finally the man and the mama panther tumbled out of the buggy and the man cut its throat. The only thing missing from this story is a big Michael Bay movie explosion. (The fate of the kittens, by the way, went unrecorded. I like to think they seized the reins of the buggy and rode off to plot their revenge.)

Not everyone found the panthers so frightening. In 1904, artist Winslow Homer, a frequent visitor to Homosassa Springs on the state's Gulf of Mexico coast, painted a watercolor called *In the Jungle* that offers an arresting image of a panther. It has climbed halfway up a wild palm. Its neck is outstretched, its mouth wide, its teeth gleaming. It's a wild thing, a thing of beauty.

But beauty could never compete with fear and greed. In case anyone lacked sufficient incentive to shoot every panther in the woods, in 1832 Florida's territorial legislature put a bounty on them, with the amount to be set by each county. In 1887 the legislature ratcheted up the pressure, setting a uniform statewide bounty amount at $5. Today that would be like getting more than $100 a hide—a strong reason to kill as many as possible.

While there are no credible modern reports of any Florida panther attacking humans, that didn't stop the humans from attacking them—and not just out of fear, either. By the late 1800s, wealthy Yankee "sportsmen" came flocking to the state's newly constructed resort hotels intent on catching as many fish and shooting as many wild animals as they could. A couple of panthers made for a fine trophy, and the bounty would help cover the cost of the trip.

But when Charles B. Cory showed up in Florida, he didn't shoot panthers for the money. He had plenty. No, Cory shot them for science.

★ ★ ★

The first time I read about Charles Barney Cory, I decided that this is the guy I want to be when I grow up. The book I was reading described him as a scientist-playboy-writer-naturalist-carouser, which is not a combination you see very often. It's certainly not an occupation that was ever mentioned at my school's Career Day.

Cory was a big bear of a man who added to his impressive appearance by sporting an elaborate handlebar mustache. His father had built up a large fortune importing wine and silks, so Cory had plenty of money to spend however he saw fit. When he wasn't entertaining various nubile young actresses (and sometimes when he was), he palled around with President Grover Cleveland and Admiral George Dewey, the hero of the Battle of Manila. He held a number of high-falutin' positions, many unpaid: curator of ornithology at the Field Museum in Chicago, president of the American Ornithological Union, and founder of the Florida Museum of Natural History near his part-time home in Palm Beach. Basically he was a cross between Henry David Thoreau and Bluto Blutarsky from *Animal House*.

While Cory was a student at Harvard, he decided one day to blow off his classes and take a trip to Florida (this was long before Spring Break and wet T-shirts). He stayed long enough, and had enough adventures, to fill up an entire book, his first of fifteen.

"With this trip to Florida in 1877…Cory began a life of freedom and pleasure in the pursuit of natural history and sport which has scarcely been equaled and which might well be the envy of many a man," a friend of his wrote years later.

Two decades later the party boy was ready to bag a panther. This was in 1895, the same year the handyman was digging up the first Calusa artifacts on Marco Island. Meanwhile the idle rich were wandering the woods taking potshots at panthers, bears, wolves and any other big hairy mammal that they happened to spot.

Cory, who lived half the year in Boston, arrived on Florida's East Coast aboard a luxurious 90-foot houseboat, *The Wanderer*. The boat, which he anchored in the New River, held twelve bedrooms, a full kitchen, a grand piano, a vast collection of fishing gear, and enough guns and ammo to wage war on a good-sized foreign country, should the need arise.

When Cory was ready to hunt, he set off with a ten-men crew that included a Seminole guide and a personal chef equipped with all the latest culinary equipment. They also had six dogs, which they turned loose first thing in the morning.

"It was our usual custom to start out at daylight and allow the hounds to run about as they pleased as we rode slowly through the woods," Cory wrote. "Every few minutes a hound would start off on a fresh trail of some animal and we would have to call in the other dogs and 'slow trail' until we came to a place where the ground was clear and soft enough to see the tracks and learn what it was that they were after... About eleven o'clock we usually returned to camp." After that it was too hot to hunt, he explained. It's possible everyone was too drunk too.

At this leisurely pace, Cory's panther hunt took two months— unsurprising, since they weren't looking for the panthers at night, the time of day when the panthers were likely to be out and about. Finally, about thirty-five miles south of Lantana in Palm Beach County, the dogs pinned down a panther beneath a fallen tree.

"I saw the panther crouching beside and partly under the fallen tree," Cory wrote. "She was not over twenty feet distant, and as she turned her snarling face toward me she presented one of the ugliest pictures I have ever seen. Her ears were drawn tightly back and she exposed a splendid set of teeth. A very pungent, musty odor was perceptible. As she turned towards me, all the dogs sprang at once... She turned on them with a quickness that was astonishing, uttering a snarling roar while biting and clawing at them savagely; but just then I fired, once, twice, three times as fast as I could work the lever, and the great cat lay kicking and aimlessly biting."

Because he was a man of science, Cory crouched over the carcass and took its measurements. This particular panther was a hair over seven feet long from end to end, and as he examined it, Cory noted its long limbs and arched nose. Later, he wrote up a full scientific description of his kill, becoming the first biologist to set down such details about the Florida panther. He declared it to be a separate subspecies of other pumas roaming the nation's woodlands, and he called it *Felis concolor floridiana*.

Then, I assume, everyone went back to party at the houseboat.

Cory's name for the cats lasted only four years, until another scientist spotted a problem. A biologist with the most wonderful name in science history, Outram Bangs, noted that the name Cory had picked had already been used for a bobcat. His elegant solution: change Cory's designation to something that honored Cory: *Felis concolor coryi*.

In other words, that snarling cat with the "ugliest face" now bore its killer's name.

Florida's hunters were very good at killing things. In 1913, William T. Hornaday, in his book *Our Vanishing Wildlife*, wrote, "In the destruction of wildlife, I think the backwoods population of Florida is the most lawless and defiant in the United States... From a zoological point of view, Florida is in bad shape."

But what took a bigger toll on the panthers was the rising tide of humans moving to Florida and filling up what had been wilderness. Chain gangs built roads that sliced across once-wild areas, opening them up to hordes of tourists in Model T Fords. Soon the new roads were followed by roadside businesses and new houses. They changed the landscape by leaps and bounds.

Each new development pushed the panthers southward, toward the state's swampy tip. In 1935, a writer for the *Saturday Evening Post* called the vast wet expanse of the Big Cypress

Swamp and the Everglades in South Florida "the last strongholds of the panther in the eastern United States." The writer, by the way, was part of a hunting party that spent six weeks tracking cats through that last stronghold. Ultimately they killed eight panthers. Oh, the things a journalist will do for a story!

That the beleaguered panthers found a refuge in the Big Cypress and the Everglades shows how tough that territory was for humans to drain and dredge and fill—or even to cross. In 1946, herpetologist and showman Ross Allen decided he needed to add a panther to the menagerie he displayed for tourists at his Central Florida attraction in Silver Springs. He took a *Miami Herald* reporter along on his hunt. Getting through the swamp "couldn't be described as walking," the reporter wrote. "It consists of stumbling through waist-high ferns, over ground strewn with vines—some of them thorn-equipped—climbing over cypress logs five feet in diameter, detouring alligator wallows, and then doing it all over again."

The panthers needed a refuge like that because the rest of the state turned seriously hostile to panthers in 1939. The Florida cattle industry became alarmed because deer ticks were infesting their cows and giving them a fatal blood disease. They started dipping every cow in arsenic every two weeks to kill the ticks. But the cattlemen didn't think that went far enough. They wanted to extirpate every last tick from the state.

How do you rid Florida of every last deer tick? Get rid of all the deer, of course! At least, that was the theory—and never mind the fact that freshly killed deer are the panther's favorite food.

Deer hunters and state game officials protested the plan. The *Miami Herald*'s outdoor writer argued that killing all the deer to eliminate ticks made about as much sense as killing all the dogs and cats to eliminate fleas. But the cattle industry held more political sway than anyone else in those days, and they got permission to arrange what can only be called an organized slaughter.

For two years, troops of armed men, eighty or so in number, charged into the woods on horseback and blasted every white-tailed deer they could find. They wiped out an estimated ten thousand of them, thus depriving the panthers of that much fresh venison. Luckily the panthers had a backup: the feral hogs descended from Soto's expedition.

Only a few people worried about the unintended consequences of the deer massacre. In late 1939, a deer hunter from New York wrote a letter in which he noted his observations from a recent trip to Florida. He said that as the deer population dwindled, the panthers began attacking cattle instead, "and consequently more are being hunted and being shot." The hunter then added, "Looks as though the wiping out of the deer may mean the end of this last frontier for the puma in the eastern United States."

At that point, most of the people bemoaning the loss of the panthers were people who liked hunting them. But attitudes toward wildlife were beginning to change. In 1936, naturalist Aldo Leopold penned an article called "Threatened Species." In it, he argued that some wildlife deserved protection, not because they were prime targets for hunting, but because they filled a necessary role in their ecosystem. Pull one out and it's like a stack of Jenga blocks—they might all tumble down.

Leopold's idea caught on. A committee of biologists chaired by Daniel Beard, future superintendent of Everglades National Park, put together a book published in 1942 titled *Fading Trails: The Story of Endangered American Wildlife*. They included chapters about manatees, ivory-billed woodpeckers, whooping cranes— and mountain lions.

In that chapter, Beard and his colleagues noted the deer slaughter, then added that Florida "still has a few cougars. One place they can be found today is in the fastness of the Big Cypress Swamp, an area where primitive faunal conditions may probably be preserved better than anywhere else in this country. Several big cougar hunts have been conducted there in spite of the fact that the animals do no harm."

Eight years later, the state agency in charge of hunting and fishing, the Florida Game and Fresh Water Fish Commission, started to worry that there weren't nearly as many panthers as there used to be. In 1950, they officially declared the panther a "game" animal, a step which allowed them to impose limits on when the cats could be hunted and how many panthers could be killed during a season.

Another eight years passed, during which the state game officials figured out that trying to regulate panther hunting wasn't working. Instead, in a panic, they banned the hunting of panthers.

One reason for their worry: No one could find panthers anymore in the Everglades. They had apparently all been killed or had fled. Everglades National Park, officially established in 1947, wanted to fix this, and they came up with an unorthodox solution—one that would have further ramifications later.

Florida is a tourist-friendly state, and its highways were for years dotted with kitschy little roadside attractions. There were places where you could see a Wild West shoot-out every day at high noon, places where women dressed as mermaids swam around an underwater theater, places where you could see (and buy) cypress knees carved into comical shapes, places full of fake dinosaurs, and places with names like The Atomic Tunnel.

One such attraction was Everglades Wonder Gardens, which in classic Florida fashion was not located in the Everglades but rather in the town of Bonita Springs near Fort Myers, on the state's Gulf Coast. It was run by two brothers named Lester and Bill Piper, and while the place was best known for its large collection of alligators, the Everglades Wonder Gardens also happened to have a few panthers.

Some had been kittens with spotted fur, babies that had been orphaned in the wild and so the Pipers took them in and raised them. Some of the cats had been kept as pets—by former circus people or cat fanciers with a taste for the exotic—and were handed over when their owners couldn't care for them any longer. The Pipers had enough panthers that they could spare a few.

Thus, in 1957, a few of the Piper cats, as they became known, were released into Everglades National Park, with still more turned loose there in subsequent years. Park officials were delighted to have panthers back roaming the place, doing what apex predators do. But that didn't help the dwindling population in the rest of the state.

In the mid-1960s, a group of nine federal biologists working for the Department of the Interior began drawing up the first list of species in need of legal protection. The final version, released in 1967, included several Florida animals: the manatee, the alligator and the Florida panther. Each had faced perils that had diminished the size of their population, but the panther was in worse shape than the rest.

Being on the list didn't do anything to protect what was supposed to be the panthers' "last refuge," the Big Cypress Swamp. Instead, it would take a near disaster to make that happen.

CHAPTER TWO

PANTHERLAND

Let me tell you about the Big Cypress Swamp.

To get there, you have to drive south on Interstate 75 until you can't go south anymore. When you get down to Naples, a glittering waterfront city, the highway bends to the east and takes you toward the toll booths for the stretch of 75 known as "Alligator Alley." If you keep going, after two hours of cruising through fenced-off watery wilderness, you'll be nearing Fort Lauderdale on Florida's east coast.

If you didn't take the turn, and instead jumped over onto US 41, you'd be driving on a much older road known as the Tamiami Trail because it connects Tampa with Miami. The Tamiami Trail cuts through the middle of the massive Big Cypress Swamp.

Along the side of the Tamiami Trail is the studio of a photographer named Clyde Butcher. Clyde is a big, burly guy with a white beard that makes him look like Charlton Heston playing Moses in *The Ten Commandments*. He has thick-framed glasses and the patience of a champion chess player. He paddles out into the swamp in a canoe that's loaded down with bulky camera equipment, including the same type of camera that Matthew Brady used to shoot battlefield photos during the Civil War.

When Clyde finds a spot that he believes would make a good photo, he ties up the canoe and eases himself out very carefully, his feet squishing into the swamp bottom. Then he sets up his old-fashioned box camera atop a tripod, and stands there, often in water up to his armpits, mosquitoes buzzing around his ears, and waits for juuuuust the right moment with just the right lighting for him to click the shutter. Sometimes it takes him six hours to get one shot.

He shoots in black and white because that brings out the con- trasting texture of the cypress knees and the wild palms. The pictures are dramatic, to say the least—a moonrise over twisted trees, a silvered wetland reflecting the enveloping sky, a field of palmettos shining in the setting sun as dark thunderclouds roll in. His massive monochromatic landscapes have earned him the nickname "the Ansel Adams of Florida."

Clyde sometimes leads swamp walks through the Big Cypress. That's the way I saw the place, splashing along in old jeans and cheap sneakers using a broomstick as a makeshift shillelagh. I was part of a group that slogged through the swamp on a cool October afternoon, stopping from time to time to marvel at jumping spiders and native orchids. We saw only one alligator, and that one fairly small, sunning itself right next to Clyde's driveway. As we waded through the cathedral of trees, we chat- ted quietly, amazed to find that the swamp was not swampy at all. The water was clear and clean and flowing slowly between our legs. When we started out, the chilly water was up to our knees, but about halfway through the trail suddenly got waist-deep, and all of us men began talking in a higher octave.

The smell was slightly funky, but not as bad as some bars I've been in. I asked Clyde to describe it and, after consulting with his wife, Niki, also an artist, he declared that the smell "is like the moist smell of a beautiful garden that has just been watered."

We saw, scattered here and there, small islands. They were thickly wooded, dark and mysterious. If we waded past any panthers, that's where they would have been hiding, snuggled down in a pile of palmetto leaves. We didn't climb out of the water and go stomping around in the underbrush looking for them. We were there in the daytime, when the panthers would have been asleep. I'm pretty grouchy when someone wakes me up in the middle of a snooze. I can only imagine how an animal with big claws and big teeth would react to being awakened. They need plenty of rest, so that at twilight they can go hunting.

The whole time I was splashing around with Clyde, I kept thinking how, forty years before, this had all been slated to be covered in concrete. Now it is, as writer Jeff Ripple once observed, one of the few places in Florida where you can stand still and hear nothing but the sounds of nature.

In 1968, the Dade County Port Authority decided South Florida needed a much bigger airport than the one operating in Miami. The authority decided to build an airport that would be bigger than the four largest airports in America combined. But where to put it?

The authority chose a spot in the Big Cypress, the swamp known as the panthers' last resort.

Henry Ford had once tried to give the Big Cypress Swamp to the state of Florida, back in the 1920s. Ford had a part-time home in Fort Myers, where one of his neighbors was Thomas Edison. He was sure the Big Cypress would make a lovely state park. But Tallahassee's officialdom said no, thanks. The state couldn't afford the upkeep, the bureaucrats said.

So it remained private property. A timber company cut down the namesake wood on 100,000 acres of it. Now people in Miami wanted to cover most of it with tarmac.

The Big Cypress, at the time, was the "world of the heron, the ibis, and the anhinga, of coot, gallinule, and pie-bald grebe, of barred owl, pileated woodpecker, and the swamp-loving warblers," one naturalist wrote. But Miami officials wanted a different kind of bird to fill the skies with thunder.

Although the big swamp formed the headwaters for the Everglades, a national park since 1947, that was no automatic dealkiller. National parks weren't considered sacred property back then, especially in the face of Human Progress on the March.

Besides, it was just another swamp, and it's not as if Florida didn't already have plenty of those. This was not an unusual move, by the way: airports in New York, Washington, Philadelphia, Seattle, Salt Lake City and Los Angeles were all built on what used to be wetlands. The land was cheap, and there were generally few if any neighbors to object.

The port authority acquired a thirty-nine-square-mile site just north of Everglades National Park and laid out plans for runways six miles long, where jets would be taking off every minute. Then, for easy access to the site from both coasts, the authority wanted a one-thousand-foot-wide transportation corridor built from coast to coast. The corridor would include a new interstate highway, a high-speed mass transit system, even a "recreational waterway" for airboats.

In classic Florida fashion, all this would be done with state and federal tax dollars, and would thus set up private developers to make a killing. The gigantic airport would spark an explosion of commercial and residential development across what pave-it-all advocates saw as soggy and valueless land.

"A new city is going to rise up in the middle of Florida," the authority chairman boasted to reporters.

And hey, too bad for the panthers hanging out in the Big Cypress like it was their own private Pantherland. They would have to flee from all the bulldozers and cement mixers as they once fled from hunters with shotguns. The question was: Where could they go? If there was no room for them in the Big Cypress, there might be no more room for them anywhere.

But then, as word spread about the site the port authority was calling "the Everglades jetport," a funny thing happened. People in South Florida became alarmed about the destruction of a swamp. Jetport advocates were stunned. Nobody had ever cared about saving a Florida swamp before. What changed?

Hunters, Native Americans, Audubon Society members and Everglades fans had formed an odd, unlikely coalition to try to keep Big Cypress the way it was. The hunters—"swamp rats," they called themselves—had camps scattered across the Big Cypress, and losing those camps would hurt like losing a family member. The Seminole and Miccosukee tribes lived on reservations in and around the Big Cypress that would be disrupted by the booming, zooming jets, not to mention all the ancillary development. The Audubon Society members valued the varied wildlife available in the swamp, and the Everglades fans feared that the new highway would cut off the flow of the River of Grass into the national park.

Together they made enough noise to grab the attention of President Richard Nixon's interior secretary as well as Congress, which held hearings. Working behind the scenes to organize the battle against the jetport was a tall, lanky aide to Republican Governor Claude Kirk named Nathaniel Reed.

The son of a New York theater producer, Reed grew up fishing in Florida's Hobe Sound. His mother claimed he emerged from the womb with a fly rod in his hand. As a youngster he was dazzled by the natural beauty all around him, and began collecting butterflies and marking down all the kinds of birds he saw. When I met him years later, Reed stood six-foot-five, and his beak-like nose and slender build made him resemble a wading bird in repose. In defending the environment, though, he could roar like a lion. While he was a staunch Republican, he had also been radicalized by Rachel Carson's book *Silent Spring*.

In 1966, Reed, a former military intelligence officer, campaigned for Kirk. He accompanied the candidate on barnstorming flights around the state in a DC-3, the men stripping off their sweat-soaked shirts upon takeoff and grabbing a deck of cards and playing a raucous game of hearts until time to put their shirts back on for the next campaign stop.

Kirk, who became Florida's first Republican governor since Reconstruction, was a man for whom the adjective "colorful" seems insufficient. He once rode a horse to a press conference, hired a private company to dig into official corruption and appeared at his inaugural ball with a woman he refused to identify by name except to call her "Madame X." (She was a German-born divorcée, and a month later they got married and stayed married until Kirk's death in 2011.) When the *New York Times* profiled him in 1967, it wrote that Kirk was "playing Governor the way Errol Flynn used to play Captain Blood—charming, daring, somewhat arrogant, seldom going by the rules."

Reed became Kirk's dollar-a-year aide for environmental issues, a brand-new position Kirk had created for reasons that were based more on personality than politics. Kirk told him: "If you want to change the things that you have been hollering about for the last fifteen years in Florida, there's a desk."

"He had no interest in conservation," Reed said years later, "but he had an interest in whoever was lowest guy on the totem pole, and at that time conservation was the lowest thing in anybody's mind in Florida. It was rape and run, avarice and greed. Make money now and do not worry about the future."

Kirk being Kirk, this was definitely not a desk job, nor easy duty. Reed once got a late-night call from a somewhat inebriated Kirk, demanding he dispatch the National Guard with a howitzer to make sure a Panamanian tanker that was leaking oil couldn't sneak out of its quarantine at the Port of Tampa. Together they took on, and angered, dredge-and-fill contractors, business-as-usual developers, and mayors whose cities were dumping sewage straight into bays and estuaries.

The jetport was a natural issue for them to tackle—big and hairy and politically dangerous, with powerful interests on both sides.

Reed's most crucial ally in stopping the jetport was a wily ex-TV reporter named Joe Browder down in Miami. Browder, who had studied ornithology at Cornell University, was an avid birder who knew his way around the wilds of Florida, but easily got lost chasing stories on Miami's city streets. Still, he knew how to push the buttons of the national publicity machine. He persuaded reporters from *Time*, *Look* and NBC's *Today* show to come down to Florida and cover the big jetport battle.

Browder had some vocal allies. One was acclaimed thriller writer John D. MacDonald, a Sarasota resident, who penned a piece for *Life* magazine contending that the project would "kill what was left of the Everglades."

Browder even approached Marjory Stoneman Douglas, whose 1947 bestseller *Everglades: River of Grass* had first brought the state's most famous marsh to the attention of a national audience. Douglas turned him down. She didn't think anyone would listen to some half-blind seventy-eight-year-old lady. People only pay attention to organizations, she said.

"Well," Browder asked, "why don't you start an organization?"

Together, she and Browder founded one of Florida's first environmental groups, Friends of the Everglades, with dues of $1 a year. Douglas denounced the jetport—and sure enough, people paid attention. That started Douglas's thirty-year career as a finger-wagging, floppy-hatted environmental advocate, a career she did not give up until she died in 1998 at age 106.

All the complaints about the environmental damage that would result just made the jetport's advocates dig in their heels. To placate the tree huggers, the director of the port authority said, they would build them a Florida version of Houston's Astrodome—just for butterfly chasing.

Browder compiled a list of 119 questions about the project's potential environmental impact. When Dade County officials were confronted with the list during a meeting, their replies to every question tended to be variations on "The answer to that question is under study."

Finally, along about Question No. 73, an angry Reed leaped to his feet and berated the county officials for wasting everyone's time and dodging their questions. The Dade County mayor responded by branding the patrician Reed and the plain-vanilla Browder "white militants," as if they were wearing tie-dyed T-shirts, waving picket signs and chanting slogans.

In the end, the "white militants" won, aided by the nation's first-ever environmental impact statement.

The report was put together by a team supervised by a US Geological Survey senior scientist named Luna Leopold, the son of *Sand County Almanac* author Aldo Leopold. The impact statement concluded that the jetport would produce 4 million gallons of sewage and 1.5 million gallons of industrial waste a day, as well as scatter 10,000 tons of air pollutants across the Big Cypress–Everglades watershed. Add on all the development that would sprout from that seed and you could see the ecological disaster spreading across the bottom half of the state.

The report contained a section on panthers—short, but packing a punch.

"Little is known about this rare and endangered subspecies since it is usually active only in the night hours," it said. "The destruction of the Big Cypress Swamp, where an estimated 75 percent of the total (Florida) population is now found, would likely bring about its extinction."

Reed used the Luna Leopold report to convince Kirk to withdraw state support for the jetport. That, Reed said later, "led to Nixon calling us all into Washington and canceling the project altogether. The federal money ended."

Without federal funding or state support, the jetport never proceeded beyond building one lonely landing strip, which remains out in the middle of the swamp—a ghostly reminder of one of the first big victories of the nation's budding environmental movement.

To make sure the jetport never climbed back out of its grave, Browder then led a drive to protect Big Cypress the way the Everglades had been, by making it a part of the National Park system. Nixon endorsed this idea. But Congress took so long to work out the details that by the time it finally agreed to pay $150 million to buy Big Cypress, Nixon had been pushed out by the Watergate scandal. As a result, the honor of signing the measure into law in 1974 went to unelected President Gerald Ford.

Thus it was a trio of Republicans—Nixon, Ford and Kirk—who made sure panthers could keep the Big Cypress.

But Big Cypress wasn't exactly like Everglades National Park. Rather than becoming a park, it became the National Park Service's first-ever "preserve." The difference sounds minor but it's not.

If it had become a park, all the hunters who fought to save it would have been kicked out. By declaring it a "preserve," the government allowed all the swamp rats to keep hunting deer and hogs and gators there, keep hanging out at their hunt camps, and keep on riding through the woods on their swamp buggies and airboats. Still, the designation guaranteed no further development would occur, particularly of the jetport variety.

Reed, meanwhile, got a promotion. He'd done so well working for Kirk that he was hired as an assistant secretary for Nixon's Department of the Interior. He said Nixon told him, "I don't give a damn about the environment—I have other priorities. I want a brilliant record, better than Kennedy's, and I don't want to be bothered by you or anybody else."

While working for Interior, Reed preserved more than 80 million acres of Alaska, publicized the dangers of DDT, and imposed a ban on the use of a coyote-killing poison called 10-80 that killed other animals as well.

But his most long-lasting accomplishment there was becoming coauthor of the Endangered Species Act, which was supposed to strengthen protection for imperiled wildlife like panthers.

The bill passed Congress by an overwhelming margin in late 1973 and Nixon signed it. Once again, panthers were included on the list of wildlife that was supposed to be protected from going extinct.

When Florida's senior game officials saw the list, they just shook their heads. They were convinced that it was too late for the panther. Florida's version of the puma had been wiped out, just like the ones in all the other Southern states.

A few people thought that was wrong. They were sure there were still a few of Charles Cory's cats skulking about. The question was, how to prove it?

The answer: hire a hunter.

CHAPTER THREE

THE HUNTER

The first time I met Roy McBride, I thought he had been dreamed up by a Hollywood casting director.

He was seventy-one then, but still in good shape, a tall and lanky man with a chiseled chin and a lock of white hair that kept falling down across his forehead like Superman's spit curl. He had the kind of a face that looked like something carved out of stone, fixed and immovable—until he suddenly cracked the granite apart with a grin. Every picture I've seen of McBride shows him wearing a battered white Stetson, and when I met him, sure enough, that's what he had on. He wore it everywhere, even indoors. He probably wears it to use the bathroom, but I didn't dare ask him.

McBride usually spends his days far removed from other people. He is notoriously tough to reach on the phone. Luckily for me, I found out he was giving a talk about tracking panthers to a roomful of biologists in a government building ten minutes from my office, so I showed up with my pen and notebook and found a seat by the back wall.

When McBride spoke, he was terse and to the point. His tenor voice seemed a bit raspy, with a strong Western twang— "these things" became "these thangs." He rarely used the words "I" or "me." McBride dislikes talking about himself. He regards tooting your own horn the way the Pope regards sin. One biologist told me that he spent two years working with McBride before finding out the man had a master's degree in biology. (The title of his master's thesis at Sul Ross State University in Alpine, Texas: "The Status and Ecology of the Mountain Lion on the Texas-Mexico Border.") Another biologist I talked to just shook his head and said, "I've known him for twenty years and I still don't know him."

The other constant about Roy McBride is his little yellow pocketknife. It showed up in a bunch of his slides that day. He used it as a measuring device when he snapped photos of panther tracks. He'd lay the folded-up knife on the ground next to the track to show its comparative size. Then, after his presentation, the conference took a break and I saw him using the knife to peel an apple for a snack. I asked if that was the same knife, and he said yes. Because I can seldom resist the urge to play the smart aleck, I asked what else he used that knife for— cleaning his toenails, perhaps? He gave me his stone-faced look and claimed he didn't remember what he'd used it for last. Then he grinned and said, "You don't want any of this apple."

McBride hailed from the mountains of West Texas, in a region that scrunches up against the Mexican border like a towel someone's shoved into the space beneath a door. McBride once called it "hundreds of thousands of square miles of habitat that really has a low human impact. Very few people live here. All of northwestern Coahuila and northeastern Chihuahua join western Texas at one point there. It is just a desert area, desert mountains. Some of the higher mountains have timber, but in general it is a real primitive form of agriculture, just grazing, or no agriculture at all. In these kind of conditions, mountain lions do real well."

That part of West Texas was so rural and remote that when McBride talked about driving into town, he meant going a hundred miles to the small community of Alpine, and along the way passing only one other house. A tad isolated, in other words.

The popular image of Texas is that it's full of oil wells and longhorn cattle. Not this part, though. Where McBride grew up was sheep country. The Spanish first brought sheep to Texas in the 1600s to provide mutton for their Catholic missions. Settlers began raising sheep for the profit they could make from the wool in the 1830s, and by the Civil War sheep had become big business in West Texas. After the war, while the rest of the South was struggling with the economic ramifications of Reconstruction, New England textile mills were offering top dollar for Texas wool. By 1930, Texas led the nation in sheep production. By 1943, Texans owned more than ten million sheep.

A major problem for the Texas flocks: predators. Sheep ranchers were constantly losing sheep to wolves and mountain lions. The ranchers tried surrounding their herds with fences and then with barbed wire, but the savvy predators still snuck through. So the ranch owners were eager to hire a hunter. That's where McBride came in.

"I lived in an area where people were trying to raise sheep and pumas killed the sheep," he told me. The choices for his future boiled down to just three: tend to the sheep, hunt down the pumas or move somewhere else. Beginning when he was a teenager in the 1940s, McBride trained himself to become a puma hunter, roving around the countryside selling his skills to the highest bidder.

He became an expert at tracking mountain lions and also

wolves, mastering a nineteenth-century skill in the late twentieth century. He knew this was not a fashionable pursuit in the age of data crunching and computers.

"Tracks are not very glitzy," he said. "Biologists today have kind of forgotten about tracks and what they might mean, but they're real useful."

Because of his tracking skills, McBride learned how the predators traveled and ate and hunted. He could almost read their thoughts. The mountain lions, he knew, were particularly rough on the herds—biblically bad, according to McBride.

"Those cats kill sheep like Samson killed Philistines," he said once.

To track them down, McBride had trained a pack of hunting dogs, Walker hounds and mixed-breeds mostly. They would track only the scent of whatever predator they were chasing, and they wouldn't start baying until they had their quarry on the run. Some of his dogs, McBride once said, "lived their whole lives, birth to death, and only knew one human being—me."

McBride and his hounds were so good, one writer claimed he "had more to do with bringing the mountain lion to the verge of extinction in Texas than any other single person." As the decades passed, McBride's reputation spread, as did the demand for his services. When there was a wily predator to catch, the cry would go up: "Let McBride do it!"

Ranchers down in Mexico began seeking out his services too. It helped that he spoke fluent Spanish. In the 1960s, a lone wolf began wreaking havoc among cattle ranches along the border between the central Mexican states of Durango and Zacatecas. The ranchers called it "Las Margaritas," because that was the name of the first ranch that it hit.

Las Margaritas began killing dozens of yearling steers and heifers, and always stayed one step ahead of anyone trying to catch it. The ranchers knew it was the same wolf because the animal left a distinctive track: Las Margaritas had lost two toes on one foot to a trap. As a result, the maimed wolf was wary of ever getting caught in anything like that again.

"The wolf seldom used the same trail twice and if he came into a pasture by a log road, he left by a cow trail," McBride later wrote. "I was sure I could catch Las Margaritas, but I couldn't get him near a trap."

He tried traps with different baits. He tried traps that had been boiled in oak leaves. He tried traps that had been carefully concealed in dirt that he'd sifted to hide any signs it was a trap. Las Margaritas wasn't fooled. McBride got him close to a trap four times, and four times the wolf got away.

"Almost a year had passed and I was now convinced that I would never catch this wolf," he wrote. "Just how the wolf could tell the traps were there is something I cannot comprehend to this date."

McBride traveled by horseback through the Mexican countryside, tracking his foe thousands of miles. Finally McBride noticed a subtle clue. Along a road frequented by log trucks, there were spots where the truck drivers pulled over and built a fire to cook. When they were done, they would put out the fire and drive on. McBride discovered Las Margaritas's tracks veered near the spots where the coals of the fire had ashed over, apparently looking for any food left behind. It gave him an idea.

"I set a trap near a road that the wolf was sure to come down if it continued to kill in the area, built a fire over the trap and let it burn itself out," McBride wrote.

To make sure there was no human scent to give away the game, McBride spread out a steer hide and stood on that while setting up his trap. Then he put a piece of dried skunk hide in the ashes and retreated.

It took a while, but finally Las Margaritas showed up to investigate. The trap beneath the dead fire snapped shut.

"Margaritas was caught by the same crippled foot and the trap held," McBride wrote. His account does not say how he killed the adversary he'd chased for so long. He only notes that "there was much celebration among the ranchers the following day."

McBride's lengthy, single-minded pursuit of Las Margaritas became the stuff of legend among hunters in the Southwest. If the tale sounds familiar, it might be because it became the inspiration for Cormac McCarthy's novel *The Crossing*.

McBride wasn't content to merely track down predators after the fact. He became interested in trying to stop coyotes before they killed. What if, he thought, he could somehow attach a trap to the sheep? That led him to invent a sheep collar that contained poison. Strap one of his collars on a sacrificial lamb and then, when a coyote bit down on its neck, the coyote died, sparing the rest of the flock. The collar worked so well, McBride patented it and went into business, selling them internationally.

He's also credited with pioneering the practice of shooting coyotes from helicopters, a method that allows gunning down a lot of animals in a short space of time. It's not without its critics—or its risks. One of McBride's helicopter hunting trips ended with the copter crashing to earth so hard it bent his gun barrel. He emerged unharmed, then dragged the injured pilot to safety.

"Roy, where are we?" the pilot asked.

"We're still in Texas," McBride drawled. "I just heard a coyote bark."

All in all, McBride once told a symposium on wolves, "I think I had the best job anybody ever had. It was worth it to see those tracks, and the things that they did."

Somehow McBride managed to balance working at that solitary job with the life of a family man. He married a special education counselor named Jere, who a Florida biologist told me looked like a beauty queen. Together they had two sons and a daughter. When they were first married, they lived in a tiny shack in a rural area so flat and dusty that, she said once, "When you woke up in the morning, you could tell where your head had been because the rest of the pillow was covered in dust."

Jere learned to fly a plane so she could ferry her husband all over creation to his assignments, but she didn't share his passion for pursuing predators. His sons did, though. One of them, Rocky, even accompanied McBride when he was pursuing Las Margaritas, learning the trade from the best mentor in the business.

After a while, something happened to McBride that changed his view of his ideal job. He lost all sympathy for all those silly sheep, and took more of a liking to the mountain lions.

An amateur psychologist might theorize that McBride changed his attitude because of the weight of guilt from all the animals he'd killed. It's more complex than that, according to Jane Comiskey, a particularly intense University of Tennessee computer modeler who befriended McBride while they were working on a study of panther habitats. She told me McBride's change of heart sprang from "him realizing our place in the world, and our impact on it."

Dan Schuler, in a 1980 book about Westerners killing predators called *Incident at Eagle Ranch*, suggested McBride had a more basic motive.

"When asked if he considered himself a conservationist, he laughed and said, 'Hell, no,'" Schuler wrote. "The fact is that he shares with other predator hunters an addiction to the work itself… The pursuit is the only thing that matters."

In other words, he wanted to save the predators because if they went extinct, he wouldn't have anything left to chase.

But what McBride told me was more straightforward. He could see for himself all the damage the grazing sheep were doing to the natural areas he'd known growing up. Meanwhile, after spending all that time trying to think like the wolves and mountain lions, he began to feel more of a kinship with them—particularly the lions.

Whatever the reason, when he got the call about tracking down any remaining Florida panthers, McBride was ready.

★ ★ ★

On the other end of the phone call to McBride was a modest, apparently mild-mannered grad student named Ron Nowak, who came from New Orleans. These days Nowak is known in wildlife circles for his impassioned defense of wolves and his attacks on his former employer, the US Fish and Wildlife Service, which he views as having betrayed the wolf.

But back in the 1960s, a different mammal caught his attention. While Nowak was serving in the air force, he ran across a 1946 book called *The Puma, Mysterious American Cat*, by Stanley P. Young and Edward A. Goldman. The book got him hooked on big cats.

"I was startled to see that there were mountain lions in Louisiana, but they were on the verge of extinction, as they were throughout the East," he told me. "In 1966 one was actually killed in Louisiana near an air force base where I was stationed at the time."

When Nowak left the service, he went back to college so he could learn more about these intriguing animals. By then, the Louisiana pumas were gone.

But someone at the World Wildlife Fund thought there might still be some in Florida. Although he was right in the middle of writing his dissertation at the University of Kansas, Nowak volunteered to help find out for sure. In December 1972, the WWF gave him a $1,700 grant to hire an expert to help him look.

He called several hunters experienced at tracking mountain lions. But he went with McBride for one simple reason: price.

"I think he was willing to work for almost nothing," Nowak explained. "He's got a tremendous interest in not just hunting. He wanted to know about the animal." Nowak told me he paid McBride $500 for his work.

McBride had some experience in this line. Before Nowak called, he'd been summoned to search for pumas in Louisiana and Tennessee, coming up empty-handed both times.

Before McBride started hunting panthers in Florida, though, he wanted to make sure Nowak could be a helper, not a hindrance to the search.

"He invited me to come to West Texas first, to show me where the panthers were and how they could be found," Nowak said.

They spent some time roaming the Big Bend National Park, and Nowak saw firsthand just what made him such a legendary hunter. As they followed paw prints through the rugged Texas terrain, Nowak was astonished at McBride's tracking skill. What he did and what he knew involved so much more than just looking at prints. To Nowak, it was as if McBride were almost a component of the landscape himself, moving through it as if it were a part of him and vice versa.

Nowak, of course, was not.

McBride "quickly realized that I was such a greenhorn—I had never done any fieldwork before," Nowak recalled. The grad student struggled to keep up with the veteran tracker. "He used to say, 'Come on! We gotta get moving!' But as we went along he came to see that I was okay."

After their stint in Texas, they packed up McBride's hounds and headed for Florida.

The terrain in Florida was about as different from what McBride was used to as it could be. Instead of mountains, the land was as flat as a billiard table. Instead of crossing desert, they were splashing through cypress swamps. Instead of being far from civilization, they were just down the road from the suburban sprawl rapidly creeping eastward. To McBride, everywhere he looked, he saw "big cities, lots of people." How could panthers live here?

As good as his hounds were, McBride wasn't sure they'd find anything at all. While the dogs' sense of smell is acute, McBride told me, the only panthers they can detect are the ones that passed by within the previous twenty-four hours. They couldn't detect something that had gone extinct.

He talked to people who were supposed to be experts. Nobody knew how many panthers there were, or whether they even existed.

McBride talked to one state biologist who "said he never had seen any tracks or any indications there were any left." Basically, the game commission expert told him that when it came to panthers, "there weren't any—that I was fifteen years too late."

Another source who talked to McBride, a biologist at Florida's Archbold Research Station in Central Florida, came to the opposite conclusion. He was convinced there were three hundred or so. McBride didn't trust that estimate, though, because that many panthers would require far more white-tailed deer and hogs than existed.

The only "official" estimate was in the Luna Leopold report on the jetport. Leopold's biologists had estimated one hundred panthers remained, with seventy-five of them making their home in the Big Cypress. The report cites no evidence for this estimate, which leads me to believe it's what biologists I know call a "SWAG"—a "scientific wild-ass guess."

The bottom line, McBride said, was that "there really was not any kind of scientific information about if they still existed, where they were, or how many were left."

McBride knew only one way to determine the truth: turn the hounds loose.

This was in February 1973, a good time to tromp around in a Florida swamp. In February the heat isn't as intense, and neither is the humidity. The mosquitoes and other bugs aren't as likely to attack human flesh. The snakes and gators are less likely to be moving around and chomping on people.

The eight dogs, trailed by McBride and Nowak, started exploring around a ranch owned by a Tampa company called Lykes Brothers. The Lykes family had controlled thousands of acres of land in that region for decades, using part of it for cattle ranching but leaving much of it untouched, making it a likely place for panthers.

The family loaned McBride and Nowak horses to ride on the hunt. The two panther hunters gradually worked their way southward to the hunt camps of the Big Cypress. The cattle ranches near the Big Cypress seemed particularly promising, they decided.

"Unlike the Big Cypress, much of the ranch country is closed to hunting and other human activity, and in this regard is more favorable for...panthers," Nowak wrote in his report to the World Wildlife Fund. He added that the area "contains large tracts of scrub forest, swamp, and other habitats well suited for panthers."

Still, McBride wasn't confident they would see even a single cat, based on his results from Louisiana, Mississippi and Alabama. "I was getting used to the idea that probably there weren't any," he said.

Yet this time, in this unlikely place, the cats were there—or rather, the signs that they had been there not too long ago. He found panther tracks. He found some scat full of bones, indicating that the panthers were eating. He found the scrape marks that the cats typically leave behind with their huge rear paws after they've urinated.

"I found evidence of some panthers," McBride recalled years later. "Not many, but a few."

Then, on the morning of February 10, the dogs caught a fresh scent.

Nowak wasn't there for some reason. He told me he couldn't remember why they had separated, just that they had. So it was just McBride working the dogs near Gator Slough, a swampy inlet about five miles west of the town of Lakeport on Lake Okeechobee in the area of Fisheating Creek, not too far from a small Seminole Indian reservation.

The dogs took off running after the thing they'd smelled, chasing it hard for a good twenty minutes, with McBride splashing along behind. He heard the dogs calling out, making a noise somewhere between a howl and whine.

That meant their quarry had climbed a cypress tree. When McBride got there, he saw it perched on a branch, peering down at the scene below.

McBride could at last get a good look at what the dogs had been after. It sure looked like a panther—a real one, not the ghost of a vanished subspecies. It looked gaunt, its fur the color of faded khakis, but it was no spirit. It was flesh and blood.

He needed a closer look. McBride had brought along a tranquilizer gun. He loaded it, took aim and fired. The dart hit home, but the drug didn't have time to take effect before the big cat scrambled back down the tree trunk and took off running again. The dogs took off after it, with McBride trailing behind.

The second chase didn't take as long as the first. When the dogs treed it a second time, this time in an oak, the critter collapsed on a limb, fast asleep. McBride grabbed hold of the trunk and clambered up the oak. Then he loaded the animal on his shoulder and carried it back down.

Sure enough, it was a Florida panther. But it was hardly an impressive specimen.

The cat was a spindly female, probably nine or ten years old. Its hide was thoroughly infested with ticks. McBride, an expert on such things, judged that it had never given birth to any kittens—a troubling sign with a female of such advanced age.

He took no pictures or measurements, just looked the cat over the way he'd done so many times out West. As the drug began wearing off, he backed away and eventually watched the mangy cat saunter off into the swamp. Later, writing up a report on what had happened, Nowak mentioned the animal's poor condition, but not that he had completely missed the excitement.

A year later, Nowak got another grant to bring McBride back.

The hunter found more panther signs than he'd found the year before, but no more panthers turned up, so once again Nowak missed out on seeing one. Still, while there weren't three hundred panthers, there weren't zero either. Nowak felt jubilant.

Even the normally stoic McBride was astonished at finding a creature that a lot of people thought was gone.

"I was amazed to find them," McBride said years later. "I mean, I got down here in this thickly settled area, and I was really surprised there were any left."

When I told him I thought it was impressive that he'd found a panther at a time when a lot of smart people were sure they didn't exist anymore, he waved a hand, dismissing my compliment as nonsense.

"It wasn't like I was good," McBride said. "It's just I was the only one looking."

That one mangy panther that McBride had found was in such poor shape, it was clearly a creature in need of protection, the kind of protection that the Endangered Species Act could offer.

But how do you protect an animal that you know almost nothing about?

CHAPTER FOUR

THE STATE ANIMAL

The first time I talked to Peter C.H. Pritchard, I couldn't get over how veddy veddy British he sounded—as British as Queen Elizabeth in a big hat, as British as James Bond saluting a Union Jack.

Despite his accent, Pritchard had lived in Florida for more than five decades, studying turtles and tortoises, writing about them and giving lectures about them. His Chelonian Research Institute, headquartered in a cheerful yellow Craftsman-style home in the Central Florida town of Oviedo, housed the largest private collection of turtle specimens in the world—around thirteen thousand items, from prehistoric to the present day. He'd studied turtles and tortoises from Guyana to the Galapagos. Three species of turtles were named for him. Pritchard is to turtles what Jane Goodall is to chimps. One of his fans and former students referred to him as "the Turtle God."

There was a time, though, back in the 1970s, long before *Time* magazine declared him a "Hero of the Planet," when the tall and lanky Pritchard was not yet thinking about turtles morning, noon and night.

Pritchard was then a vice president of the Florida chapter of the Audubon Society. The editor of the chapter's magazine, *The Florida Naturalist*, asked him to write a series of stories about various endangered species found in the state. One of them was the Florida panther. When he started making phone calls for the panther story, he made a discovery.

"I was very struck by how people I had been directed to 'knew' a lot about the panther, but they each had a different spin on it," he told me. Worse, he said, was the fact that even though the panther had been classified as endangered, "it didn't seem to lead to any action."

Pritchard had seen a puma in Guyana a decade before, just a fleeting glimpse as it raced across a trail ahead of him, but the sight of it left a vivid memory. He wanted to do more than just write about its Florida cousin. He wanted to become a catalyst for saving it.

Pritchard talked his Audubon colleagues into letting him convene a meeting that gathered all the Florida panther experts together in one room so they could discuss and debate their findings. Pritchard, of course, would be there taking copious notes for his story.

"It was rather self-indulgent on my part to bring in all these experts to educate me," he said, chuckling.

One biologist invited to the conference wrote later that he thought Pritchard was being generous by calling everyone "experts." Most of them clearly were not. One person there had seen a wild panther in the past three years—McBride. Many of the others were activists or government officials for whom the panther was only an abstraction.

And then there was the flashy, outspoken Frenchman named Robert Baudy.

Baudy was a barrel-chested man with dark, wavy hair that he combed straight back from his huge forehead. He had piercing eyes and the self-confidence of someone who has repeatedly stepped into a lion's cage and survived. Newspaper reporters often described him as "dashing."

The son and grandson of animal trainers, Baudy had been brought to the United States in the 1950s by gossip-columnist-turned-variety-show-host Ed Sullivan to exhibit his monkeys and tigers on *The Ed Sullivan Show*. From there he went on to tour the country with his whip and his animals.

By the 1970s, Baudy retired from show business to settle in rural Central Florida and operate what he called Savage Kingdom—apparently a spoof of Disney's Magic Kingdom. Within its high fences he kept a collection of big cats: lions, tigers, panthers and jaguars, among others. Outside the gates he posted signs inviting area farmers to give him any horses or donkeys that had keeled over or were about to breathe their last. Baudy's cats needed a lot of meat to eat, and Baudy wasn't averse to shooting an old horse in the head if that's what it took to feed his menagerie.

Baudy disliked government regulations and government officials. He frequently announced, in his thick French accent, that no one working for any state or federal agency could do anything right. Of course, many of the other attendees at Pritchard's conference were state and federal employees, thus making Baudy even more certain he was meant to take the lead. Pritchard politely described the Frenchman as "the most free thinker of the bunch."

Pritchard's assembled "experts" spent two days in March 1976 sharing information about the big cats. They did this at an unlikely venue: the oldest Unitarian Universalist Church in Florida, a chapel built on what had been a three-acre orange grove in Orlando.

No panthers showed up. About twenty men and women signed in as attendees, but of the dozen speakers on the agenda, not one was female or anything other than Caucasian. Nobody brought along a Polaroid to shoot photos, but, given the year, I picture the men all wearing double-knit bell-bottom slacks and long sideburns or even beards. The women probably wore cowl-neck sweaters or polyester pantsuits with their Farrah-feathered hairdos. Everyone's collar was as wide as an interstate highway.

One by one, the speakers stepped up to the lectern and spelled out their views on panthers. One contended there were still a hundred of them out roaming around. McBride said he doubted there could be more than twenty. Without actual data, though, they were all like the blind men in the fable about the elephant: each held a different opinion of what the creature looked like because each had his hands on a different part.

The group stayed late into the evening discussing what they had seen and heard and speculated about. They were spellbound by McBride's stories about tracking big cats across Texas and Mexico. Despite Baudy's contempt for bureaucrats, Pritchard recalled that many were dazzled by his air of sophistication. He even gave them a tour of his facilities and showed them species of cats that most had never seen before.

Baudy insisted it was time to take drastic measures to save the panther. He wanted to capture a few from the Big Cypress, pen them up at his Savage Kingdom and breed them together to produce a passel of new cats. The way he talked about it, Savage Kingdom could crank out new panthers just like a Detroit factory line rolling out new cars. Baudy fancied himself an expert at captive breeding and made sure the others knew it.

"Quite a few species maintained at our compound are the

second, third and even fourth generation of captive-born animals," Baudy told the group.

But first, he said, someone should capture, measure and closely examine at least five panthers from the wild, just to make sure that Florida panthers were really different from their western counterparts—an issue that would come up again and again.

Nobody else was quite ready to launch a captive breeding drive. In fact, a top official in the US Department of the Interior's Endangered Species Office took the opposite stance. He told the group that the best approach to panther recovery would be "a form of benign neglect," Pritchard wrote later. "He reasons that any panthers that survive today did so without any deliberate help from man."

Set aside some land as protected habitat for the panther, this official suggested, and then "leave it the hell alone."

The most important person at the meeting wasn't Baudy or McBride or Pritchard or even the do-nothing guy from the Department of the Interior. No, the most important person was a five-foot-eight biologist named Robert C. Belden. His friends called him Chris.

And he was almost completely out of his depth.

Chris Belden was in his late twenties then, with a bachelor's degree in forestry and a master's in wildlife management. He'd fallen in love with the outdoors while earning the rank of Eagle in the Boy Scouts, the top rank a boy can earn, a sign of his determination and organizational skills. At his Eagle ceremony, when he was fourteen, Belden declared his intention to become a biologist.

Belden has expressive brown eyes and thick, dark hair that flops down over his forehead on one side. At the time, he was growing what would become a thick, dark beard. He's the kind of guy who always weighs his words carefully before he talks, and when he opens his mouth he speaks with a slow Tennessee drawl.

He was hired in 1974 as the staff mammal expert for Florida's wildlife research lab in Gainesville, a Central Florida college town north of Orlando. His employer was the Florida Game and Freshwater Fish Commission. When Pritchard invited the game commission to send a panther expert to his conference, Belden's boss tapped him to go—even though Belden had never seen a panther in his life. He figured being ignorant wasn't much of a handicap, though.

"At the time, I didn't know anything about Florida panthers and neither did anyone else," Belden explained years later.

The game commission had no real panther experts for the simple reason that nobody hunted panthers anymore. Although technically every animal in the state belonged to the people of Florida, the game commission didn't care about most of them. It paid attention only to the ones that were hunted—deer, quail, turkeys and so forth. The notion of protecting a nongame species from going extinct was pretty much a foreign concept.

Quickly, Belden pulled together a report for the conference by rummaging through the lab's cabinets for any old studies or sightings he could find. He sorted through the documents, evaluating whether they were believable or not.

He concluded that only a handful of the reported sightings were real panthers. Most were not. Some people claimed to have seen a "black panther," something that at that point existed only among '60s militant groups and Marvel comic books. Sometimes what people thought was a panther turned out to be a bobcat, which is smaller and has a stump of a tail. Sometimes what they had claimed to see wasn't even a feline—it was a big dog, or a fat raccoon. The panther reports were a good indicator of the unreliability of eyewitness testimony.

Belden, in a report he co-wrote with another game commission biologist, noted that they had found only seven confirmed reports of a panther. One of them was the one from McBride and Nowak's search (although he complained that McBride hadn't documented his discovery with photos or measurements).

The bottom line, Belden said, was that while panthers might still exist in Florida, no one knew whether there was a viable population. Those few survivors might be the last of the big cats, not the nucleus of a group likely to survive into the future. He also warned against overestimating how many panthers still wandered Florida, calling it "fatal" to their future.

There was another Department of the Interior official at the meeting, and unlike his colleague, he believed in doing something about the panthers. He announced that being listed as endangered was only the first step to saving an animal like the panther. The next step would be to figure out what steps would be required to get the panther *off* the endangered list someday, a process known as "recovery" of the species.

Coming up with those steps would require forming a committee to write what's known as a "recovery plan"—and he put Belden in charge of doing just that. Despite his lack of expertise, Belden was the designated representative of the state's wildlife agency, so in the world of bureaucrats, that made him the leader. Other members selected to work on the recovery plan included Pritchard and Baudy—but not McBride, who was headed back to Texas.

The first step, they agreed, was to figure out where the panthers were. So the methodical Belden set up a Florida Panther Record Clearinghouse and asked everyone in Florida to let him know about any new panther sightings. He even wanted to hear about panther tracks or dead panthers found anywhere.

He gave interviews to reporters and even wrote a piece for the *Florida Wildlife* magazine encouraging people to contact him and do their bit to protect panthers from going extinct.

He was quickly inundated with reports, nearly all of them bogus.

"People reported tracks that had been made by dogs, bobcats, otters, alligators, and raccoons," Belden said. "They sent in pictures of house cats. They found panthers, dead on the road, that when I got there turned out to be deer, foxes, and, one time, a brindled pit bull terrier swollen up like a fifty-five-gallon drum."

To figure out which sightings were real and which ones weren't, Belden decided he needed to learn how to spot the signs of a big cat. Like Nowak before him, Belden spent a week in Texas trailing after McBride.

"He wanted to know where I found them and that sort of thing," McBride recalled. "He indicated he was going to start looking for them. I encouraged him to come to West Texas and learn what the tracks looked like, and urine markers, and droppings and so forth, so he could conduct investigations in Florida."

Belden's search was painstakingly slow work, but it produced a huge side-benefit. By going public with his search, he sparked the public's imagination. His quest helped make the panther a popular figure around Florida.

Stories about Belden's search for panther sightings were usually accompanied by photos of the beast looking sleek and alluring. Florida's settlers had once feared this cat, but now the suburbanites and city dwellers who had filled the state became fascinated by this elusive creature. Everyone wanted to help Belden find one. It became the animal kingdom equivalent of *Where's Waldo?*—and nobody hates Waldo.

Their interest in the panther would, in a few years, pay off for Belden and his fledgling project.

Here's how much Belden's quest changed things:

In 1978, a hunter named Doyle Watson shot a panther in the Big Cypress and then hid the carcass in a freezer at his father's ice business in Homestead. When a deputy questioned him, Watson claimed he had shot the panther only because it had been charging at him and his girlfriend.

A judge ordered the medical examiner to check the evidence.

Belden told me he skinned the cat and then stood by while the coroner examined the panther's wounds. The angle of the bullet showed that it had been shot while it was running away, proving that Watson was lying. Watson was fined $500 and sentenced to thirty days behind bars. That was the stiffest penalty available under the law.

A few years before, he might have been given a medal. The public, now enamored with panthers, expressed outrage at the outcome. In response to the public outcry, the Florida Legislature made the killing of a panther a third-degree felony, punishable by a fine of up to $5,000 and as much as five years in prison.

By 1979, Belden had collected more than a thousand reports from all over Florida, most of them about animals other than panthers. The ones that he could verify as real were nearly all from three places: Big Cypress, Everglades National Park and a thickly vegetated area north of Big Cypress known as the Fakahatchee Strand, home to the greatest concentration of wild orchids in North America, including the famed ghost orchid. The Fak, as its fans call it, had been partially logged by a timber company and then slated for development by an unscrupulous builder. Once the company's shenanigans were exposed, though, its executives agreed to trade the land to the government so it would become a state park—thus saving a little more habitat for the panthers.

To Belden this was clear evidence that the best place to look for live panthers was in those three areas. He was ready to do more than just sit and wait for reports. He was itching to get out in the wild and find some panthers himself.

Belden also wanted to do more than just find the cats once. He wanted to find them over and over, to plot where they went, where they hunted, where they bedded down and where they bred and birthed their young. He wanted to capture panthers and strap collars around their necks that were attached to small battery-powered radio transmitters. Then he could go back again and again, detect their radio signals and plot their travels across the landscape. This would become known as the panther telemetry program.

Biologists had not been using radio signals to track wildlife for very long. One of the first successful tests, involving white-tailed deer in Minnesota in the early 1960s, required the scientists to design and build their own antenna. In 1970 a biologist in Idaho with the mellifluous name of John Seidensticker became the first to fasten radio collars to cougars. He followed their wide-ranging movements for more than two years. Seidensticker was able to locate the same marked animals over and over, figure out which cats had killed what, and even monitor their social interactions with each other.

Belden figured the same approach ought to work with Florida panthers, although he was a little worried about the effect that the heat and humidity might have on them while being pursued by a pack of dogs.

But first Belden had to convince the panel of experts that this was a good idea. One member, Baudy, raised so many objections that two years passed before Belden finally got permission. Even after Belden started catching cats, Baudy told a newspaper reporter that it was "the most poorly planned capture plan of a rare species that I have ever seen." The reporter noted in his story how much the two men loathed each other: "Neither will admit that the other knows anything about the Florida panther."

When Belden at last got a green light to start catching panthers, he immediately called in McBride.

"He employed me for thirty days or so to see if he could catch a few cats—and we did," McBride said.

On February 10, 1981, nearly five years after he was first classified as a panther expert at the Audubon gathering, Belden finally got to see his first panther in the wild.

It nearly killed him.

★ ★ ★

McBride once explained his approach to a panther hunt this way:

"We do not go out expecting to actually see panthers. We initially go out and look for evidence that they have been there. I calculated one time that if a panther moves six or seven miles in a night and its strides are nineteen to twenty-two inches long, he would leave something like nineteen thousand or thirty-eight thousand tracks. Of course, all of them would not be visible. Some of them would be on hard surfaces. But out of that number, at least some would be expected to be maintained by some kind of soft medium, like mud. There is going to be evidence left. What you are really looking for is evidence that the animal lives there. We did not go by actual panther sightings. We went by evidence of their existence."

Once they found the evidence, of course, then they could track where the panther had gone and try to follow it.

They hunted panthers in the cool of the morning, to make sure the cats didn't get overheated as they fled the dogs. Belden set out about 5 a.m. with another biologist, Bill Frankenberger, checking for panther signs along the old logging trails in the Fak. McBride was already running his dog pack, searching for any panther scent, working by himself because the dogs weren't used to having any other humans around.

Two other state biologists were helping out, a curly-haired guy named Tom Quinn and a woman named Deborah Jansen. Female field biologists such as Jansen were a rarity at the time, but she could easily hold her own with any of the men. She stood five-foot-four, with blondish hair, an athletic build and, at least on the surface, the placid demeanor of someone who never seems surprised or excited—although when she went on that first panther hunt, she was as hyped up as a kid full of cotton candy riding on a roller coaster. She was particularly excited about working with McBride, whom she described later as "a magnificent man."

She hailed from Wisconsin, and still spoke with that same clipped speech pattern. As a girl she used to stuff frogs and snails in her pockets to bring home. Her dad was a salesman, her mom an English teacher who was squeamish about spiders but who still encouraged her daughter's curiosity about nature. Because of that curiosity, and also the need to prove herself to the men, she would often volunteer for extra duties, even if it meant staying out in the field longer than anyone else. Technically she wasn't supposed to be on Belden's capture team, but when she heard what was going on she had jumped at the chance to help out.

Everyone on Belden's team toted walkie-talkies so they could communicate, but the devices had only a short range. As a result, Belden arranged everyone in a pattern that would allow them to relay messages to each other if necessary.

At 8:25 a.m., Jansen radioed Belden and Frankenberger to relay a message she'd gotten from McBride: the dogs had caught the scent of a cat and were in hot pursuit. At nine she radioed again to say that they had treed their quarry, and passed along McBride's instructions on where to meet.

They all convened at an old water oak that was surrounded by dogs. Sure enough, fifteen feet up above them perched a panther.

Belden was almost overwhelmed with excitement to see in real life this thing he'd been studying for so long. He noted its cinnamon-buff fur flecked with white, the long tail with a crook at the end. He snapped a blurry photo showing the cat peering down at them and not looking at all frightened, merely a bit annoyed.

McBride, as the most experienced marksman in the group, aimed the tranquilizer gun and shot a dart into the panther's rump. Belden, watching from below, saw the panther's jaw drop. To his dismay, the big cat did not fall from the tree. Instead, it stretched out on a limb and dozed off.

Someone would have to climb up and get it.

At that point everyone turned to Belden and pointed out that hey, you know, this was his research project, so therefore he should be the one to climb the tree, right? Belden had no counterargument. He grabbed hold of the trunk and began shimmying up toward his snoozing quarry.

"I got up about ten feet but couldn't go much further as the top of the tree was dead and it appeared weak," Belden recalled later. "I tied a rope around the trunk and let it down for Roy and Bill to pull on, hoping they'd be able to shake the panther out."

Before they could start shaking the tree, though, McBride hollered, "He's coming down! You better get out of there!"

Sure enough, the groggy panther had roused itself enough to start scrambling down. Alarmed, Belden started doing the same, trying to stay ahead of the cat, when suddenly the panther lost its balance and "was hanging right above my head by only his front claws, and they were slipping."

Belden jumped.

"No one knows who hit the ground first—me or the panther," he wrote.

The panther tried escaping, but it was too woozy to get very far. After it wobbled about a hundred feet, McBride grabbed hold of its tail and wouldn't let go. Then Belden plunged in another tranquilizer dose. The panther at last went down.

Belden and his crew didn't know how much time they had, so they hurried. Their primary mission, of course, was strapping on the leather radio collar. Belden tackled that, taking care that the strap wasn't on too tight or too loose. Too tight and it would hamper the panther's breathing. Too loose and the cat might be able to scrape it off.

Next they weighed the cat. It turned out to be a one-hundred-twenty-pound male, about ten years old. Then they inked small tattoos in both ears so they could identify it. They used a needle to collect a blood sample, and followed that up by taking a sample of its poop.

Once the collar was on, Belden stood up and snapped a photo

of his crew with their prize. In the photo, the panther is clearly knocked out. Roy McBride, wearing his Stetson and what looks like a high school warm-up jacket, is leaning over the cat, plucking ticks off its hide and dropping them into a jar. He's being assisted by Deb Jansen, a grin on her face as big as if someone had just told her she'd won the lottery. Quinn, the other male biologist, squats next to her, looking a little baffled about what to do next.

After thirty minutes the panther began to stir. Everyone pulled back, including the dogs, far enough to be out of sight, except for Belden and Jansen. They stayed to document how the panther recovered and how it might react to wearing a collar. Once it was sitting up, and apparently fine with its new neckwear, they packed up and went to join the rest of the crew.

"Somehow it was easy walking out" of the swamp, Belden wrote afterward. "I didn't care about pushing through the brush, getting cut by thorns, or sloshing through water up to my knees. My spirits were high. The capture went smoothly and the panther was in good condition. I knew that in the months ahead we would learn more about Florida panthers than had been learned in the last fifty years."

Ten days later, on February 20, they nabbed a second one, another male, this one weighing 108 pounds, and went through the whole process again—except for the part about falling out of the tree. Soon they were making regular trips out into the swamp to monitor the two panthers' movements. They didn't have swamp buggies or airboats for traversing the wilderness, as they did later.

"We just walked," McBride said. "Chris would give me a walkie-talkie, and I would start out in some area [where] we had found sign and I would work the area with the dogs. Chris would drive around on the other side to pick me up. That is how the telemetry program got started."

The radio collars transmitted a signal that they could pick

up with handheld antennas. Using those signals, Belden could chart where the panthers went and what habitat they seemed to prefer. He was convinced this would lead to a solution about how to save the panthers.

The one person who thought this was all wrong was, of course, Baudy. He accused Belden and the other biologists of playing cowboy. They were having fun adventures at the expense of saving the panthers, he contended.

But their "adventures" paid off in an unexpected way, thanks to a group of schoolchildren.

First, let's talk about the polar bear.

In August 1981, a Florida state representative named Bill Bankhead filed a bill for the next year's session that would officially designate a Florida state animal. Bankhead, a Republican real estate man, had to put in the name of some animal for the bill to serve as a placeholder for the final selection. Rather than stick in something that was a possible selection, such as the manatee, he filled that space with the word "polar bear."

This, of course, led to such poker-faced headlines as "Polar Bear Florida's State Animal?"

At that point, the state's frequently verbose education commissioner stepped in. Ralph Turlington—nicknamed "Ralph Turtleburger" by some wags who thought his head resembled that of a turtle—wanted the state's schoolchildren to pick the state animal, not the state's legislators. He drew up a ballot that featured as candidates the alligator, the manatee, the Key deer and the Florida panther. He left a space for write-in votes. Then he had his staff send it out to schools around the state.

There's nothing like an official request from the state education commissioner to motivate local school officials to participate in democracy. Hundreds of thousands of kids around the state were handed ballots to fill out. Some kids selected a preferred candidate among those Turlington offered. Others cast write-in votes for the dolphin, the rattlesnake, the camel, the salamander, even the monkey. (Believe it or not, there are monkeys in Florida. They were turned loose on an island by the guy running a jungle cruise around Silver Springs in the 1930s. He didn't realize the monkeys could swim.)

In the end, though, the clear winner at the end of voting in December 1981 was the Florida panther, thanks to the stories about Belden's efforts to track them down. It received more than 211,000 votes, far more than its nearest rival, the manatee, with 137,000. The gator got just 13,000 votes, the deer a mere 8,000.

Bankhead, as promised, amended his bill to substitute the panther for the polar bear, and then the typical Florida political shenanigans began. A baby-faced state representative from Leon County named Andy Johnson insisted that "the obvious choice" for state animal was the gator, despite how few kids had voted for it. He said he intended to push the gator instead of the panther. The schoolkids countered this with a letter-writing campaign. In February 1982, Bankhead said he was being bombarded with eighty letters a day "from students who are just irate that we may not honor their choice."

In the end, the panther triumphed. Bankhead's bill passed without a change and Governor Bob Graham—a lawyer whose family made its fortune in development—signed it into law.

By choosing a wild animal hardly anyone had ever seen as the state's unlikely mascot, Florida's schoolchildren raised its profile. Its official status prodded state legislators and bureaucrats to boost funding for Belden's research. The panther study breezed into 1983 with what appeared to be smooth sailing ahead.

Then disaster struck.

CHAPTER FIVE

MOUTH TO MOUTH

After Deb Jansen earned her master's degree in wildlife science in 1978, she went to a wildlife science conference determined to get people's attention. She was one of the few women present, so that helped. It also helped that at the time she had a sort of blond Afro—not the look sported by any of the other female conference attendees.

But just to make sure that absolutely nobody missed seeing her, she walked around the conference wearing a big placard that said, in hard-to-ignore green-and-blue letters, "M.S. IN WILDL. LOOK'N FOR A JOB."

She got plenty of job offers, but they weren't for the kinds of jobs she was looking for. They came from consulting firms that wanted her to sit in an office and compile reports about field studies written by men. Jansen wanted to be the one in the field, tromping around in a swamp, wading in the surf, collecting the data firsthand.

She finally got her chance with a temporary job doing crocodile research at Everglades National Park. Florida is the only place in the world that has both alligators and crocodiles living together in peace (with each other, not with us humans). The crocs are on the endangered species list. The alligators used to be, but by the 1980s they had completely bounced back.

Jansen didn't shy away from going out into the River of Grass to study the crocs.

"You just couldn't find anybody willing to work harder," one male biologist said years later. "She just gave everything she had all the time."

Eventually she landed a full-time job with the game commission in South Florida. Technically she was doing something called "game management," helping to keep tabs on the deer and other species that hunters cared about the most. But whenever she could, she joined the panther capture team to help with their work.

And that led to her putting her mouth onto the mouth of a panther.

The first two panthers that Belden and his team caught were officially designated (in a manner that Dr. Seuss would recognize) as Florida Panther 1 and Florida Panther 2, or FP1 and FP2 for short. Jansen was there for both.

The team caught six more panthers the following year and equipped them with radio collars too. Tracking their movements provided oodles of info that Belden and his biologists had never had before—once they figured out how to keep up with them.

At first, Belden spent sixteen hours a day driving around the Big Cypress and the Fakahatchee Strand in a red Ford pickup truck, jouncing around over the old logging trails and stopping every mile. At each stop, he'd get out and reach for the telescoping mast that was mounted in the bed of the truck. He'd expand the mast to raise an H-shaped antenna twenty feet in the air and rotate it 360 degrees, trying to pick up a signal from one of the collars. If he heard nothing, then he would crank the antenna back down, get back in the truck and drive another mile, then stop and do it all over again.

Ninety-nine times out of a hundred, the antenna picked up no signals at all.

Finally, after about six months, Belden and his team figured out that this was mostly a waste of time. They couldn't track this wide-ranging predator from the ground. They needed to be up in the air, soaring above the rugged terrain.

Some biologists frown on chasing their radio-collared study subjects from above, rather than experiencing the landscape along with whatever animal they're studying. They abhor the intrusion of a droning modern machine in a natural setting.

But with panthers, a ground pursuit had proven all but impossible. The animals cover too much of the swampy ground for a human to keep up any other way.

Belden got the funding to rent a pilot and a small plane. Flights would take off from the Naples airport and then fly low and slow above the tops of the wild palms and cypress trees. Belden or one of his biologists—Jansen helped out when she could—would ride in the passenger seat, listening for signals from the antenna, now strapped onto a wing strut. Then they would chart on a map where the ping came from.

"When we started flying," Belden recalled later, "we could locate all the cats nearly every day. That's when we discovered how mobile they are. It was nothing for one to move twenty miles in a night."

That wasn't all they discovered. Belden's tracking team learned that in summer, the panthers traveled mostly at night and then slept during the day. In winter, they sometimes moved during the daylight hours too. It changed the way they hunted the cats.

They began building a picture of the panther population—mostly male, and most of them aging. It was not a picture of a healthy group with a long future ahead.

One thing Belden learned firsthand was that the panthers' greatest predator was the automobile. Not long after collaring the first two cats, Belden saw his third panther. It was lying dead on a desolate stretch of US 29.

"I came across it about two hours after it was killed," he recalled later. "The animal was still tender and dripping blood. I guess it was one of the two females we figure are in the Fakahatchee population."

A veterinarian examined the carcass and discovered that this was a far more tragic event than it first appeared. The dead panther had been pregnant with four kittens.

Tracking the animals wasn't easy on Belden's home life. He had a house in the Gainesville area, where he and his wife were raising two young daughters. He'd spend a week at home with them, then spend several hours on the road driving down to Naples. He would devote the rest of the month down in South Florida to chasing panthers, then head back home to start the cycle all over again.

Meanwhile, Belden's fame spread. The fact that his team had found a puma east of the Mississippi, an animal that some experts thought to be extinct, caught hold in the public imagination.

Soon Belden was in demand as a speaker. Newspapers and magazines wrote about his work. They even published his photo. A TV show called *The American Sportsman* tagged along on one of the panther hunts, spreading Belden's fame nationally. He was The Hero Who Found The State Animal.

But then something went wrong.

At first it was something small. One of the cat's collars needed fresh batteries. To replace them would require recapturing that particular cat. No big deal, right?

And so the team headed out to recapture FP3. You know, the cat that's stuffed and on display in Tallahassee. The one where everything went sideways.

It happened on a Monday, of course.

The calendar said January 17, 1983. January in Florida is never as cold as January in New York or Wyoming. On this particular day, the morning temperature started in the fifties and slowly climbed into the low sixties. Belden's crew that day included Roy McBride, Deb Jansen, Bill Frankenberger and Scott Sanders. Their search for FP3 took them into the rutted logging trails and thick brambles of the Fakahatchee Strand.

About 11 a.m., McBride's dogs treed the seventy-pound female in a thirty-foot-tall live oak tree. Nobody had a clear shot from the ground, so Sanders took the tranquilizer gun—a pistol version, much lighter to carry than the rifle—and climbed the tree. When he got about eighteen feet off the ground, he finally had a good view of the panther, so he took aim and fired. The dart went into the back side of the animal's right hind leg, and the drug took effect in four minutes.

"She stood wobbly on a tree limb and laid down and wedged herself in a crotch of the tree," Belden wrote in a report.

Sanders wrapped a rope around the cat's flank and dropped the other end over a limb for Frankenberger to grab. Somehow, though, he had left too much slack in the rope. When Sanders began lowering the unconscious cat, "the panther free-fell with the rope slipping and grabbing around her hind feet," Belden wrote.

As they lowered the cat the rest of the way down, "blood was dripping from her nose," he wrote. Once the cat was on the ground, they discovered "she was no longer breathing and there was no pulse."

Both Frankenberger and Jansen jumped in and tried reviving the panther with mouth-to-mouth resuscitation, just like a lifeguard with a drowning victim. They huffed and puffed, but to no avail.

"She was dead," Belden wrote.

I asked Jansen once about her attempt to get a dying panther to live.

"Oh, that was so long ago!" she said. "It was just sort of a desperate attempt to see if I could get the breath back in the animal."

The thing to remember about that event, she said, was that they had never dealt with a situation like it. Nobody knew what to do: "Every one of us were inexperienced."

Their leader, Belden, felt miserable. He had seen one dead female panther from the Fak, and now his team had killed the second one. He was sure it was all his fault. He was the one who had filled the dart with the anesthetic. He had used the exact same dosage that they had used when capturing FP3 the year before. What had gone wrong?

He slung the dead cat up onto his shoulders and began walking out of the swamp, leading his dejected team toward a reckoning.

"At that point," he said years later, "I felt like I was carrying the whole subspecies on my shoulders. If the panther went extinct, it would be my fault. For all we knew, those eight panthers were all that was left, and I had just killed one."

When Belden emerged from the swamp, he deposited the carcass in the back of a truck. Then Frankenberger drove it north to the University of Florida, where a veterinarian would examine it to figure out why FP3 died.

Meanwhile, Belden went to the office and made his report to his superiors.

His bosses were not happy. The assistant director of the agency noted to a reporter that losing one animal out of eight was "on the order of a fifteen percent loss. While that may be acceptable for some animals, I don't think that's acceptable for these animals."

Belden's glowing public image quickly lost its luster. He and his panther capture program became a target for critics who accused them of harassing those poor cats for no good reason. The *Miami Herald* ran an editorial that called the death of FP3 "an outrage," and argued that it was time to just leave those pathetic panthers alone. Didn't the animals have enough to put up with? Why chase them with dogs and shoot them with darts if they were so close to extinction anyway? Just let them go, for Pete's sake!

Baudy, of course, was ready to lead the charge against Belden, pushing once again for captive breeding instead of scientific investigation. But the most prominent voice decrying the death of FP3 came from someone with even greater influence: Everglades doyenne Marjory Stoneman Douglas.

To her, putting a collar on any cat was "stupid and reprehensible," according to John Rothchild, a Miami journalist who helped her write her autobiography. She was sure she knew all about panther behavior from her experience with domestic cats, particularly one named Jimmy that slept atop her books.

"If Jimmy hates collars, so would any other cat," she told Rothchild. "Cats are bothered by collars, especially the roaming-around kind. A collar can get stuck on a branch and strangle a cat."

In response to the uproar, the game commission suspended Belden's panther-capture program. His bosses announced they would be forming a panel of experts—yet another panel—to review everything that Belden had been doing and make sure it was proper.

The review didn't take long to find that everything Belden's team did was proper, allowing the capture team to head back into the woods. But then Belden got in hot water with his bosses again.

The *Miami Herald* ran a front-page story on the panther program. In an interview, Belden declined to comment on whether one way to save the panther for future generations was to limit how many deer that hunters could kill. But the reporter noted that in the official Panther Recovery Plan that he'd written was a recommendation that areas where the panthers lived be closed to hunting "until such time as we know more about panther management and how to prevent people from shooting them." The plan specifically called for closing the Fak to all hunting.

Florida's game commission, which sold hunting licenses, depended on the financial and political support of hunters. The people the governor appointed to serve on the game commission were usually hunters themselves. By suggesting that deer hunting might threaten panthers, Belden had violated a major taboo.

The head of the game commission told the *Herald* that he strongly disagreed with Belden, saying "the evidence does not support at this point closing any of the area to hunting." Any attempt to close off hunting in panther habitat would create an angry backlash against the animal, he warned.

"While the vast majority of hunters certainly would not take any action, a few may be so resentful it could cause death to the panthers," he said. "It's not worth the risk."

Belden's bosses removed him as head of the capture team and ordered him to stay out of South Florida. He was no longer allowed anywhere south of State Road 70, a highway that runs across Central Florida. He was, in effect, banned from Pantherland.

Even two years later he was still under a cloud. On an evaluation, his boss wrote, "One important concept in regard to wildlife management is that politics and wildlife management cannot be separated. Chris needs to accept that fact." Another superior wrote, "Mr. Belden does not seem to have a good understanding of the relationship and responsibility of his work to the agency program of which he's a part."

"After I left South Florida I fell into a deep depression," he said years later. "My marriage almost fell apart." Then he read Norman Vincent Peale's book *The Power of Positive Thinking* and realized that "all of those things had happened for a purpose. The people, the events, the panther, were all instruments directing my life." At that point, he said, he bowed his head and accepted Jesus Christ into his heart.

You could say the loss of FP3 led to Chris Belden being saved. But it had a much broader impact on the future of all panthers.

The University of Florida veterinarian's report, when it was completed, didn't specify what went wrong with the capture of FP3. It just said, "The cause of death cannot be ascertained based on tissue findings. It is likely that it is related to an untoward effect of the anesthesia."

But the official game commission verdict was that the dart had hit the cat's femoral artery, delivering its dose of drugs far too quickly. The cat was dead before it fell to the ground.

Before reinstating the capture program, the game commission officials decided to make a major change in the makeup of the team. Instead of just keeping it as a hunter and several biologists, they would add someone new to the mix—someone whose sole responsibility was to ensure the safety of the panther itself.

They would add a veterinarian.

And that's how a woman from the Pacific Northwest wound up discovering the greatest threat to Florida's panthers.

CHAPTER SIX

THE TURBO-VET

To replace the Tennessee-born Chris Belden, the game commission promoted another slow-talking Southerner, Mississippi native John Roboski. The agency could have promoted one of the people on the capture team who had experience, but no. The job went to a guy who had never been out in the swamps chasing cats.

Roboski needed the job. He'd been working toward a doctorate at Auburn University but was deep in debt. He and his wife had two children, so he craved a steady paycheck. He had never expressed an interest in panthers before, which led to questions about his qualifications. One of the capture team members even asked him, "How did you get picked for this?"

"I have a reputation for being able to get things done," Roboski replied.

Twenty-five years later, he could still vividly remember the first panther he saw in the wild: "We chased this old female down. I can still see her standing way up in a cypress tree. She was so gaunt, she really looked thin. We left her in the tree."

By then, the team had begun carrying a net to catch any panthers that fell out of the trees after being darted. But the net wasn't foolproof. It would sag when a panther landed in it, to the point where an injury might occur.

Around this time, Roboski hired a big, jovial Georgia-born biologist named Walt McCown to work with the team. McCown, the son of an accountant and a librarian, had fallen in love with biology as a kid while wandering the woods behind his suburban home. He was fresh out of grad school when he was hired. The minute Roboski mentioned panthers, "he had me," McCown recalled. "Big, fierce things always intrigued me."

During capture season, they would start work around 4:30 a.m., he said. Then they'd be on the go for hours on end, cruising along in swamp buggies, searching for any panther sign on the muddy trails. They'd work until the sun dropped below the horizon and they could barely see to find their way back home.

As the new guy, McCown drew the duty of climbing the trees and lowering down any tranquilized panthers that didn't fall out on their own. The fifth time he had to clamber up a tree like a crazed lineman on a power pole, the panther he was after suddenly jerked awake and kicked itself free of the tree limb it was on. As it tumbled down through the branches, headed for the ground, McCown told me, "I watched this panther falling and I watched my career falling too."

The crew down below was ready with the net, but they were standing in three feet of water. The panther hit the net but the speed of its descent made the net dip into the water, splashing water all around. The panther was uninjured, but it could have easily drowned or broken bones in the fall, McCown said.

That's when he and Roboski agreed that they needed to do

something about those rough landings. They sat around brainstorming ideas and finally came up with an inflatable "crashpad" made from trash bags that were sewn together (later versions were made from sailcloth and parachute cord). A panther (or a panther biologist) could land on it safely just like a stunt man falling off a building onto an inflated cushion. The crashpad became a part of the standard equipment that they hauled into the swamps while tracking the cats. They were already toting so much gear, Roboski said, that "we looked like one of those earliest Darkest Africa expeditions."

But the most important addition to the team wasn't its cocky new leader, the bear-sized tree-climber or the new piece of equipment. It was the woman who came to be known as the Turbo-Vet.

Her name was Melody Roelke. She had curly brown hair that fell to her shoulders, intense brown eyes and an inability to sit still. She was prone to speaking her mind. She was the capture team member who dared to ask Roboski how he'd gotten his job—even though she was brand-new herself.

She grew up on a farm in Oregon, but her parents weren't farmers. They were artists from California who had no earthly idea how to take care of the animals they owned. For instance, they kept their lambs inside the house. Roelke grew frustrated at not knowing how to care for them properly and began reading up on it. That's what led her to become a veterinarian.

Roelke married young, and somehow the marriage survived the grueling rigors of her time at veterinary school. Then she got a job at a clinic in Roseburg, Oregon, that was just down the road from a place called Wildlife Safari, a foundation trying to breed cheetahs in captivity. After a year at the clinic she went to work for Wildlife Safari. Her first day on the job, she helped deliver a cheetah cub.

"It was my job to hand-rear it," she recalled. "I took it home and it slept in our bed." Perhaps, she said, "that was the beginning of the end of our marriage."

At Wildlife Safari she learned to work with all kinds of big animals—not just cheetahs but also tigers, wildebeests, even elephants. She learned to shoot a tranquilizer dart and she learned all about captive breeding. Every day when she drove to work, she told herself, "I'm the luckiest person in the world."

Then her luck changed.

In 1982, Wildlife Safari had forty cheetahs. It often bought, sold or traded animals with other zoos and wildlife facilities. These days such trades require keeping the animals in quarantine to ensure they don't have diseases, but back then such a precaution was rare. One day a male and female cheetah arrived from another facility. They fell ill with a fever and died.

Then the same disease swept through the rest of the cheetah population, killing half the adults and three-fourths of the juveniles. The speed with which the virus moved through the cheetahs, and the fact that it killed so many, indicated to Roelke that the cheetahs lacked the genetic diversity to fight off the virus. Their genes were so similar, Roelke told me, that it was like they were all the same cat. When one fell ill, they nearly all fell ill.

Tests by some visiting scientists had shown that the genetic problem was likely among the Wildlife Safari cheetahs. Now here was proof of the danger of a lack of diversity.

Wildlife Safari had lined up a sale of some of the remaining cheetahs to another facility. Roelke, fearing they might spread the disease to other breeding populations, told the zoo director about the problem.

"I couldn't keep my mouth shut," Roelke said. "The next thing I knew I was out of work."

Fortunately, she saw an ad for another job: a wildlife medicine residency at the University of Florida. She took it even though it meant a pay cut. Then, after the death of FP3, state game officials asked her to join the capture team chasing panthers in South Florida. She would be in charge of all aspects of the panthers' medical exam, starting with the tranquilizer and continuing until the cat woke up and took off. Her job was to make sure nothing like the FP3 disaster ever happened again.

They gave her one rule to follow.

"The edict that was given to me as the vet for the team was, 'Don't hurt anybody,'" she said.

Getting Roelke to talk to me about her time spent working with the panthers wasn't easy. She had moved on, mentally and physically. She had also moved around—to Africa, among other places—and she'd remarried and had a child.

Yet despite all the years that had passed since her panther work, I could still hear the passion burning in her voice. I could also hear traces of the pain and frustration she had felt.

The panther capture team had its own style, its own vibe, one that set it apart whenever its members encountered anyone from outside their circle. In their uniform shirts, in their constant conversations about the mechanics of catching cats, in their musky-smelling post-capture odor, they did not resemble the other denizens of South Florida.

This was particularly true in a little town just south of the Fak known as Everglades City.

The town of about five hundred bragged that it was "Florida's Last Frontier," but the residents weren't cowboys. Virtually every able-bodied man in town had the knee-high white boots and burly arms that marked them as professional crabbers. They knew their way around all the clam beds and oyster bars of the Ten Thousand Islands, one of the most extensive mangrove estuaries in the world.

Whenever the capture team was around, the crabbers made it clear they weren't welcome.

"The local people down around Everglades City weren't particularly fond of what we were doing," Roboski told me. "Nothing threatening, but we'd get some comments when we'd walk in this little eating joint called Jane's... A lot of us didn't look like we fit in down there. We looked like a bunch of college professors or guys in uniforms."

What the capture team members didn't realize at the time was that all those clannish, hard-eyed crabbers were distrustful of government employees for one simple reason: they were running a massive drug-smuggling operation.

Between 1983 and 1990, narcotics detectives busted some three hundred people in the greater Everglades City area for smuggling marijuana through the Ten Thousand Islands. Some got popped for drugs, others for evading taxes on the hundreds of thousands of dollars in profits they raked in. Not everyone involved in sneaking in "square grouper" got caught. Even today there are rumors of strongboxes full of cash buried in backyards.

The smugglers were more than just suspicious of government employees. They also blamed the government for forcing them into smuggling. They contended they had been pushed into a life of crime because the National Park Service banned all commercial fishing around the edges of Everglades National Park, which had once been their prime crabbing grounds.

The panther capture team members had no one to guide them in dealing with the locals or negotiating socially awkward situations. They were pretty much on their own. The nearest boss was in another town across the state. Even though nobody was checking up on them, though, they didn't slack off. They all busted their butts running through the wilderness, chasing after panthers through mud and thorns and thickets.

"There were times when we were literally up for days at a time," Roboski said.

If they did get any sleep, it didn't last long. They'd be guzzling coffee at 3 a.m., "with cobwebbed heads and bodies that moved by habit through the dark," one account of a 1984 capture reported. They'd climb into trucks that were hitched to trailers carrying off-road swamp buggies, then head out to the Fak or some other spot where they could disembark in the predawn darkness. Then they'd back the buggies down a ramp, load up and head out, bouncing past the ghostly cypress trees as the sun rose, slowly lighting up their way.

If they got word that McBride's dogs had treed a cat, Roboski would rise up, holding a telemetry antenna in one hand like the Statue of Liberty raising her torch, trying to pick up a signal from the one dog wearing a radio collar. Then they'd all take off in that direction, trying to catch up.

Often what they found at the end of their soggy trail was a decrepit old cat so skinny its bones looked ready to poke through the skin. Roboski, McBride and Roelke would slosh around the base of the tree in ankle-deep water, debating whether to go ahead with the capture. Each had a veto. Sometimes, remembering the furor over FP3, they knew their best move was just to walk away.

Sometimes they'd go ahead with the capture, and dart the cat. One of the biologists, usually McCown, would have to climb the tree and throw a rope around the doped-up panther and lower it to the crash bag. Then Roelke would swoop in and examine the cat, taking samples galore, before it could wake up and wander off.

Catching cats was tough, dirty work. Spend the day chasing them through the swamp and the crew would emerge coated in mud and smelling like a panther—a wild, funky scent that would cling to their skin and hair and clothes for hours afterward. But the adrenaline rush made the work during the other months of the year seem tame by comparison.

"I lived for the capture season," McCown said. "It was challenging physically, intellectually and sometimes emotionally."

He was particularly enamored with McBride, treasuring the time he got to spend with the legendary tracker. McCown compared it to being a rookie ball player sharing a dugout with Ted Williams. He came to admire McBride as a man who knew how to chase down wild animals, and yet was also widely read in both science and literature. A lot of what McCown learned from McBride, he had to piece together on his own because McBride was so notoriously closemouthed.

"I learned a lot just by shutting up and watching him," McCown told me.

One of the things he learned was persistence. "He was out there every day, every day, every day, even in the pouring rain, even when he was so sick he was throwing up over the side of the buggy, he would still be out there, every day," McCown said. "We'd be wading through the water in the rain and the dogs looking up at you like you're nuts, and he'd still be out there."

The lesson in that? "You can't determine the outcome of the day, but you can determine the effort," McCown said.

Each time they went after a panther was different, McCown said. A thousand things could go wrong, "and if you could think of a hundred of them you were a genius," he said. For instance, there was the time one woozy panther clawed a chunk out of a biologist's backside.

More often, they'd go out and find nothing at all.

"It's amazing the amount of effort and work that went into just capturing a single animal," Roelke told me. "By the end of my first year we had captured just nine. We would go six weeks without catching any."

They only chased the cats in the cooler months, for the panthers' own safety. The rest of the year, they looked at other aspects of panther life. For instance, they would check the health of raccoons, bobcats and other animals that the panthers would eat if they had no deer available. Or they would plot out the spots where the panthers frequently crossed highways that sliced through the Big Cypress. That led the state to change the speed limit on US 41 and Alligator Alley, lowering it from fifty-five to forty-five miles per hour between dusk and dawn, when the panthers prowl. That slight reduction looked good on paper but did little to stop cars and trucks from flattening the occasional cat.

For the capture team, the long hours and the isolation bred an atmosphere where everyone—except the perpetually reticent McBride, of course—cracked jokes or pulled pranks.

There was the time some other scientists visited to do a study on white-tailed deer. They set up spotlights in some trees to help them spot the deer at night. The capture team was helping out. The restless Roelke accidentally sat on a tangle of wires for the spotlights. Someone had apparently peeled back the insulation right in the spot where she planted her keister.

"The lights went out and she's hopping around even more" from the shock, Roboski said, chuckling at the memory. "That's how she developed the name 'Sparky.'" Later, she picked up another nickname tied to her constant blur of movement: the Turbo-Vet.

Before one excursion into the swamp with a visiting writer, two of the burly male biologists were trying to spook him with stories about all the gigantic venomous reptiles they would encounter.

"Good day for cottonmouths," warned McCown in an exaggerated redneck accent, fondling the machete he often carried while on a hunt. "I've seen twenty or thirty of those snakes in a half hour. So big, all they'll do is fall on you and they'll kill ya."

McCown came up with some of the cleverer pranks, such as attaching a radio collar to a teddy bear and hiding it near another biologist's house.

"We were like a small combat unit or a baseball team that travels together," he said. They had to crack jokes and pull pranks to relieve the tension, he explained.

Some of the tension existed because Roelke was different from the other capture team members. They were all white Southern men, used to talking and acting in a certain way—unlike Roelke, who grew up a California girl from an artsy background. The men had been trained as wildlife biologists, and so their approach to dealing with animals—as a group of study subjects—differed from hers, as a veterinarian concerned with the health of individual animals. Perhaps the biggest difference was that none of the guys had the amount of experience that Roelke had in dealing with big cats.

"She knew a lot of stuff that the rest of us had never even read about," McCown said. She wasn't shy about sharing that knowledge, and did not always do it in the most diplomatic way. Sometimes, McCown said, "it seemed like there were more experts than there were panthers, and they were more than willing to share their opinion about how you should do your job." He admitted that he was guilty of doing a similar sort of kibitzing too.

Some of the pranks had a darker edge, suggesting a macho resentment. Roelke once found someone had peed on her car's tires while it was parked. Another time she was doing an autopsy on a white-tailed deer and when she cut it open, she discovered someone had stuffed a dead snake down its gullet—a venomous water moccasin.

Amid all the pranks and jokes and nicknaming, though, Roelke was pursuing something serious. First she tackled the mystery of FP3.

"When I first started," she told me, "I was reviewing a tape of an old *American Sportsman* show, because they were there for the first capture of FP3. So I'm watching this animal on the ground, and it's barely breathing. Me, looking at the animal, I can see she's very, very deep in terms of how the anesthetic affected her."

She knew then the dosage was too high: "Then the next year they capture her again and use the same dose. She never left the tree alive. That dose of the drug was too much for her."

She didn't blame Belden for what happened, though. Most wildlife agencies of the time trusted their biologists to handle the tranquilizer dart duties instead of sending trained vets out, she explained. Sometimes animals died from the wrong dosage, she said, "but it was just a part of doing business. But if you've got a species where there's only thirty left, and you kill one, that's bad."

She said the game commission "left Chris out to dry. It was not his fault."

That wasn't the only mystery she wanted to solve. She was also looking for signs that the panthers were having the same problem as the cheetahs in Oregon: "I came on board already looking for evidence of inbreeding."

She found it pretty fast.

Let's talk about kinks.

No, not the "whip me, beat me, hurt me, make me write bad checks" kind of kinks. I'm talking about the kinks in the tails of the panthers. When Chris Belden pulled together data on what made the Florida panther subspecies different from other pumas, he noted three characteristics:

1. A kink in the end of the tail that bent it at a dramatic ninety degree angle.

2. A whorled cowlick in the fur in the middle of its back.

3. White flecks scattered around its neck.

Belden listed these as primary identifying points for Florida panthers, because every panther he and his team caught had those same three characteristics.

But remember Charles Cory, the playboy who first identified the panther as a separate subspecies? Cory's description of the panther he shot made no mention of those three characteristics.

To Belden, that was because his description was vague. To Roelke, though, that was a flag that was as red as a stop sign.

Eventually the panther biologists figured out the white flecks were the result of ticks nibbling on panther flesh, so that one requirement was tossed out by Belden's successors. But they clung to the other two, the kinked tail and the cowlick.

The cowlick wasn't all that bothersome to the panthers. It's a benign pattern in the fur, not something dramatic. But a kink that bends a cat's tail at a ninety-degree angle so precise it could be used in a math textbook? That was wrong on the face of it. The five vertebrae that form the kink would not have bent that way naturally, Roelke decided.

"I knew those were markers of an underlying bottleneck" in their genetic makeup, she said. A bottleneck happens when the population of a species or subspecies drops so dramatically that what remains no longer has a diverse gene pool. She'd seen the same thing with the cheetahs.

To test her theory, she toted so much equipment out on the captures that Roboski joked that she could perform field surgery on any member of the team. Once they captured a panther, she collected samples of its skin, its blood and its poop. With every capture, she would put some of her samples into a Federal Express package and ship them to a geneticist at the National Institutes of Health in Frederick, Maryland, named Stephen O'Brien. She had met him while checking what was wrong with the cheetahs, and now she turned to him again to determine if another big cat had the same problem.

Roelke was so intent on solving this mystery that when she took vacation time, she didn't leave the panther puzzle behind. Instead, she told me, "I would go to British Columbia, to Colorado, to Chile, and work with the biologists there. That way I was able to collect comparative samples."

But there was one set of pumas that she couldn't get her hands on, even though they were right next door to where she was working.

Everglades National Park had panthers roaming around, but park service officials didn't want them captured. They would not give the capture team permission to run around the park after their cats. They were afraid of another FP3 happening in the park, harming its reputation.

The park superintendent, in a letter to state officials, argued that the Everglades panthers were "the least disturbed (by man) of all the remaining population. I feel strongly that it is important to protect this undisturbed aspect as much as possible."

They allowed McBride to snoop around, without his dogs, to see whether he could find any signs of panthers. He estimated there might be five or six—in other words, about a quarter of all the panthers in Florida.

What no one realized at the time was that they were different from all the other panthers.

In June 1985, after two years of running the capture team, Roboski had had enough. He turned in his resignation.

"It got to the point where I had kind of figured out we needed more people working on the project," he explained. But the commission was spending $250,000 a year already and couldn't offer a dime more, its leader said. In 1983 the commission set up a fund to collect private contributions to pay for panther research. By early 1985, the fund had raised a grand total of $120.

Meanwhile, Roboski said, the long hours took their toll on his health and his marriage. "I had a young family, and I could see that my work was having an effect on that."

After he quit, though, months went by with no one in charge of the capture team. They struggled on as best they could, leaderless.

Finally, in December 1985, game commission officials promoted another biologist to take charge. Once again, they picked a man. Once again, they chose someone who had zero prior experience in dealing with panthers.

But this time they picked a biologist who—unlike Roboski—came in with some very strong ideas about the panther program. When I interviewed Roboski about his time at the game commission, he had nothing but complimentary things to say about McBride, Roelke and the rest—except for one person.

When I asked Roboski if his successor discussed the panther program with him, maybe asked for some pointers or perspective that would be helpful, Roboski replied: "No, he did not." And that's all he would say.

CHAPTER SEVEN

THE NEW MR. PANTHER

The new capture team leader was David Maehr. He had a big smile, a big laugh and a head full of dark hair. He might seem easygoing unless someone disagreed with him. Then that person would find out Maehr wasn't one to back away from an argument.

"The man liked to argue, and the subject seldom mattered," one newspaper columnist who knew him noted. "Whatever your opinion, he tended to take the opposite side."

Belden and Roboski had both been laid-back leaders, whereas Maehr seemed more driven, more competitive, "a go-getter," recalled Walt McCown, who liked him a lot. Unlike Belden and Roboski, Maehr turned out to be a prolific writer. McCown said Maehr could "sit down in an afternoon with a legal pad and write an article and with very few edits get it published."

Maehr was so sure of himself that he wasn't shy about dis-
agreeing with people with far more experience with panthers,
like Deb Jansen or Melody Roelke. He would even second-guess
Roy McBride. He didn't pay much attention to edicts from his
superiors at the game commission, either.

"He thought he was God's gift to the world," Roelke told
me. "No matter who came up with an idea, it was his. I'd been
on the project for about four years when he showed up. He had
absolutely *no* interest in anything I had learned."

Maehr's first trip out to catch a panther was also his first day
on the job. What happened that day gave a hint of what was
to come.

They were going into the Fak to find a panther that already
had a collar. They needed to replace the batteries before the signal faded. The team took along a writer who was interested in
seeing how panthers are caught. When they got far enough into
the swamp that they had to leave their swamp buggies behind,
Maehr hung a radio collar on a tree branch. At the end of the
day, he explained, they could follow its electronic blips back to
the buggies like bread crumbs in a fairy tale.

McBride's dogs treed their quarry after a short chase. Maehr,
because he was the man in charge, reached for the tranquilizer
gun to bring the cat down. Later, Maehr would call this an in-
advertent breach of capture team etiquette. He wrote that he'd
learned afterward that shooting the tranquilizer dart was usually McBride's job.

The cat they had captured was a female that seemed "sick,
scrawny, and scarred," the writer noted. The panther was between nine and eleven years old, with cuts under one eye and
on the inside of one leg. Her ribs rippled under the fur.

"She's in bad shape," Roelke announced, taking charge of
the medical exam. "But, still, she looks better than last year."

Roelke was dressed for the day in torn jeans, sneakers and a thermal underwear top. She explained that in the Fak, the panthers all had low body weights. They were all anemic.

"Points to some sort of nutritional problem," she said.

As Roelke took all her samples, another member of the team bolted on a new collar with fresh batteries. It also had reflective panels designed to make the panther more visible to cars and trucks when it crossed the highway. Then they set up a little tent over the panther, a tent that Roelke herself had designed for when panthers were recovering from being darted.

They left the panther in the tent while it awakened. Roelke kept going back in to check on the cat's progress. Each time, the cat would raise its head and stare at her and make sounds like it was drunk. Once, as it regained its senses, it slashed at her and left a bloody scratch at her wrist.

"Doesn't bother me," Roelke told the writer.

Finally, with the sun going down and the Fak fading into darkness, it was time. Roelke pulled the rope attached to the tent to open the front door. Then she shook the canvas sides to persuade the panther to scamper out. Recovered, the panther bolted (as the writer put it) "in one extravagant, explosive charge."

Then it was time for the team to head back to their swamp buggies through the deepening twilight. The sky was lit by a full moon but the Fak was full of deep shadows. Maehr took the lead, sloshing through the dark water, following the signals from the collar he'd hung up. They staggered along through the uneven terrain for more than an hour, longer than they had spent hiking in. Yet still there was no sign of where they had parked the buggies. The writer wrote later that he began to wonder if Maehr had gotten them lost. He began worrying that soon they would become gator food.

Suddenly, without a word, one of the other biologists—the only Florida native in the group—broke off from the pack and veered in a different direction. After a moment's hesitation, the others followed. In ten minutes they were climbing into the buggies.

Eleven years later, Maehr wrote a book about Florida panthers. In it he told the story of his first day on the job and his first panther capture.

He didn't mention anything about how he had led everyone the wrong way.

Despite his outward confidence in his abilities, even Maehr acknowledged that he had no background in chasing wild pumas.

Nothing he'd learned at Ohio State, where he got a degree in wildlife management, or the University of Florida, where he got his master's, had equipped him for what he was now doing.

None of his prior work experience was much help either. His first job out of college was working as a mining inspector for Ohio's environmental agency. Six months later, he changed sides, taking a job as "environmental supervisor" with one of the coal mining companies he had been in charge of inspecting.

At the University of Florida, his master's thesis was on bird abundance at closed phosphate mines. When he landed a job with the Florida game commission, he was hired to study fur-bearing mammals, such as bears. Bears, needless to say, are not like panthers, except that they are fur-bearing mammals. Nevertheless, each time Maehr shifted to a new species, he adapted.

His game commission bosses liked the job he was doing with the bear research. They offered him a promotion to a desk job. He turned it down, explaining that he didn't want to give up fieldwork. They offered him the panther capture team leadership position. He turned that down too, at first. He was convinced that the capture team was a joke, chasing bedraggled old cats around, documenting the extinction of a once-proud species. He'd rather stick with bears.

Besides, some other game commission employees warned him against it. They told him about "the political nature of the work, dishonesty among supervisors, severe working conditions, and unpredictable co-workers," Maehr wrote later.

But finally his bosses convinced him to move to South Florida and take the panther job.

"I figured if I was going to preside over an extinction event, it might as well be in an interesting place," Maehr wrote.

To him, though, the job was more than merely stepping into Roboski's shoes. He wasn't just leading the capture team—he was saving it. The months without a leader had taken their toll on the team's work, according to Maehr.

The number of panthers wearing radio collars had dropped to just two, the monitoring and field activities had nearly hit a standstill and nobody was looking at what the panthers might be doing on privately owned land, he wrote in his book.

The team also hadn't gone up in the air to fly around and check the radio signals in quite some time, Maehr noted. Biologists who didn't mind climbing a tree to fetch down a wild panther balked at going up in a tiny Cessna and flying low over a wilderness landscape. Once you've hurled into a barf bag in a small plane, you never forget that smell.

Maehr went out and hired another Southern boy, this one a folksy, moon-faced North Carolina native named Darrell Land. Maehr assigned him to do the flights three times a week.

More than thirty years later, with his mop of brown hair going gray, Land was still climbing into a plane three days a week to fly around and record the radio signals. I rode with him one fall morning in 2018, zooming over the Big Cypress at five hundred feet, only the tops of the wild palms visible above the morning mist. They seemed so close that I could almost touch them.

Land, listening for the radio pings in his headset, would signal the pilot with his left hand: a tilt to the right meant circle to the right (we never circled to the left). Pointing down meant drop down to get closer to the signal. Hand flat meant level off. When the fog burned off, we could see a vast stretch of green, dotted with snowy white figures. Those were egrets feeding on whatever they could find in the water. We never saw the panthers, but the signals picked up by the plane's antenna said they were there.

When Maehr hired him as a panther biologist, Land had just finished his master's degree at the University of Florida. He had no experience with mammals of any kind. He was studying woodpecker nesting habits and working at a state park. He was green as grass.

"Did I even know Florida panthers were in Florida? I don't think I did," he told me. "Cats do like birds, so I guess that was the connection."

Land had to learn the job while doing it. In addition to flying over Big Cypress and the Fak, he helped Maehr and the other two biologists with panther captures, which he dubbed "collar and foller," because they would collar the cats and then follow them around. He also assisted with studies of deer and bobcats to see how they interacted with the panthers.

But even a novice like Land could see they were missing out on key information about the panthers because they couldn't get into one important piece of habitat: Everglades National Park. The park superintendent's opposition was like something from the Old Testament, he said: "Thou shalt never catch a panther here."

The capture team had another problem, one that Maehr was well qualified to tackle. Ever since the furor over FP3's death, they had fallen out of favor with the public.

Hardly a month went by without a Florida newspaper running a letter to the editor accusing the team of cruelty for chasing the cats around to collar them, Maehr wrote in his book.

Without a favorable public image, the team couldn't get a boost in financial support from the game commission. It was another reason why the capture team job had initially struck Maehr as pitiable and distasteful.

Maehr set out to change that. He invited lots of journalists and government bigwigs to go along on panther captures or to ride along on the aerial radio checks. He traveled the state giving talks to civic groups. He wrote columns and op-ed pieces about how important their work was. He published scientific papers about all the data they were collecting. To him, Belden had failed the panthers by not publishing every scrap of information the team collected in its first years. Maehr would not make that mistake.

Maehr's promotional efforts slowly restored the shine to the panther hunters. Among the people he befriended: Carl Hiaasen, the popular *Miami Herald* columnist and wacky Florida crime novelist. But even Hiaasen knew Maehr could be controversial.

Maehr "ticked off some people," Hiaasen wrote. "When reporters asked a question, he'd answer bluntly and with little regard for what his bosses might think. He was perpetually exasperated by the lead-footed bureaucracy of wildlife management, and he'd say so. Dave didn't care about diplomacy. He cared only about saving the panther."

But that wasn't the way his bosses and some of his colleagues saw it. To them, Maehr was focused on promoting himself, not promoting panther research. They believed that getting research published with his name on it was his top priority—not trying to use that research to benefit panthers.

"He was so eager to be 'Mr. Florida Panther' that he would take a little bit of data and publish it," said Deb Jansen.

Maehr's determination to publish publish publish "has caused divisiveness within the research team you administer as well as complaints from other staff," Maehr's boss wrote in one of his evaluations.

The irony is that the person doing the really crucial panther research wasn't Maehr. It was the Turbo-Vet.

★ ★ ★

About the time Maehr started leading the capture team, Roelke began carrying a new piece of equipment out into the field. The instrument is called an electro-ejaculator, and you should be glad they don't often use it on humans.

This is the down-and-dirty side of biology that you never hear about in high school. Veteran biologists employ a host of tools and techniques for collecting samples from their study subjects. Trust me when I say that a lot of them are not exactly pleasant to contemplate.

Without getting into details, let me just say that, as with many UFO abduction stories, the electro-ejaculator involves the use of an anal probe. In this case, it's designed to help biologists collect multiple samples of semen.

Roelke, mindful of what had happened to her Portland cheetahs, had been wondering about what kind of shape the panthers' spunk might be in. After all, the animals the capture team had knocked out were physically decrepit and often malnourished. Once she examined what the electro-ejaculator produced, she didn't like what she saw there either.

"Right away it became extremely apparent that the Florida panther was in trouble," she told me. "They had maybe a quarter of the diversity of other panthers. Their sperm quality was the worst seen in any male I had ever examined... It just looked absolutely horrific."

Low sperm quality meant the panthers would have a hard time reproducing. The lack of diversity meant that even if they did reproduce, they might be creating genetic defects that could doom the subspecies.

She used a field microscope to show Maehr what was wrong, putting the pearly drops onto a slide for him to examine. He wrote later that he spotted "a few slowly jittering sperm cells seeking an egg to fertilize." At first he conceded that this was alarming.

But then Maehr dug up some research from Oregon that showed that, among pumas out West, sperm viability varied by season. The little swimmers did better in some parts of the year than in others. Or maybe, he theorized, their testosterone levels were controlled by the proximity of female panthers. If the male got near a female, then those lazy little spermatozoa would go from wimpy dog paddlers to Olympic-class racers just to get to the female's eggs.

Either way, the super-confident Maehr convinced himself that this was nothing to worry about, and waved away Roelke's warnings.

Maehr's main concern was habitat. Every day when he was driving to and from work in Naples, he saw more and more construction going on. Concrete trucks and dump trucks full of fill dirt rolled across the landscape, following the lines of bull-dozers cutting through palmetto prairies and cypress swamps. Every day they made the habitat for this wide-ranging predator a little smaller. Every day they chased even more of its prey away. That, to him, seemed like the real threat, not some dewy squiggles on a slide.

But then the team finally got permission to catch cats in the Everglades, and suddenly everything changed.

CHAPTER EIGHT

MEDICINE MAN

In the late fall of 1986, after a tremendous amount of prodding by federal biologists at Everglades National Park, the park's superintendent relented. The panther capture team would at last be allowed into Florida's most famous national park.

For more than a month, they scouted around on the pinnacle rock pinelands and sawgrass prairies for cats without finding any. The search was not an easy one. In his book, Maehr called the Everglades terrain harsh and unforgiving.

Failure just made McBride more determined. Before dawn, while the rest of the sleepy-eyed crew was sipping coffee and wolfing down pastries, McBride would be out working his dogs, searching for a scent or a sign. Finally, in early December, Mc-Bride's dogs treed the first panther ever to be captured in the park.

By the time Maehr and the others arrived on the scene, the

horizon had begun to glow, silhouetting their quarry against the gradually lightening sky. As the sun rose, though, they saw something none of them had seen before: a Florida panther with a tail as straight as a stick.

Once they darted it and brought it down on the crash bag, they could see that this was no trick of the light. This cat had no kink.

Oh, how I wish someone had taken a photo of the looks on their faces! Science is all about making assumptions that are proven wrong and then starting over with new assumptions. But this one, this belief that all panthers had kinks in their tails, was so fundamental to the job that they were doing that I imagine everyone on the ground taking a big, shaky gulp of air as they readjusted their expectations.

Everyone but Roelke, that is. She'd known it all along.

The straight tail wasn't the only difference from the other panthers they had caught. The Everglades cat's fur was lusher and softer, with no whorl. Also, it seemed quite healthy. This cat was apparently eating better than those in the Fak and Big Cypress.

In the next three months the team caught two more Everglades panthers with straight tails, showing that that first one was no fluke. By then Roelke had determined that the Everglades cats also had a subtle genetic difference from the ones found in the Big Cypress and the Fak. But how could that be?

A search of the park's own records supplied the solution. The key lay with a couple of brothers living in a small town on the state's west coast, a place known as Bonita Springs.

Lester and Wilford "Bill" Piper started out as bootleggers in Detroit. They did quite well until they made a few too many enemies. At that point they decided to move to Florida for their health.

The brothers, as one historian told me, were "mountain men without a mountain," rough-hewn characters who could build anything they needed and were adept at dealing with wild animals. First they built a shack by the Imperial River in Bonita Springs when that town was only a wide spot in the road. Because Bill Piper enjoyed collecting reptiles, people often stopped by to see his latest acquisition. The show was impressive—and free.

In 1936, the brothers opened a makeshift zoo on the Tamiami Trail, the town's main thoroughfare, which also connected Miami and Tampa. For Tampa-bound tourists who had just driven across the Everglades, a stop in Bonita Springs offered a chance to grab a bite to eat and visit the Pipers' attraction. They called it Everglades Wonder Gardens, a place to marvel at the odd and unusual animals of the vast marsh.

The Pipers' top star then was Big Joe, billed as the largest North American crocodile ever found. Joe had been netted by a Key Largo fisherman, and in his prime measured fifteen feet long and weighed more than a thousand pounds. He lived to be 75, and then the Pipers stuffed and mounted him so he could continue drawing oohs and ahhs from the tourists.

Hollywood steered more customers to the Pipers after their bear, Tom, played the role of the wily Old Slewfoot in the Gregory Peck–Jane Wyman movie *The Yearling*. The Pipers ran national ads about Tom that helped put little Bonita Springs on the map for tourists.

When I visited the place in 2010, the admission had climbed to $15. After I forked over my cash, though, I stepped into something like a time machine. I was transported back to a pre-Disney Florida, when the state's two-lane highways were dotted with cheesy roadside attractions with names like "the Aquatarium" or "the Cypress Knee Museum."

Most of those places were bulldozed long ago, the victims of changing traffic patterns and changing tastes. But not Everglades Wonder Gardens, which was drawing 50,000 visitors a year while still maintaining that pre-Disney vibe. A winding walk along its shady concrete path took me past exhibits built of lumber and chicken wire, not steel or aluminum. The sun peeked through a canopy of banyans and fruit trees. The displays featured alligators galore, snarling crocodiles, lolling black bears and dignified flamingos. There was even a Florida panther, the one I mentioned before that constantly paced its enclosure, plotting its escape.

In 1986, around the time the Everglades panthers were first being captured, the Humane Society of the United States blasted the Everglades Wonder Gardens as a "freak show," rating it among the worst captive-wildlife attractions in the nation.

Yet the Everglades National Park records credited the Pipers as the saviors of the Florida panther in the park.

Here's what happened: At some point in the 1940s, the Pipers acquired a few panthers for their menagerie. Three times during the '50s and the '60s, Everglades National Park officials notified the Pipers that the park was bereft of big cats. At their request, the Pipers turned some of their cats loose in the park to replenish the wild supply.

But the Piper cats weren't all purebreds. Although the Pipers denied it, Roelke determined that one of those Piper cats had a non-Florida origin. She suspected a South American puma had somehow gotten into the mix, freshening up the gene pool. That would explain the straight tail and the smooth fur.

This discovery did not make her popular with her coworkers at the game commission. It raised too many questions. Mixed-breed animals didn't get protection from the Endangered Species Act or funding from the US Fish and Wildlife Service.

"People were scared," Roelke told me. "In no uncertain terms, I was told—out in the middle of the Big Cypress, miles away from anyone else—I was basically told that I didn't have to publish that data. It was not a pleasant situation."

Meanwhile, though, she wondered about the ramifications of the Piper cats. What did the original purebred panthers really look like? To find that answer, she sought the help of another woman, one who was an expert in navigating the past.

A lot of the people who flock to Gainesville on weekends are headed to The Swamp. It's not an actual marshland. It's Ben Hill Griffin Stadium, home of the Gators, the University of Florida's football team. But some people, the ones who could not care less about who gets bragging rights in the Southeastern Conference, skip The Swamp and instead head to the Florida Museum of Natural History.

The museum started in 1891 when a professor named Pickel spent his own money buying collections of minerals, fossils and human anatomy models to put on display. Other professors donated their personal collections too. By the 1930s the museum held half a million specimens. Now it fills three buildings. Its holdings include one of the world's largest collections of butterflies and moths.

On the day I visited, I skipped all the public displays—even the butterflies—and headed for the basement lair of Candace McCaffery and Laurie Wilkins. They worked deep in the bowels of the museum's old quarters in Dickinson Hall, across the street from the campus police headquarters. The hallway outside the entrance to their domain was lined with unopened boxes of African tribal artifacts confiscated from an illegal trader and donated by the authorities.

In the warehouse-sized room where the two women were working was a weird menagerie of bobcat skeletons, whale bones and stuffed platypuses. I saw a big lumpy package covered in packing tape, sitting in the middle of one aisle. It turned out to be a manatee carcass they had just received in the mail. Far in the back, next to the wall, was a baleen whale's massive jawbone.

The main thing I wanted to see, though, was their panther collection.

McCaffery was the museum's mammalogy collection manager. She had reddish hair going gray and she wore glasses, a fleece jacket, a red flannel shirt and a pair of faded jeans. She was delighted to take me around the collection.

The first thing she showed me was a row of tall white steel cabinets. She opened the doors and, to my surprise, they contained dozens of panther pelts. They hung there in rows just as if they were in Cruella de Vil's coat closet. I reached out to touch them, stroking the soft fur. Each pelt terminated in a pair of clawless, boneless paws, big and heavy and black.

"Each one is assigned a number in our database," she explained. "We have thirty-nine fields of information for each specimen. Since we have so many, we try to organize them by number. We use steel cases to keep potential insect problems out."

The only one that's not in their collection, she told me, is FP3, the one that wound up stuffed and on display in the museum in Tallahassee. McCaffery said she did not know why that one cat was treated differently from the others. She had never located any paperwork that explained the diversion. Was it supposed to be evidence of wrongdoing? An object lesson? A memorial to the whole subspecies as it spiraled down the drain? Perhaps someone in Tallahassee thought it would be the last one they'd ever see. She couldn't say.

And then we got around to the bones.

The museum had box upon box of panther bones sitting on six-foot-high steel shelving and stretching out so far it reminded me of the warehouse at the end of *Raiders of the Lost Ark*. The boxes held specimens dating back to the 1940s. McCaffery let me peek inside one of the boxes. It contained long leg and thigh bones, flat white shoulder blades and, in little plastic baggies, a collection of tiny bones from the paws, as well as the claws. The skull was smooth like ivory, the teeth still looking very sharp.

Every time a panther dies in Florida, its carcass is dissected by a veterinarian to determine the cause of death. Then the carcass goes to the museum.

"I skin them and clean them," McCaffery said, which struck me then and now as a remarkable statement, although she did not think so. "Then we have a dermestid beetle colony that finishes the job."

The dermestid beetles are sometimes known as "flesh-eating beetles" or "skin beetles." The museum keeps them in an enclosure outside the museum, she said. They swarm over the panther carcass and pick all the bones clean of every last scrap of meat and gristle. After they're done, McCaffery washes and fumigates the remains, to make sure all the beetles are gone. If the beetles got into the museum, they'd eat everything in sight, she explained.

Once we'd finished looking at the bones, she took me over to meet Wilkins, who was technically retired but regularly showed up for work at the museum as if she were still on the payroll. Wilkins was a petite, birdlike woman, with a mop of dark hair streaked with silver. She wore a rough-looking poncho, robin's egg blue.

She was the woman Roelke had turned to for help in determining what was happening with the panthers' genetics. To answer her questions, Wilkins had trekked around the country to examine the coats of all the puma specimens at other museums and compare them.

"It was a labor of love," she told me with a faraway look in her eye. "I was trying to do something that had never been done before. I was trying to quantify *color*."

Rather than just eyeball each pelt and make a judgment call on each one's shade, she toted around a big contraption called a "spectrophotometer" that had been invented for use by the paint industry. Built by the Milton Roy Company in Rochester, New York, the "Color Scan" machine compared color samples and differentiated one shade from the other in a definitive way. To get one of these machines, she called up the distributor, and he donated a demonstration model. Today the machines are small and do their job in the blink of an eye. The prototype that Wilkins carried was bulky and hard to maneuver, and it was anything but quick at making its analysis.

"I had this big machine, and I drug that thing around," she said, smiling at the memory. "I worked in the cold room at the Smithsonian, on a broken leg—and at night." That was so the sound of the machinery wouldn't disturb any other researchers, she explained.

She even trekked to the Field Museum in Chicago to look at Charles Cory's original type specimen—the panther he shot and then measured and used as the model for the entire subspecies description.

"That was something," Wilkins recalled. "The Field Museum didn't know what they had." To her disappointment, Cory's pelt had been on display for so long it had faded. But the loss of color didn't change one of its distinctive characteristics, she said: "It had a very clear cowlick."

None of those specimens, of course, had a kink in its tail. That was clearly a recent development in panther evolution.

Wilkins also helped Roelke with her questions about why the Big Cypress and Fak cats seemed so malnourished compared to the ones in the Everglades.

"I examined so much panther scat that one day somebody in the parking lot called out, 'Hey, it's the Scat Lady!'" she said, laughing.

The conclusion: the Everglades cats had plenty of deer to eat because the park service allows no hunting there. In Big Cypress and the Fak, though, the hunters blasted away at the white-tails, cutting into the panthers' prey base, exactly as Chris Belden had feared.

Roelke railed at game commission officials that they were let-

ting the state animal starve. But then something happened that
made the other part of Wilkins's research more vital than ever.

Sometimes when panther carcasses show up at the natural history museum, the cause of death is still a mystery.

"We'd clean them and skin them and find prior injuries that
had healed," McCaffery told me. Most of them were killed by
being hit by cars, or by being attacked by other panthers.

Sometimes, though, the museum staff found something more
troubling.

"Some of them had been shot," McCaffery said. "We found
bullet holes in their heads."

Wilkins decided to do more than just look for holes. What she
found made the pro-hunting game commission uncomfortable.

"We borrowed a metal detector to see if there was any evidence, and found a bullet," Wilkins told me. "The panther had
been shot." But then, she said, "we found *another* bullet. I spoke
to the head of the game commission, told him about the metal
detector and what we found, and he said, 'Hunters are *not involved* in this in *any way.*'"

Sometimes, though, the identity of who shot a panther was
no mystery at all.

In October 1984, a deer hunter named Elmer Brooker was sitting in a tree stand fifteen feet off the ground in a wildlife management area near West Palm Beach when he spotted a tawny
cat passing by the tree. Brooker, a heavy equipment operator,
was what's known as a "primitive weapons enthusiast." He was
carrying a black-powder shotgun. He aimed at the cat and fired,
spraying buckshot into its head and shoulder.

Later, two other hunters passing by the tree stopped to look
at what Brooker had killed. A voice called out from the treetops, "You guys ever see a Florida panther?"

They reported him to the game commission for breaking the
law, and he was arrested. When he pleaded guilty, the reason

Brooker gave for killing a panther—a female panther, at that—
was his upbringing.

"The gist of what he said to the judge was, 'you're trained
as a youngster to be scared of panthers,'" the clearly disgusted
prosecutor later told reporters. "But it wasn't like the panther
was going to run up the damn tree."

Brooker faced a year behind bars, but the judge—himself an
avid hunter—refused to put him in jail. Instead the judge sentenced him to probation.

While Brooker's case was playing out, a far bigger one was
grinding its way through the courts. It involved a far more
prominent defendant: the head of the Seminole Tribe of Indians, one of two Native American tribes living in South Florida.

James Billie's true title was "chairman," but he preferred being
called "chief." Billie is a virtual compendium of only-in-Florida
attributes: he was born on a chimp farm. He once wrestled alligators for a living. After serving in Vietnam, he cut a couple of
country music records, and earned his license in cosmetology.
His married life was, shall we say, complicated. Under his leadership the tribe opened a gambling casino, the first such Indian
gaming hall in the country and the one that set a precedent for
the others that soon followed. Among other things, the casino
sold a hot sauce with Billie's name on it.

One December night in 1983, Billie and a buddy were driving through the woods on the tribe's reservation, about fifty-
five miles north of Fort Lauderdale. Something scampered past
the truck. The truck's headlights reflected back from a pair of
eyes set low to the ground. Billie fired his rifle, then climbed
down to see what he'd hit. It was a panther.

Unlike Brooker, Billie did not just leave his cat lying dead on
the ground. He loaded it on the truck, took it back to his home
and skinned it. He stretched the skin between some poles to dry
it. He saved the skull for display. Then he cooked and ate the
meat—including the heart.

Billie had plenty of enemies on the reservation. One of them alerted the state game commission. A pair of commission investigators showed up at Billie's home and confiscated the skin and skull. Billie told them that he was immune from their laws because the panther was killed on Indian land. He said killing a panther and eating its heart was part of his tribe's religious practices.

They arrested him anyway.

The news of Billie's arrest made the *New York Times.* The reporter talked to a Seminole medicine man, a cousin of the chief's, who said the accused was in training to become a medicine man. He said the panther offered powerful medicine for healing—for instance, the panther's claws, scratched lightly on the skin, could help relieve such degenerative diseases as muscular dystrophy. Parts of the tail, he said, are put in a mixture to rub on boys' limbs to make them run faster and jump higher. The skin, the paper reported, is used as "part of a secret religious ritual held deep in the Everglades in June."

The Seminoles have long been represented by an attorney named Bruce Rogow. He is a law professor who looks like a walking stereotype of law professors, with his bald head, beard, wire-rim glasses, neatly tailored suits and carefully arranged bow ties. Among other things, Rogow had shepherded his clients through launching their gambling hall. The Seminoles had once been dirt poor, subsisting on sales of tourist trinkets and tickets to gator-wrestling shows. Now, thanks to gambling, they were raking in plenty of dough.

Rogow knew Billie well, always a plus for a defense attorney. When I interviewed him, Rogow referred to the chief as "kind of an unfettered fellow," which is akin to saying Al Capone had a little trouble with his taxes. Rogow said that during their discussion of trial strategy, he told Billie right up front, "I don't think I'll let you testify."

"Why not?" Billie asked. He said he didn't understand why

he'd been charged with a crime for killing and eating a panther. "White people eat pussy. Why can't I?"

"*That's* why I can't let you testify," Rogow told him.

The facts of the case were never in dispute, Rogow told me. The panther was dead. Billie had killed it. Both prosecution and defense agreed on that. But he still believed he could get Billie acquitted, so they rejected any suggestion of a plea deal.

Rogow initially argued that Billie's killing of the panther was a religious act, and therefore protected under the First Amendment. He also attacked the search of Billie's home, the handling of the evidence and every other aspect of the investigation. His objections failed to dent the prosecution's case, but they delayed the trial for so long that three years passed. In the meantime, federal officials, watching the clock tick down to the end of the statute of limitations, finally filed a federal charge against Billie too.

Both cases went to trial in 1987. First up was the federal case, which was tried in West Palm Beach. Rogow said his focus in picking the jury was to look for "slightly liberal" people who might be more sympathetic to a minority defendant. He had his client pack the courtroom with Seminoles wearing their traditional tribal garb. Meanwhile, he shifted the defense strategy to focus on the same question that Laurie Wilkins had been trying to answer: What *is* a Florida panther?

Wilkins took the stand and testified about her search for the answer. She brought along five different puma skins and laid them out for the jury to examine. She talked about the characteristics that made a panther a panther, and talked about how Billie's panther matched those characteristics.

"It was very dramatic," Wilkins told me.

But Wilkins's testimony convinced some of the jurors that picking out a true panther was a difficult proposition for a layman. Billie's panther had a kinked tail and a cowlick, but those panthers found in the Everglades didn't have those—so which one was the true panther? Billie had fired quickly, without taking a careful look at the whole animal. How could he have possibly known he was shooting a real Florida panther if an expert needed a paint-matching machine?

The prosecution's experts testified about using a DNA test to determine that Billie's cat was a bona fide panther. But Rogow turned that around, asking if the state had ever done such a test on any other panthers. No, the state had not. Rogow then questioned whether the test had been done properly and if the results were correct.

The defense attorney had so muddied the water that, after seven hours of deliberations, the jurors couldn't agree. Some voted for conviction, some against. Finally they announced that they were deadlocked and the judge declared a mistrial.

"I don't think anyone felt he knew he was shooting at a panther," one juror said afterward.

Federal prosecutors vowed to try Billie again and this time get a verdict. In the meantime, though, Billie's state case went to trial. This one wasn't in well-populated urban West Palm Beach. Instead it took place in rural LaBelle. Accordingly, Rogow adjusted his jury-selection strategy. He knew potential jurors in LaBelle might be more sympathetic with a hunter who shot something he shouldn't have.

"I wanted a jury full of poachers," he told me.

Once again, Billie packed the courtroom with Seminoles in their colorful outfits. Once again Billie's attorney questioned whether the panther that was shot could be identified as a panther. This time, though, Rogow also attacked how the game commission handled the evidence seized from Billie's home. A game officer, looking to get the flesh off the bone, boiled the skull on his stove "like a pot of spaghetti," Rogow told jurors in his closing argument. And the hide, stuffed into the officer's freezer, had been handled in a way that "sends shivers up your spine."

This time the jury stayed out a little more than an hour. This time, there was no mistrial. They voted to acquit.

"I think the big thing was the botching up of the game commission," the foreman told reporters afterward. "They were terrible."

When the verdict was announced, Billie sat calmly with his chin propped on his fists. Then he turned to his attorney, shook his hand and said something to him. The newspapers reported that he told Rogow, "Sho-na-be-sha," which is Seminole for "Thank you." But Rogow told me that he made up that quote just to placate the reporters. The truth, he said, is that Billie told him, "You really taught those motherfuckers a lesson!"

The next day, the feds dropped their case against Billie too. He was free of all criminal charges.

Not long after the case ended, the head of the US Department of the Interior visited the reservation. Billie gave him a tour, then climbed into the tribe's own helicopter to fly the man to his next appointment. As Billie steered the chopper over the treetops, the official said, "I always wanted to ask you about that panther case. You ate the panther. What did it taste like?"

Without cracking a smile, Billie replied, "Oh, it was a cross between bald eagle and manatee."

Even as their work was being questioned in court, Maehr and the capture team were still pursuing their research. To Roelke, the genetic questions were paramount, but Maehr kept insisting that they needed to know more about habitat.

Maehr was willing to pursue that question wherever it led—including to a place he wasn't supposed to go.

In 1988, just five months after Billie's exoneration, Maehr decided to capture a panther that needed new batteries in its radio collar. There was just one problem: the panther had last been detected on Seminole land.

Maehr decided to go after the cat anyway. He did so without

telling tribal officials that the capture team was coming. He also didn't inform his superiors about this politically ticklish pursuit.

With McBride's dogs baying around them, they stood at the base of the tree where the panther had been trapped. Then Maehr did something bizarre.

"At the tree, Dave as the leader of the capture team swore everybody to silence," Roelke told me. Stunned, they all agreed. Then they darted the cat, brought it down, changed the collar batteries and turned it loose.

To cover up what he'd done, Maehr put in his field notes that the capture occurred somewhere off the reservation. But the cover-up didn't stick. Someone blabbed.

About two months after the secret capture, Maehr's boss—the same one who had transferred Belden to North Florida for daring to suggest deer hunting is bad for the panther population—gave him a written reprimand. He was found guilty of conduct unbecoming a state employee and falsification of records. Trespassing on the Seminoles' land hurt what Maehr's boss called "a sensitive and perhaps tenuous relationship" between the state and the tribe.

"More importantly, you directed subordinate staff and staff that were under your leadership to participate in the activity and then provided me with false information regarding the true capture location of the above-mentioned panther," the boss wrote.

It would not be the last time Maehr would be accused of faking his panther data.

CHAPTER NINE

BOTTLENECK

In a way, Dave Maehr was right. The loss of habitat really was the panthers' greatest threat—in the long run.

That's true for all big cats with a tendency to range far and wide. Around the world, lions, tigers and pumas are losing a battle to survive because they're losing habitat and losing their preferred prey. They thrive only in places that still meet the definition of "wilderness"—a word derived from the Old English term *wilddeornes*, which means "the place of wild beasts." Humans have wiped out oh so many of those places, and killed oh so many of the wild beasts—sometimes for food, sometimes to eliminate a perceived threat, sometimes just for fun, sometimes to convert that habitat into homes for humans. Once they're gone, few people even notice how the beasts have disappeared.

In Florida, the panthers were battling more than just a loss of land to more and more development. The state's fastest growing areas tend to feature two kinds of mass transit: very little or none at all. As a result, each new person moving to Florida brings along a car or two, and so as the population swells, so does the traffic volume. Dirt roads become two-lane blacktops which become busy highways, making them that much harder for wide-ranging panthers to cross safely. In the mid-1980s, panthers were being run over at the rate of about one every other month.

In November 1984, though, something unusual happened. A car zooming along the Tamiami Trail through Big Cypress hit a panther and, for once, *didn't* kill it. As usual, though, the driver didn't stop.

A Naples restaurateur driving a produce truck spotted the injured cat lying by the side of the road. He reported what he'd seen at the next highway patrol station, and the capture team scrambled to pick up the mangled cat.

It was a male, and in bad shape. Both its rear legs had been run over. One had suffered a compound fracture. A jagged bone protruded from a bloody hole in its skin. A layman might call it more dead than alive.

Now the capture team faced a choice. They could simply euthanize the poor thing—put it out of its misery and move on. On the other hand, McBride had recently put together an official estimate of the population, based on captures, scrapes and other signs, that said there were no more than thirty panthers left. With so few to begin with, and cars wiping out so many of them, why kill another one?

They took it to a Naples veterinary office for an initial exam by Roelke and another vet. Then they loaded the tranquilized panther into a plane and, with Roelke riding along, flew it up to Gainesville. Eight University of Florida veterinary specialists operated on it for five hours. Three days later, they did a second operation, putting steel plates into the injured legs.

Everyone now referred to the injured cat as Big Guy, as in "How's the Big Guy doing today?" It spent weeks recuperating in the animal hospital in Gainesville, living a schizophrenic existence. In the daytime, amid a chorus of barking dogs and other noisy animals in close quarters, Big Guy seemed placid, even laid-back, Roelke told me. Yet when meal time came, the cat absolutely refused to eat. Wouldn't touch any food whatsoever, and they could not figure out why.

Then, when night fell, Big Guy went wild.

He kept trying to escape. He jumped and jumped, over and over, making such powerful leaps that he bent the metal plates in his legs, Roelke said. The vets had to operate again, this time inserting the kind of plates used for horses. He also chewed on the chain link fence holding him in, biting down on the metal so hard he snapped off his canine teeth.

The stress of being snatched out of the wild and put into close confinement was clearly taking its toll. Roelke volunteered to care for Big Guy personally, the way she had cared for the cheetahs at her last job. When Big Guy was turned loose in a large pen at the game commission's offices in Gainesville, he stopped trying to jump and chew his way out, but he still didn't want to eat.

Roelke came up with a way to feed him anyway. She put the meat on a J-shaped hook at the end of a pole, then passed it through a hole in the fence. She knew the right body language and vocal inflections to challenge Big Guy and make him hiss at her. When he opened his mouth to respond to her, she would drop the food right into it.

They released live prey into Big Guy's pen, but that didn't work too well. He caught a hog, pinned it beneath his powerful paws, then chomped down on its neck in the usually fatal way. He held his mouth on that spot for the usual length of time for a panther that's just captured something to eat. When he let go, he expected to feed on the dead hog. Instead, the hog got up

and ambled away. Big Guy really needed those canine teeth he'd
lost. The vets eventually gave him some replacement chompers
made of titanium.

Roelke worked one-on-one with Big Guy for so long that
he began to "talk" to her, she said. Whenever the cat saw her,
he'd make a low, throaty sound like "a little chortle," Roelke
said. "When I walked into his pen, he was making a vocaliza-
tion to me."

His behavior fascinated her. She regarded it as a window on
how panthers would behave in the wild. His behavior changed
how all future panther captures were handled, she told me. No
more leaving them in tight quarters in the animal hospital.

In spite of Big Guy's clear desire to be free, game commission officials did not want to turn the cat loose when he was
healed. His metal plates made him an unsuitable candidate for
release, they said. Instead, they were finally listening to Robert Baudy's advice.

They wanted to use Big Guy to launch a captive breeding
program for panthers—aided by an unlikely ally.

Despite Belden's distaste for Baudy, they actually agreed on
one thing: eventually, captive breeding needed to be addressed.
The panther recovery plan that Belden and his team had cobbled together addressed the potential need for it, but only when
all else had failed.

Belden's recovery plan envisioned a multiyear approach, with
lots of checks and balances to make sure that there would be no
mistakes. Fieldwork by the capture team would lay the groundwork, as biologists learned everything they could about the big
cats before any attempt at breeding occurred.

They were being cautious (despite Baudy's clamoring for swift
action) because captive breeding is not a step to be taken lightly.
It represents the ultimate intrusion of humans imposing their
will on the fate of a wild creature, an attempt to engineer their

reproduction to guarantee their future. Captive breeding is regarded as a last-ditch effort to save a species. It's generally expensive to pursue and the odds for success are seldom good.

For instance, the most recent attempt at captive breeding an endangered species had ended before it ever started. The dusky seaside sparrow, a tiny bird that inhabited the marshes of Central Florida, once had flocks that numbered in the thousands. By the mid-1970s, though, the sparrows' numbers had fallen so far that only a handful remained. By the time all the government agencies involved gave their permission to launch a captive breeding program in 1980, all they could find were five birds—every single one of them male. That was the end of the captive breeding attempt. The last dusky died in captivity at Disney World in 1987.

So the people running the game commission didn't think they had time for Belden's cautious plan. To them the panthers were already on the verge of becoming the next dusky seaside sparrow—an unacceptable fate for Florida's official state animal.

"Panthers were viewed as a lost cause," Maehr wrote in his book. "Despite a wash of good news from the field, agency anxieties led to changes in strategy." For those nervous Nellies, he wrote, "no plan is swift enough."

Besides, they had a bird in the hand—Big Guy—and a good place to put him that wouldn't cost the state a dime.

The place was about as far north in Florida as you could get without crossing over into Georgia. It was called White Oak Plantation, and its seven-thousand-acre spread was full of exotic animals, such as barasingha from India, shelducks from Australia and red lechwes from Africa. Its original owner in the late 1700s and early 1800s was a Quaker named Zephaniah Kingsley Jr., who saw no conflict between illegally importing slaves from Africa for sale to other slave owners and meanwhile "marrying" several female slaves who bore him children. He actually believed in what he called "good slavery," which means treating your human chattel nicely while denying them their freedom.

Now the plantation was owned by the Gilman Paper Company. Its CEO, Howard Gilman, would fly down from New York in his private jet every weekend to ride horses and hunt bobwhite quail. Between his visits, the plantation's staff stayed busy breeding endangered wildlife as a source for zoos. They would also exchange their animals with other breeding facilities to refresh their genetic material. They regarded their work as "keeping the modern ark afloat," although they generally had more than just two of each species they were saving.

White Oak spent $200,000 building a pen for Big Guy that would simulate his natural habitat, as much as anything in the rolling hills of North Florida could mimic the steamy swamps of South Florida. State officials toured the place and gave their blessing, and so Big Guy was shipped to White Oak to be put out to stud.

There was only one problem. Unlike Zephaniah Kingsley, Big Guy had no interest in creating any progeny.

The capture team caught a decrepit female panther in the Fak and shipped her to White Oak to breed. Big Guy refused to have anything to do with her. McBride went to Texas and caught some female cougars and brought them back to White Oak. Big Guy liked one of them, but seemed unsure what to do about that. He would follow her around, but that was it. Panthers are generally more physical.

"It's kind of a peculiar relationship," a game commission spokesman told a reporter. "The female doesn't ovulate without help from a male. He has to go up to her and bite her on the neck. Then the female will give off a certain cry and odor to attract the male, and then they start pawing and biting and biology takes its course."

But Big Guy wasn't in a nibbling mood, not even with titanium canines, and so his intended mate didn't get into the mood either. The game commission sent out a press release announcing that the pair had "co-mingled," a ham-handed effort to imply they had had sex when of course they had not.

The only thing weirder was that game commission officials had decided they didn't like the name "Big Guy." Instead they began trying to convince everyone to call the captive cat "Jim." Every time I read that name in the records of the case, I crack up. It makes me think of Dr. McCoy barking at Captain Kirk on the TV show *Star Trek*: "Dammit, Jim, I'm a panther, not a sex machine!"

Instead of going along with "Jim," some wags dubbed the cat "Big Gay" because he had no apparent interest in females. That was wrong too, though. At long last, after all the non-nibbling and co-mingling, Big Guy copulated with a female cat.

And then…nothing happened.

What went wrong? To Roelke, the answer was both obvious and depressing. It tied back to her observations in the field about male panthers' sperm.

"Big Guy's sperm were not capable of binding to and penetrating the egg," she told me.

That discovery was a wakeup call about just how imperiled the panthers were. Even if they were all captured and put into zoos to breed in captivity, the cats might not be physically capable of bearing any healthy kittens.

Big Guy would live out the rest of his life at White Oak, becoming so docile that his keepers could walk into his enclosure without fear of being attacked. He died in 1994, having never sired a single kitten. But because he was accessible, he did become the most photographed panther in Florida history. He produced more images than offspring.

As Roelke had suspected all the way back in 1983, the panthers were suffering from serious genetic problems. The population was so small now that relatives were breeding with each other—fathers with daughters, mothers with sons, brothers with sisters. That's why their genetic diversity was so low, and why such genetic defects as kinked tails and cowlicks were cropping up.

Now Roelke was seeing even more serious defects: male panthers with at least one and sometimes two undescended testicles, for instance, as well as both males and females with small holes in their hearts. The undescended testicles could prevent them from being able to impregnate females. The holes, known as "atrial septal defects," could just plain kill them.

To her what was happening was obvious. The panthers' genetic diversity was so low they couldn't break the cycle of defects on their own. Instead, as reproductive failures grew, the population would drop even lower, and the defects would get worse, until finally the last panther, frail and alone, slunk away into extinction.

But she couldn't convince the men in charge that she knew what she was talking about.

"Inbreeding in wildlife has never been documented!" Maehr told her (a claim that scientists I spoke to said was false). Furious, Roelke snapped, "You just pay attention."

But Maehr had no time for that. He was too busy dealing with the latest of his bosses' brainstorms for launching a captive breeding program:

Capture every single panther left in the wild—just like the dusky seaside sparrow. But thanks to Chris Belden, nobody knew quite where to put them.

CHAPTER TEN

"EXTINCTION IS GOD'S PLAN"

Chris Belden had been exiled to North Florida, where pan-thers were as common as snowy days. But he just couldn't leave panthers behind.

The recovery plan he had worked on for so long didn't begin and end with the panthers down in South Florida. It called for finding them a new home somewhere else, so they could spread out. Ideally the panthers would end up with three separate colonies, each one well apart from the other two. That way if some disease began to spread through the ranks of one group, or some other disaster hit that wiped one group out, then the other two would be able to carry on. If someday there were three colonies of about 250 cats each, then and only then could the panther be taken off the endangered list, the plan said.

Unlike South Florida, North Florida wasn't feeling the same

kind of development pressure. There were still plenty of open spaces, plenty of forests that had yet to be clear cut, plenty of marshes that had yet to be filled in, paved over and built on.

Belden determined that North Florida still had some potentially perfect panther habitat. Even better, a big chunk of it had been preserved by the federal government.

Between the tiny town of Lake City and the sprawling metropolis of Jacksonville lay the Osceola National Forest, created by President Herbert Hoover in 1931—nearly 200,000 acres, of which 13,000 acres were cypress-sweetgum swamp. Closer to Orlando, there were the 387,000 acres of Ocala National Forest, its boundaries first set in 1908 by President Teddy Roosevelt. The Ocala forest contains the world's largest contiguous sand pine scrub forest. Although they weren't directly connected, they were close, with some still-undeveloped land in between.

A panther would have room to roam there.

But Belden didn't rush to turn a bunch of cats loose in those federal forest tracts. He was always a careful man, and after FP3, he became more careful still. He consulted experts from other wildlife reintroduction projects so he would know what mistakes to avoid. He surveyed landowners and hunters in the area to make sure they wouldn't object, or worse, start shooting. He even got one of North Florida's notoriously smelly paper companies, Buckeye, to offer to pay cattlemen up to $10,000 to cover any loss of livestock from the reintroduced cats.

Finally, he was ready. Ideally, Belden would ask McBride to catch him a few panthers, turn them loose in North Florida and see whether they liked it. But South Florida couldn't spare any panthers. There were too few of them left. What if something went wrong? What if another FP3 happened—or worse, several of them?

Better to test out the terrain with a relative of the panther, the Texas cougar. The cougars were close enough to panthers to be kissing cousins. That's why two had been imported to breed with Big Guy. It wasn't their fault that Big Guy wasn't much of a Romeo.

In spring of 1988, McBride caught seven Texas cats—three males and four females—and brought them to Florida. They were each sterilized so they wouldn't deliver any litters while wandering through North Florida, causing a confusing legal situation. Then they were fitted with radio collars so Belden could track their progress from the air.

The cats were trucked through the White Oak Plantation woods to a spot not far from the Osceola National Park. Fresh venison placed outside their cages tantalized them with a mouth-watering scent. Then, at last, the biologists opened up the cage doors.

"At first the animals were reluctant to leave their accustomed confinement," a witness wrote. "After ten minutes, one of the females moved out and started to eat. Gradually the other cats wandered off into the woods." Not all the cats, though. One female stayed in her cage until two in the morning, then finally bolted toward freedom.

On paper, what followed was a big success.

In real life? Not so much.

Remember that these cougars had been plucked by McBride from a dry, mountainous landscape and then turned loose amid rolling hills, pine forests and thick cypress swamps. Yet because panthers, cougars and pumas are such adaptable animals, these transplants quickly settled into their new home. In no time they had figured out how best to traverse the land and hunt their prey.

"They did really well for a while," Belden told a reporter a year later. "They set up social structures and territories."

If they could keep that up, it would prove that Belden was right, and this was perfect habitat for panthers from South Florida.

But then hunting season started.

People with guns began roaming the woods, ready to start blasting at a moment's notice. They were supposed to be hunting deer, but not everyone is scrupulous about shooting what's in season.

Just like that, two of the Texas cougars were shot dead. Their radio collars began sending what the biologists call a "mortality signal," which means they have stopped moving and are unlikely to ever move again. There was a necropsy, of course, but no one could figure out who did it and so no one was ever charged.

Bear in mind that there have been no documented panther attacks on humans in Florida in the twentieth (or twenty-first) century. There was no real reason to shoot those animals. But they were gunned down by modern Floridians just as if their pioneer forebears had been the ones toting the guns.

Then a third Texas cougar died from unknown causes. Its carcass was found floating in a river.

The other four, as Belden put it, "kind of freaked." The hunters ran them right out of the territory they had just established. One was found snoozing in a tree near Jacksonville, sixty miles from where it had been turned loose. Another made it all the way to Georgia.

They rounded up the survivors and shut down the experiment. In April 1989, Belden told a reporter that the future now looked "pretty bleak" for the future of panthers. He added that the main problem with the experiment wasn't the cougars. It was "too many people."

In a report on what happened, Belden wrote, "We cannot recommend the introduction of Florida panthers into northern Florida at this time. Instead, we recommend further study of techniques for establishing viable populations that are compatible with the expanding human population."

But he didn't give up. A few years later, his agency set even more Texas cougars loose in North Florida.

This time the experiment really went off the rails.

★ ★ ★

Once again, Belden tried to smooth the way. He got an assistant, the bearlike Walt McCown, and together they distributed brochures explaining the purpose of the experiment. They persuaded the state's biggest bank to pay up to $10,000 to cover any livestock losses. They invited representatives from fifty-eight hunt clubs to a meeting to discuss what was going to happen, so that this time their members would know not to shoot the big cats.

"A little bit of groundwork was laid with the citizens, but not nearly enough," McCown said years later. "We should have undertaken a couple of years of public engagement before starting. But it was just me and Chris in a couple of pickup trucks, trying to perpetrate this audacity."

Once again, the male cougars were all sterilized before being released so they wouldn't impregnate the females. Once again, they all had radio collars attached for tracking.

The cougars numbered nineteen this time—a big increase from the previous attempt. And, in an even bigger departure, nine of them were not caught in the wild by McBride. Instead, they were raised in captivity at White Oak Plantation. Some were kittens, released along with their mothers.

Given that Belden's agency was considering a captive-breeding program at the time, they needed to see how captive-raised cats would do in a North Florida setting. They were all given names that consisted of the letter T (for Texas) and a number.

In one way, the captive-raised cats did great. They adapted more quickly to their new home than the wild mountain lions did. On the other hand, they weren't nearly as shy around people as the wild ones, and that led to problems.

Reading Belden's rundown of what happened to each of the cougars is a little like reading an after-action report on the Battle of the Little Bighorn.

By the end of the experiment, seven cougars had been killed

in a variety of ways. Two were shot with arrows, one fatally. Another was crippled by a rifle bullet. Biologists had to euthanize it. One of the kittens they were tracking ran up a tree while being chased by McBride's dogs, but when it was hit by a tranquilizer dart it fell into a creek below the tree. It died three days later—its fate an echo of FP3 because once again the tranquilizer didn't deliver the dosage with the right timing.

Meanwhile, though, the cougars had done lots of damage too. They had slaughtered deer, calves, elk, hogs, a horse and one unlucky house cat that wandered outside at the wrong time.

One captive-raised cougar, T-33, was a colossal public relations disaster. It repeatedly got too close to people, frightening them. It attacked no humans, but did kill a hog, a horse and that one house cat—as the cat's owner watched in horror—before Belden and his crew swooped in and captured it.

And although all the male cougars were supposed to get vasectomies before being released, T-33 somehow fathered kittens by at least three female Texas cougars. The experts figure that that happened because even after a vasectomy, a cougar still has active sperm present for a few days—although how T-33 could impregnate that many cats in that short a space of time remains something of a mystery.

Biologists had a hard time keeping tabs on T-33's kittens because, unlike the other cougars, they had no radio collars or other tracking devices. One turned up as far south as the Central Florida town of Waldo—the state's most notorious speed trap—where it became known as "the Waldo Cat." The capture team finally caught the Waldo Cat, removing it from the wild.

Despite all the problems T-33 caused, it completed the experiment unscathed. A far more tragic fate befell the one designated as T-39.

T-39 was trying to cross into a fenced area outside Lake City when its head became caught in a snare. The snare was anchored to a fence post. As the animal tried to pull away, the noose tightened. The female cougar "pulled the fence post out of the ground and drug it several hundred yards before the snare cut through her neck column," one witness said.

I talked to the man who set the snare, Lake City accountant Michael Carter. He and his wife, Colvin, owned a hunting preserve stocked with at least ten thousand deer, elk and other animals that paying customers could stalk and shoot.

Carter said he bought the snare because he was trying to catch coyotes preying on his animals. He was not apologetic about snaring T-39 by accident. According to him, the cougars had also been treating his herd like the buffet line at Golden Corral. The Carters were convinced they lost half their deer to the cougars, but failed to persuade the state to reimburse them for more than thirteen of them.

The state paid the Carters $1,000 each for the loss of their deer. What price will the state pay, the Carters asked, should a panther kill a small child? To Carter, it was foolishness to try to bring back an animal that last roamed the state when Florida was largely undeveloped. Put panthers in North Florida now, he predicted, and they would all be gunned down by frightened residents.

"I'd be hard-pressed not to shoot one if I found him killing my livestock," Carter told me.

His wife, when I interviewed her, was just as blunt. If you turned loose a panther in suburban Tampa, she said, "people would go nuts. It's all right to have them in the Everglades, but it's not all right to have them in our backyard."

The Carters weren't the only ones who felt that way. Outraged area residents collected petitions calling for the state to stop turning loose big predators near their homes. They formed an organization called Not In My Backyard, a triumph of literalism over cleverness in creating an acronym. They also expressed their anger at the game commission's official representatives.

"I never before had so many offers to have my ass kicked," McCown said.

Seeking to placate the angry mob, Belden's bosses brought in professional mediators to hold public listening sessions. It didn't work. Instead of settling everyone down to thrash out their differences like civilized creatures, the meetings degenerated into shouting matches. Some people argued that Florida should stop spending all this time and money trying to save panthers. They contended that "extinction is God's plan."

It marked a stark reversal from the days when the panther was so beloved by schoolchildren.

Belden accepted another public thrashing with his usual quiet demeanor and retreated to write his reports. After exploring the question of whether North Florida could be the host of its own panther colony, he could see that the answer was "Yes, but..."

"The bottom line: it's biologically feasible," Belden said. "But there are an awful lot of social problems that have to be overcome." And nobody had any idea about how to do that.

As for the cougars, they became a further embarrassment for the game commission. The survivors were rounded up and then the commission sold them to an animal dealer in Texas. What state officials didn't anticipate was that the animal dealer then sold them to a place like the one the Carters were running, home to "canned hunts." That's where the owner turns rhinos, tigers and mountain lions loose so paying customers can shoot at them. At least one of the cougars was shot during a canned hunt, according to Maehr.

"It was stupid," he said. "They disposed of the animals in the easiest way they could, instead of going to a zoo or an animal retirement place... Go visit, get letters of reference and find out the cost. Then get a written agreement that they'll keep them there until they die a natural death."

Even the Waldo Cat wound up headed for a canned hunt, until animal activists got wind of it and raised a fuss. Then a state legislator jumped into the middle of things, announcing he was on a "mission" to save the Waldo Cat from captivity. He demanded a legislative hearing to investigate how the state had fouled up.

"We can't just wash our hands from what has happened to these animals," he said, with just a trace of a harrumph in his voice. Did I mention he was running for reelection?

In the face of blistering criticism, state officials hurried to buy the Waldo Cat back. They found him a safer home among the menagerie of animals on display at Silver Springs, where, despite being a Texas cougar, it was put into an area dubbed "Panther Prowl." Nobody from the public knew the difference.

Meanwhile, despite Belden's results, the push for a captive breeding program was going full-steam ahead. His bosses were determined to produce more panthers, even if they had nowhere to put them all.

CHAPTER ELEVEN
THE VORTEX

Fifty. That's how many panthers Dave Maehr was supposed to capture. That's how many would be needed for a successful captive breeding program, he was told in 1990.

This was, of course, impossible. There weren't fifty Florida panthers in Florida. McBride had found signs of no more than thirty. Cars and trucks had flattened so many that the number was probably lower than that now.

No one said it out loud, Maehr noted later in his book, but the effect of using so many panthers for captive breeding would be to eliminate every single breeding panther from the wild. They would destroy the wild population to save it.

Clearly the game commission's leaders were in panic mode. The state animal was about to vanish into oblivion, just like the dusky seaside sparrow. They had to do *something*, right? Granted, they didn't want to capture all the panthers all at once, but over several years. But the end result would be the same: putting every single one of the wild animals into a zoo, to be cared for at taxpayer expense for the rest of their lives.

This was the downside of getting the public interested in the fate of the panther. Every time a car splattered a panther's guts across a highway, the newspapers and TV stations reported it. Every story on a panther death mentioned how few remained in the wild. Every death seemed like a major subtraction from the population. The underlying tone of each story, Maehr wrote, was that it was only a matter of time before an eighteen-wheeler hauling Budweiser flattened the last of the panthers.

Nobody ever mentioned that there were new kittens being born each year too, Maehr complained. To him, the new births were sufficient to replace all the mature panthers that were being run down by heedless humans.

Meanwhile, federal officials had begun taking the threat of lost habitat seriously. In 1989, the US Fish and Wildlife Service spent more than $10,000,000 buying twenty-four thousand acres of land from the family that Collier County is named for. They used it to create the Florida Panther National Wildlife Refuge, guaranteeing that at least a little bit of Southwest Florida would never be paved over.

The feds were so serious about preserving the Panther National Wildlife Refuge for panthers that they chose to build no visitor center on the land. They also decided not to let tourists in. There's no gift shop selling stuffed panthers. At the refuge, the gates stay locked all year round.

To visit, I had to drive down to the last exit on Interstate 75 before it becomes Alligator Alley and cuts across the Everglades to Fort Lauderdale. I had to wend my way through parking lots for a Holiday Inn Express, a Super 8 motel, a Shell station, a few mini-warehouses and a Cracker Barrel restaurant. Finally I was able to park at my destination, a four-story hotel the color of Pepto-Bismol.

The parking lot was full of panel vans, the signs on the side showing that they were for installing insulation, cable and fire alarms at all the new subdivisions being built in panther habitat. Not far down the road stood a battered yellow sign that said "Panther Crossing." It was surrounded by concrete barricades for road repair and new construction. I had a hard time picturing any panthers crossing on that spot.

Inside the hotel, I found the desk clerk on duty was a dark-haired woman with black nails and the kind of eye makeup that some people call "smoky" but that looked more like "charred." She was wearing a necklace adorned with a small silver replica of brass knuckles, with a cutout in the center that was shaped like a heart. I was tempted to ask her what that meant. Instead, I asked her for directions to Suite 300, where the Fish and Wildlife Service was a permanent guest.

This was the headquarters of the Florida Panther National Wildlife Refuge.

Just inside the glass door of Suite 300, there's an office that looks like any other wildlife refuge visitor center, complete with a bunch of colorful brochures and a glass display case containing a stuffed panther. But even there, you can't quite forget that you're not in a refuge but in a Florida motel surrounded by fast food joints.

The refuge manager, a thin, graying, twinkle-eyed lady in a khaki uniform, told me the wildlife service had moved into this hotel in 1992 and slowly expanded to have offices on three floors for their fifteen employees. One biologist had a full-fledged motel room, complete with a shower, she said. The rest had desks in what had been converted to office space.

The manager told me it was "interesting"—her word—to work out of a hotel next to a major interstate highway. The refuge staff had noticed a seasonal change in the clientele. During the winter, she said, they saw lots of snowbirds visiting from the North. In other seasons, she said, they saw a lot of young women in skimpy outfits standing around in the parking lot— ladies of the evening, working the trucker routes.

The refuge's chief biologist, Larry Richardson, took me out to the refuge in his government-issue Ford F-150. Larry had glasses, graying hair and the manner of an enthusiastic science teacher. As we bounced along old logging trails, scaring up flocks of wild turkeys, he told me about how he'd been one of the first people hired by the refuge back in 1989. Over the next twenty years, he joked, "I've watched this go from nothing to almost-nothing."

Richardson started out as an expert on deer, not panthers. He told me he did his master's thesis on their "acoustic behavior." When I said I didn't know deer made any sounds, he opened his mouth and made what I can only describe as a plaintive beep.

"They bleat, they grunt," he explained. His thesis became wildly popular with the hunting crowd. "You go in sporting goods stores and they've got these calls now, and they use the names I gave them, like 'The Snort Wheeze.'"

We tromped through thick, black muck to look in the trees for delicate little native orchids with names like "cowhorn" and "jingle bell." We were stared at by a buck and two does that didn't seem to be at all scared of us. We startled a three-foot al- ligator, and then a six-footer half in its hole. We saw scat from an even bigger gator. It was a gray curl, like a crescent roll crossed with a waffle cone. I was kind of glad we didn't meet that one.

By saving the refuge for panthers, the National Park Service was saving land for all these other plants and animals too, he pointed out. But it took a while for the panthers to trust it as a place where they could find prey and hide from hunters.

"When I got here in 1989, I rarely saw a panther," Richardson told me. By 2009, at least five were known to live on the refuge land, with more passing through on their way to somewhere else. They were stopping off to snack on the four hundred or so deer whose population Richardson had carefully cultivated.

But he worried that this oasis was being isolated by the development rapidly eating away at the habitat around it.

"We don't want the panther population resigned to an island," he said. "But you could kind of say we're an island."

Opening the refuge was only one step the feds took. The next was hiring the International Union for the Conservation of Nature and Natural Resources to study the situation and make recommendations. The IUCN had assembled a team of experts who "came to function as an endangered species fire brigade which careens from crisis to crisis with state-of-the-science advice," as one writer put it.

The team was led by a biochemist named Ulysses "Ulie" Seal, whose expertise had already been brought to bear on saving the black-footed ferret out West. Seal had a day job working at a Veterans' Administration hospital in Minneapolis, where he did research on prostate cancer. But his passion wasn't curing cancer—it was trying to save endangered species. That occupied the rest of his time. He published more than two hundred sixty scientific journal articles that looked at everything from wolf nipple measurements to badger urine.

Seal had a big, bushy beard, a booming voice and a boisterous manner that some people thought made him resemble Santa Claus. When he entered a room, he immediately became the center of attention. His coworkers found him charismatic. Some other biologists who had to deal with him during an endangered species crisis found him insufferable.

"Sometimes he turned people off," said Seal's second-in-command, a geneticist with the Chicago Zoo named Bob Lacy. "The force of his personality would take control of where the conversation was going."

For the panther problem, Seal and his team held a three-day

workshop at a hotel ballroom in Naples. The first day fell on Halloween, but there were no treats for the attendees, just a lot of work.

Seal brought in specialists in genetics, reproductive physiology, population biology and wildlife biology. They put their heads together with Florida's panther experts—Belden, Roelke and Maehr from the state game commission, and Deborah Jansen, who had taken a job working for the National Park Service at Big Cypress.

Missing from the group was Roy McBride. For some reason the one man with the most knowledge about the lives of panthers was left out of the planning for the panthers' future. McBride would never forget the oversight. At a conference twenty years later, I heard him grouse about biologists fiddling with computers in air-conditioned offices instead of trusting data collected in the field.

When the meeting began, the tension in the room was palpable, Lacy told me. He and Seal had heard that at least one of the field biologists had refused to share any information about panthers with the outside experts, only to be told by their bosses that they would share their data or face disciplinary action.

The most strenuous objections came from Maehr, Lacy said. To him, Seal's experts were exaggerating the genetic problems facing panthers. He contended that if they could just provide the panthers with the habitat they needed, that would solve all of their problems.

To Lacy, some of this was Maehr's ego getting in the way of his judgment.

"He was viewed as Mr. Panther," Lacy told me. Having Seal waltz in and take charge of a discussion of the future of panthers "was a direct challenge to his authority."

On the other hand, Lacy said, Seal and his colleagues viewed Roelke as having done the most crucial work of all by finding the evidence of genetic problems. Roelke told me she was relieved by the support from the outside experts.

"By that point Dave had managed to turn the entire capture team against me, because I was in favor of captive breeding," she said.

You don't see any of this drama mentioned in the minutes of Seal's meeting, but the account still makes for fascinating reading. Just after the group convened, Roelke dropped a bombshell. One of the Everglades panthers had died under mysterious circumstances, she said. It wasn't run over. It wasn't killed by another panther. It hadn't been shot by a poacher. Finally an examination of the cat's liver turned up something disturbing.

The liver contained a lethal dose of mercury.

Where did the mercury come from? Apparently from the panther's regular diet of raccoons, which had been eating lots of fish from the Everglades canals. A check of other panthers from that vicinity found that they, too, had absorbed mercury into their systems, albeit not a lethal dose—not yet, anyway.

Where was it coming from? Eventually the source turned out to be air pollution. The smoke from metals mining and smelting, coal-fired utilities and solid-waste incinerators produced it, and then as it floated through the air, Florida's summer rainstorms would snag it and the rain drops would then deposit it in the Everglades. A secondary source: the 400,000 acres of sugar cane farms on the edge of the Everglades. They set fire to their fields every fall at the start of their harvest season to burn away the sugarless, leafy portions of the plant. Then machines move in to grab the sugar-filled stalks. The muck beneath the crops contains mercury too, which means the smoke from the fires carried even more pollution into the Everglades.

This was disastrous news. It meant that one of the panthers' key habitats was poisoned. With the Big Cypress and the Fakahatchee Strand seeing development creep closer and closer to their borders, ranches and groves being converted to subdivisions and strip shopping centers, and now the Everglades turned deadly, soon the panthers would have no place to call home.

Seal began asking questions of the various experts, and each answer became fodder for a computer program that Lacy had come up with. The program was named "VORTEX," as if it were some sort of James Bond villain's doomsday device.

Actually, the name came from a biological term, "the extinction vortex." As the population of an endangered species—or in this case, subspecies—dwindles down to a certain level, it hits a point where it begins spiraling toward extinction at a faster and faster pace. Inbreeding causes a loss of genetic diversity, fueling an inability to reproduce, which diminishes the size of the population even more.

"Once a species is on that downward slope, it's hard to pull it back out," Lacy told me.

The VORTEX program was designed to figure out whether the species or subspecies being studied had hit the point of no return. If it had not, then the program would suggest ways to avoid it, no matter how improbable or legally questionable. Seal's motto was find the alternative, then figure out if it would work.

In this case, as one news account reported, "VORTEX spat out an ominous answer."

Unless the government got busy with a captive breeding program, and soon, there was an 85% probability that the Florida panther would die out in 25 years. Period.

The rest of the session involved the panther experts calling the roll of all the cats they had captured and figuring out which ones might be capable of producing offspring in captivity. Which ones were considered "founders" of the panthers' genetic lines, and which ones were their offspring? Which ones had shown problems in the past? Which ones would go to White Oak plantation for breeding, and which ones to the Miami Zoo, which also wanted to help? There was talk of maintaining a "stud book" to trace each cat's lineage, and of how to go about reintroducing their kittens to the wild.

Despite Maehr's continued objections, state officials signed off on the Seal group's recommendation to launch a large captive breeding effort.

"Florida Panthers to Be Bred in Zoos to Prevent Extinction," the *Miami Herald* announced on its front page.

But the call to go out and capture lots of cats faced two major problems. One of them involved Roelke's research. The other resulted from the public reaction.

With every capture, Roelke was finding bad news among the male panthers. Not only did they have poor sperm, but she was also seeing that more and more had only one testicle, or even no testicles at all.

That particular genetic defect is known as "cryptorchidism," not because flowers are involved but because orchid roots resemble male sex organs. "Crypto" is the Latinized form of the Greek word *kryptos*, which means "hidden, concealed, secret." In other words, the panthers' testicles hadn't appeared. Panthers with no testicles were sterile. By 1990, nine out of ten male kittens that were born had that condition, Roelke said.

"It was like they had hit a biological brick wall," she told me.

One day a car flattened another panther. What Roelke found when she examined the animal proved to be another signal of how far gone the panthers were.

"I found a dime-size hole between the upper chambers of the heart," Roelke said. "Usually if a hole's in your heart, you die."

She marked it on her report as "ASD" for "atrial septal defect." Once Roelke found ASD in one cat, she found it in others.

"We collected a cat hit in the road and brought him in for rehab," she said. "He had a heart murmur. Suffice it to say suddenly we started finding lots of animals with this very heart condition."

Roelke had been shipping skin and semen samples she'd taken from each panther to genetics experts at the National Cancer Institute. These were people she had first worked with when she was studying cheetahs, and she trusted them to make a thorough analysis. They found that the panthers "were all genetically compromised," the leader, geneticist Stephen J. O'Brien, wrote.

A healthy animal population would have genetic differences among each animal But the genetic variations between panthers in the samples was "the lowest of any North American puma subspecies, and nearly as low as what we had seen in cheetahs," O'Brien wrote. "Florida panthers were showing signs of close inbreeding and shedding of intrinsic genetic diversity, a red flag for an endangered species."

In public, Roelke supported the idea of captive breeding of the panthers. But in private she wondered: If we do captive breeding with *these* panthers, won't we just be creating more cats with serious genetic defects? How does that help save the subspecies?

Persuaded by Seal's VORTEX verdict, federal officials were ready to sign off on the idea of catching wild cats and breeding them in captivity to replenish the population. In December 1990, the Fish and Wildlife Service officially approved the plan Seal's group had come up with. But before it could issue the permits allowing Maehr's capture team to start rounding up panthers, someone slammed on the brakes.

Her name was Holly Jensen, and she was a nurse working in the intensive care unit at Alachua General Hospital in Gainesville. She also had a private practice as an acupuncturist, and she had a side job as trail boss at a horseback riding camp. She grew up in the town of Rockledge, not far from what became the Kennedy Space Center, but before the invasion of space cadets turned it into a boomtown.

"It was the most fabulous place to live," she told me. "There was wildlife everywhere. You could surf or waterski or swim or walk in the woods. We'd ride bikes everywhere. It was the most beautiful place imaginable."

From a very early age, Jensen discovered a passion for nature. When she saw another kid shooting at birds with a BB gun, she'd say, "Stop or I'm going to have to hit you." Then they'd be rolling around on the ground throwing punches.

Soon, though, along came the space program, bringing a flood of engineers and their families. Fast-buck builders quickly turned sleepy Brevard County into Urban Sprawl Central.

"Watching everything in the world you loved covered in concrete was very hard," she said with a sigh.

When she got older, she threw herself into animal welfare causes. She joined People for the Ethical Treatment of Animals, the Animal Liberation Front and the Fund for Animals. When she heard about the plans for captive breeding of panthers, she knew it sounded wrong.

"They wanted to take all the founder animals, the gene pool, into captivity and then try to recover them," she said. "They were going to take them out, spend all this money rehabilitating the species, and meanwhile all the places where they would live would disappear."

That wasn't her only objection.

"The whole way they were going to do captive breeding was to take the most important animals out of the wild," Jensen said. "They had the best genes. They were the best hunters. They had the best immune system. These animals were like the last of their kind. Why would you take the greatest warriors out of the wild?"

Jensen pulled in the New York–based Fund for Animals, an organization founded by animal rights activist Cleveland Amory that kept its attorneys busy suing over cruelty cases and endangered species decisions. Amory particularly despised hunters, and so his organization had successfully pushed a vote in California that banned the hunting of pumas in that state, and was working to try to ban it through the rest of the country. Lest you think the Fund to be an entirely humorless bunch, you should know that it ran a sanctuary for injured rabbits called "Hope for the Hopless."

Jensen and the Fund for Animals filed a lawsuit against the Fish and Wildlife Service. The suit contended the federal agency had not addressed the impact of removing so many cats from the wild, or the chances of successfully reintroducing them. They said the agency was in such a rush it hadn't fully considered every angle.

"What's the point of doing captive breeding of panthers if you've got no place to put them?" the attorney for the Fund for Animals asked.

The lawsuit demanded the feds do a full-fledged environmental impact statement similar to the one that stopped the Everglades jetport from being built, a process that might take two years to complete.

Negotiations ensued. In the end, the agency reached a settlement with Jensen: in exchange for the feds doing a supplemental study on panther habitat, Jensen agreed that she would not object to them capturing six kittens. No adults. No catching every cat in the wild. Just kittens, period.

Not everyone saw this as a victory for the panthers the way Holly Jensen did. As the second study finished up in fall 1991, the state's largest newspaper ran an opinion column by its former environmental reporter headlined, "Florida Panthers Perish Amid Endless Bickering." The opening paragraph took an even more dramatic tone: "While the bureaucrats are preparing their reports, the big cats are dying in the swamp. While the lawyers are arguing their cases, the big cats are dying in the swamp. While the legislators are looking the other way, the big cats are dying in the swamp."

The writer was angry because while the feds drew up their

study, the last two panthers in Everglades National Park died. In all, six of the "founders" died before they could be captured.

But when Maehr finally ventured out to capture the kittens selected for use in the captive breeding program, something even worse happened.

CHAPTER TWELVE

THE CAPTIVES

Dave Maehr stood in the middle of a thicket of palmetto and listened.

The capture team, after a diligent search in the underbrush, had found the mother panther's den. They knew the kittens were inside. They knew they had to creep up on the den and pull the kittens out.

The only question was: Where was the mom?

Capturing panther kittens turned out to be a lot trickier than capturing an adult. To catch an adult, McBride would spot tracks or other signs, the dogs would sniff out a scent and off they would go, chasing the critter up a tree. Then it was just a matter of shooting a tranquilizer dart at the cat and bringing it down to the ground safely.

But you couldn't tree a kitten, or even find a sign of one outside the den.

To find a kitten, the team first had to figure out if any kittens even existed. That meant checking radio-collar signals until they found a female panther that had stopped moving around. A female that stayed near one spot was most likely a mother with a den. Inside the den, she would be raising her little ones, leaving only occasionally to go hunt some food for them.

Once the team located a mama cat like that, the team would head out early in the morning and follow the mom's radio signal. The blip-blip-blip sounds would lead them to her vicinity. Then the team would creep up to within fifty feet or so and try to figure out where the den might be.

Even if they found it, they couldn't just go charging in and grab the kittens. Sticking your arm in a den while the mom was there was a good way to get your arm chewed off. So they had to wait—and listen for the blips—that indicated she had headed out to stalk some prey.

Once she was gone, they had to move quickly, sneaking in, snatching up the kittens, racing back out before she returned with their food.

As with a regular capture, though, a thousand things could go wrong. The first time Maehr and his crew went out to catch some kittens, the steering failed on one of their swamp buggies. By the time they got it fixed, the day had fled.

Another time, they made it out into the field and found the den, but when they snuck up on it and reached inside, they found two male kittens. Game commission officials had decreed that they could not take two males at a time. They could only take a female and a male, for balance. So they had to put those two back.

Once, when Maehr brought along a reporter for the Fort Lauderdale paper, the team reached the den too late in the morning to catch any kittens. The mother had already returned from hunting and would not be leaving again for quite some time. They stuck around, hoping to catch a break, only to see their adventure turn into "a daylong lesson in heat stroke," the reporter wrote. Desperate for shade, the team members crawled behind spindly slash pines or burrowed down under the buggies. Finally, as the sun set, they gave up.

The next day at 7 a.m., Deb Jansen went back alone. She soon radioed the rest to say the mother was still in the same spot. At 3:30 p.m., the rest of the capture crew gathered at a rendezvous point not far away, hoping for something to change. Finally, the radio crackled with Jansen's urgent call: "She's moving."

When they got near the den, Maehr checked the radio signals to make sure the mom was still on the hunt, then announced to the group, "Okay, we're going in."

Single file, they made their way through a dry prairie, then waded knee-deep through a marsh. They circled the suspected den location, each team member sliding up to it from a different direction, eyes darting around, searching for the kittens.

At last they spotted them: two little balls of striped fur about the size of the average house cat. One was male, one female. Their eyes were barely open, and they mewed at their captors. The team looked them over and except for a kink in one tail, they appeared to be fine, the reporter noted.

Just then, though, there was a crackling sound in the nearby underbrush, and the reporter asked, "Who's monitoring the radio?"

No one, it turned out. They had all gotten too excited about the kittens.

Everyone rapidly retreated from the den, returning to the swamp buggies, toting the two kittens. Everyone but Jansen, that is. She stayed behind to watch how the mother reacted.

Sure enough, when the mom returned to the den with the prey she had killed for her brood, she freaked out. The mama cat spent hours searching in and around the den site for the missing kittens. Finally she gave up. Three days later, she abandoned that den.

When the reporter asked about the cruelty of robbing a mother of her young, Maehr admitted it would be hard on the mama cat, and hard to explain to animal lovers.

"These animals have feelings," he said. "We're all telling ourselves it's for the good of the animal."

But in an exam room far from the prying eyes of any reporter, Roelke discovered that it was all a wasted effort.

This should have been a moment of triumph for Maehr and the panther team.

The Florida Legislature had authorized the sale of special "Protect the Panther" license plates to raise money for research on the big cats. They were modeled on the "Save the Manatee" license plate that had been released the year before to raise money for research on the state's official marine mammal. License plates are an odd way to finance scientific research, but both proved to be extremely popular, raising tens of thousands of dollars for important work.

Thanks to Maehr's constant promotion of the panther research program, complaints about the scientists putting collars on the cats had diminished, and soon there were far more panther license plates on cars than actual panthers. (It's possible some of those cars with panther plates later ran over actual panthers, but nobody's ever proven that.)

Meanwhile the Florida Department of Transportation—after extensive prodding by state wildlife biologists—had begun building underpasses beneath some of South Florida's major highways, allowing panthers to cross without being splattered across the pavement. Some critics openly questioned whether the panthers would really use the underpasses, even though the DOT (after still more prodding) put up fences to block them from crossing any other way. But then biologists put up motion-sensor cameras that caught plenty of photos of panthers crossing under Alligator Alley. They weren't alone, either. The cameras snapped pictures of bobcats, white-tailed deer, bears, turkeys, raccoons, various wading birds and even alligators using the underpasses. (Also appearing on camera at one point: a prankster dressed in a gorilla suit.)

And now, to cap it all off, the captive breeding program, long discussed, was at last beginning.

But as Roelke had feared, the kittens that Maehr's team had captured weren't suitable for breeding.

"This is the epitome of our failure to rescue the Florida panther," she explained. "The first male that was brought in to captivity...a month later I went to White Oak and the first thing I evaluated was this kitten. It turned out this animal had no testicles that had descended."

To say Roelke was upset is to put it mildly.

"I became a raving lunatic," Roelke told me.

Sometimes it can take up to eight weeks for a male panther kitten's testicles to descend. But after that period of time had elapsed, the kitten's testicles still had yet to appear. The next step: operate on the poor kitten.

"He underwent surgery for five hours in Gainesville," Roelke said. It didn't work, she said: "The testes were too far up."

So that meant that the first kitten the capture team had brought in couldn't reproduce. He ended up living out his entire life in captivity at the Lowry Park Zoo in Tampa. He never produced any offspring.

The next one, she said, was even worse. Its heartbeat sounded like a washing machine, a sign that it was suffering from the same ASD Roelke had detected in older panthers. Desperate, she took the kitten to Gainesville, put it under anesthesia and subjected it to open-heart surgery.

The kitten died on the operating table.

To Roelke, that marked the end of all hope for the panthers, not to mention the end of her personal effort to save the panther.

"It was obvious to me we had lost the game," she said. "I had put in nine years of my life and I felt the panther was done."

She blamed the resistance of Maehr and the rest of the game commission and federal wildlife officials. Their reluctance to accept her warnings that the panthers were facing a genetic crisis had caused this. She also blamed herself for not pushing harder.

The only way a captive breeding program might have worked, she said, is if one had started back when Roy McBride caught that first panther near Fisheating Creek. The panthers weren't too far gone at that point, Roelke said.

"We dragged our feet," she said. Meanwhile the genetic problems got worse. The panthers "didn't have holes in their hearts when I started."

In the end, Maehr and his team caught three newborn kittens and seven juvenile panthers between the ages of three and six months old. The ones that survived all lived out the remainder of their lives in captivity. But in one of the most bizarre bureaucratic blunders in Florida history, no one ever gave the green light for them to breed.

The discovery of the genetic problems among the captives prompted everyone in charge to act as if they'd forgotten the breeding program even existed. Years later, when I asked people about it, nobody could tell me who had dropped the ball. No one had any written orders saying, "Don't do this." It just… evaporated.

One excuse I heard that sounded plausible: in the rush to get the kittens into captivity, nobody had considered what would happen if they succeeded in breeding hundreds of cats. Just as Holly Jensen feared, nobody had planned ahead for where the offspring would live. Nobody had figured out how to pay for their upkeep until they were grown enough to be released into the wild. Without money to pay for the program, it stalled.

That was the bearish Walt McCown's take on it.

"There was a plan to remove them, but the plan sort of stopped there," he told me. "There was no plan or budget for their care, feeding, and breeding."

No one considered the consequences to the wild population, either, he contended. The ones that were taken were the kittens that might have had the chance at replenishing the population in the wild, while "the ones that were left were the ones you wouldn't *want* breeding."

Talking about it years later, he said, "It still bothers me... We took a whole generation out."

Because the captives had spent nearly their entire lives in cages and enclosures tended by humans, they couldn't even be released back into the wild, McCown said. No adult panther had ever showed them how to hunt, how to feed, how to survive.

"It would be like dropping off a couple of stockbrokers in the Amazon rainforest and saying, 'Good luck!'" he said.

Eight years after Maehr's team first grabbed a kitten from a den, the bureaucrats belatedly gave the green light for the cats to breed. By then it was too late. They were too old.

In a way, the kittens weren't the captives. They were just collateral damage.

The people in charge of saving the panther were the captives. They were prisoners of an idea—the idea that if all else failed, they could always fall back on captive breeding. They thought they had the time and the brains and the resources to save the panther. Now they were learning how very wrong that idea had been.

Roelke and McCown weren't the only ones who had a tough time dealing with the failure. Another veterinarian named Carolyn Glass had occasionally filled in for Roelke in accompanying the capture team to catch the kittens. Glass was deeply shaken by the discovery that the kittens were unsuitable subjects for captive breeding, Roelke said.

Not long afterward, Glass drove her state-issued truck into a garage at the game commission's Gainesville office building, then closed the garage door. She ran a hose from the exhaust pipe to a window in the cab, rolled the window up as far as it would go, climbed into the truck's driver's seat and cranked the engine.

McCown had just moved into his new office in Gainesville to help Chris Belden with the North Florida habitat test. While he was putting books on his bookshelf, a coworker ran in and told him that Glass was missing.

Right after that, he said, "I heard a blood-curdling scream."

Everyone ran to the garage, just ten feet from McCown's office, where someone had found Glass. She was already dead. In addition to inhaling carbon monoxide, he said, she had started an intravenous drip of euthanasia drugs into her arm.

"She was dressed in her uniform, in her agency vehicle," McCown told me, his voice husky and low. "I think there was a message there... Endangered species [work] attracts people with problems, or provides problems for them if they don't already have them."

Amid all the dismay and despair, though, one more option to save the panther appeared—a last, highly unlikely chance to set things right.

CHAPTER THIRTEEN

HAIL MARY

In 1975, the Dallas Cowboys football team was losing to the Minnesota Vikings in a divisional playoff when the Cowboys' quarterback, Roger Staubach, begged for divine intervention. With twenty-four seconds left in the game, he dropped back, launched a desperate fifty-yard spiral downfield and then muttered a "Hail Mary" prayer as he watched it fly.

The ball found its target, receiver Drew Pearson, who caught it just inside the five-yard line and ran it into the end zone for a touchdown. Thus the Cowboys beat the Vikings and the phrase "Hail Mary pass" entered America's pop culture lexicon.

"I could have said 'Our Father' or 'Glory be,'" Staubach said years later. "But I don't think 'Our Father' would have carried on."

In 1992, Florida's panthers needed a Hail Mary pass.

The panther experts gathered once again at White Oak Plantation. The owner had installed a bar, a classic one from Chicago that was rumored to have come from Al Capone's favorite gin joint. It was on the same hall as the bowling alley. Right next to the bar and the bowling alley was a lecture hall with expensive wood paneling and a set of tables spread around.

That's where the experts now congregated, although they probably felt more like sitting in the bar and drowning their sorrows.

As they filed into the lecture hall at White Oak on October 21, 1992, they each wore a grim look. Captive breeding had failed. The kittens selected as having the best genetic background turned out to be just as messed up as the others. Panthers were teetering on the brink of extinction and the bright minds studying the problem had not only failed to save them, but had actually made things worse.

Outside the weather was gorgeous. The chance of rain was zero. The high temperature was a cool (for Florida) sixty-six degrees, meaning no mosquitoes to bother you on a nature hike. But inside? Nothing but storm clouds.

The clock was ticking down to zero. The game was nearly over.

Given the chance to sit anywhere in the room, everyone divided into their own tribes: biologists at one table, bureaucrats at another, computer geeks at a third and so on.

The tension felt palpable, and much of it centered on Maehr.

Deb Jansen and the other members of the National Park Service staff had repeatedly demanded that Maehr notify them when he took a capture team into Big Cypress. Jansen was doing her own capture work now, and didn't want Maehr interfering.

But her demand was one that Maehr had repeatedly ignored— to the point that his boss had sent him a scorching memo about it. Yet he continued with the same behavior. The state's own capture team was on his side.

"The average Joe could go there anytime—but *we* had to ask permission," McCown told me. "I didn't understand that."

Maehr's team members were also mad at Roelke. Despite Maehr's objections, she had pushed the captive breeding idea, to the point of selecting which kittens should be captured. Roelke was convinced that Maehr had turned everyone against her. When her old partners on the capture team looked at her, she said, the looks they gave her made her feel like "the evil Antichrist."

Roelke was so upset that she was ready to not only leave panthers behind, but leave the country. She had accepted a job in Africa as the chief veterinarian for Tanzania's national park system. She was scheduled to leave for the new job before the conference began, but she postponed her trip for this one last White Oak discussion.

As she looked around the room, she saw signs of nothing but defeat.

"They all shook their heads and said, 'It's over. It's done,'" she recalled.

Roelke had at least one friend in the room: Stephen O'Brien, the geneticist from the National Cancer Institute, who had started working with Roelke on cheetahs and now collaborated with her on panthers. He considered her work crucial to diagnosing what was wrong with the panthers and figuring out how to save them.

But he could see, too, how distressed she was at how things had worked out. At one point in the meeting, he said, she leaned over to him with tears trickling down her cheeks and said, "At least they're finally listening to me."

That left the big question: Given the failure of captive breeding, usually the last option to save a dying species, what could anyone do to pull the panthers out of their extinction spiral?

This was the dusky seaside sparrow story all over again, only worse. This wasn't some drab little bird. This was Florida's state

You could argue that the most significant panther in Florida history is stuffed and on display in front of the state library in Tallahassee. The plaque on the display says nothing about its history.

Wealthy playboy Charles Cory shot a Florida panther, measured it and described it as a puma subspecies. Later, the panther subspecies was named for him: *Puma concolor coryi*.

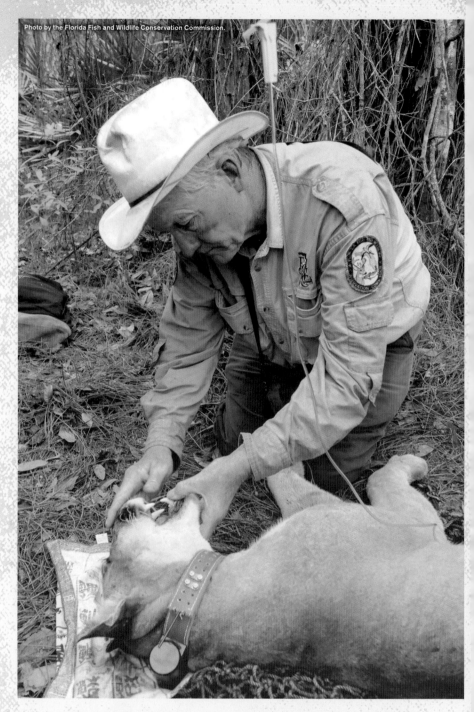

When panthers were included on the first endangered species list, some Florida officials said they were already extinct. The World Wildlife Fund hired a Texas cougar hunter named Roy McBride to find any that were left.

Roy McBride collects ticks from Florida Panther 1—the first Florida panther officially captured by state biologists—with the assistance of a beaming Deborah Jansen. Chris Belden, who nearly killed himself trying to get the cat out of a tree, took this 1981 photo.

Chris Belden attached radio collars to panthers to track their movements, and then he drove around in a truck with an antenna trying to pick up the signals. Eventually he figured out an airplane would work better.

Deborah Jansen, who once tried to save a dying panther with mouth-to-mouth resuscitation, holds a pair of panther kittens from the Big Cypress National Preserve, where she's been the top panther expert since 1987.

Florida's schoolchildren picked the panther as the official state animal over the alligator and manatee. A caged panther watches the Legislature vote to approve the selection in 1982.

Photo from the Florida State Archives.

Photo by Tim Donovan of the Florida Fish and Wildlife Conservation Commission.

So many panthers that Belden caught had kinks in their tails that biologists believed it to be an identifying characteristic. Melody Roelke knew it was the mark of something more alarming.

A Florida panther treed by hounds seeks refuge in a treetop in the Big Cypress National Preserve. This was the point at which a tranquilizer dart fired at FP3 sent it tumbling to the ground, dead, changing the panther capture program forever.

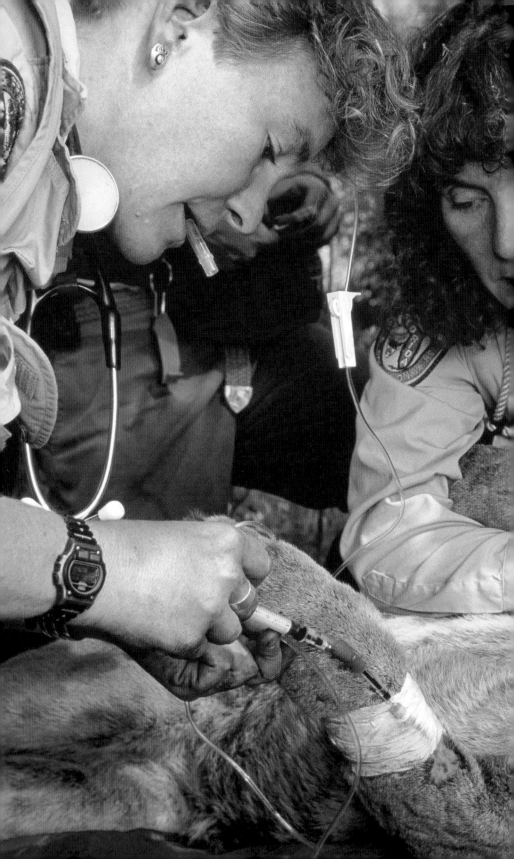

Veterinarians Carolyn Glass (left) and Melody Roelke (right) take samples from an unconscious panther. After making her disturbing discovery, Roelke had a hard time convincing the male biologists that they needed to do something about it.

Photo courtesy of the *Tampa Bay Times*.

Dave Maehr, seen here with a crash bag used in capturing panthers, revived the reputation of the panther capture team. He also worked hard to boost his own reputation as Mr. Panther.

Photo by the author.

Darrell Land shows off a panther skull he keeps in his office. Hired by Maehr to fly around and plot the radio signal locations of panthers with radio collars, he was still at it thirty years later.

Everglades Wonder Gardens, a roadside zoo run by ex-bootleggers Lester and Bill Piper, helped keep panthers in Everglades National Park. Later, the Piper cats provided a clue to how to deal with the problem Roelke discovered.

Photo from the Florida State Archives.

Larry Richardson was hired in 1989 at the brand-new Florida Panther National Wildlife Refuge. Over the next twenty years, he said, "I've watched this go from nothing to almost-nothing."

Computer modeler Jane Comiskey knew there was something wrong with Maehr's science, but she didn't realize how much was wrong until she redid his study herself.

Roy McBride captured eight female Texas cougars to be turned loose in Florida to breed with panthers. The cougars' release into the wild, seen here, was basically a Hail Mary pass.

Photo courtesy of Andy Eller

Andy Eller, seen here standing in the Fakahatchee Strand, knew his bosses at the US Fish and Wildlife Service were relying on junk science to approve development in panther habitat. He tried to stop it.

2017-11-22 5:19:17 AM   M 2/5

FWC4546   Photo courtesy of the Florida Fish and Wildlife Conservation Commission.

A pair of panther kittens flee the flash of a trail camera north of the Caloosahatchee River. You could argue that they are now the most significant panthers in history.

animal, the mascot of schools galore, the icon on scores of license plates.

The only thing left to try, the only option for a "Hail Mary" pass, was something no one had ever tried before. Something nearly unthinkable. It could potentially save the panthers—but it might also unravel the legal protections surrounding them.

The record is unclear about who first brought it up.

Nobody I talked to was sure about who was desperate enough to mention it. O'Brien thinks it might have been Roelke. That makes sense to me. She was always outspoken, and now that she was leaving, she had no reason to hold back. She would never see these people again. Why not speak her mind? But Lacy thinks it was Ulie Seal, always an advocate for pursuing an idea to its logical conclusion, no matter whether it was legal or wise. That makes sense too.

Whoever it was, the two-word phrase he or she uttered was something no one had wanted to think about.

Genetic augmentation.

Usually when people in Florida talk about "augmentation," they're talking about plastic surgery—specifically breast or butt implants. Florida has a big market for that kind of augmentation. Billboards lining US 19 on part of the Gulf Coast tout the docs who can give you deeper cleavage. Meanwhile vans drive around Miami adorned with wraparound paintings of women with voluptuous buttocks barely contained by thong bikinis, suggesting this bounteous booty can be yours—for the right price, of course.

But this isn't that kind of augmentation. Genetic augmentation doesn't make your body parts bigger and squishier and sexier. Instead, it's all about fixing a fouled-up gene pool by introducing something fresh and new.

How do you genetically augment the poor Florida panther? By bringing in some other kind of puma to breed with it.

Ulie Seal's rescue team had first discussed this a year earlier at a conference on panthers in Washington, DC. They dismissed the idea pretty quickly because it would cause nothing but problems. Bringing in outside animals could erase local adaptations, disrupt the native animals' social structure and spread parasites. One other consequence: "Creation of a false sense of management accomplishment."

Moving animals or plants for any reason "is fraught with danger and should be strongly discouraged," they concluded. Nevertheless, they agreed then, there might be a rare set of circumstances that could constitute an exception to this rule.

Now, facing the failure of captive breeding, they had to ask: Is this one of those exceptions? Yes, they decided, it was—mostly because they had no other choice.

They recognized that this solution was legally questionable. A panther bred with some other kind of puma might produce offspring that would not be protected under the Endangered Species Act.

The act gives the Fish and Wildlife Service the power to protect species, subspecies and distinct population segments, as well as their habitats. What the act does not address is half breeds— genetic hybrids. By pushing the purebred panther to become more of a melting pot for puma genes, corporations or special interest groups could cite that as a reason to knock the panther off the endangered list. They could use it as an excuse to open the already shrinking habitat for rampant development. There could even be a return of the hunting season.

The lack of rules covering hybrids is the reason why no one tried crossbreeding the dusky seaside sparrow before it disappeared. The half breeds would lack any legal reason to keep people from shooting them.

Yet, as that example showed, keeping a bloodline pure to maintain legal protection was a pointless exercise if the animal ceased to exist. There would be nothing left to protect.

At that point, O'Brien said, having acknowledged the dire reality they were all facing, there was a shift in the debate. Instead of arguing over whether to bring in another kind of puma to breed with the panthers, they started arguing over *which* puma to use.

The choices: North American mountain lions versus South American pumas.

To O'Brien, logic dictated going after the puma subspecies with the healthiest genes. The South American pumas met that requirement, he said. For proof of how well they would mix with panther genes, he contended, look no further than the Piper cats in the Everglades. Their clean genes saved the fading panthers in the River of Grass, producing hybrids with no kinked tails or vanishing testicles.

But others pushed for sending McBride back to Texas to capture some of the cougars he had spent decades pursuing. Although American pumas had a generally poor sperm count, there were other, historic reasons to favor Texas cougars. What we now call the Florida panther once ranged across the whole South. In those days, the Florida cats probably bred with the occasional Texas cat. Their habitats overlapped, and so at some point their genetic material had probably mingled.

One person who wasn't debating South versus North American pumas? Maehr, who still didn't see the need for this discussion, O'Brien said.

"He was in denial about the data," O'Brien said. "He thought it was just hand-waving by a bunch of scientists who wanted to make themselves famous by publishing a lot of papers."

Even five years later, in his book, Maehr made it clear he remained unpersuaded. He continued arguing that genetic augmentation was unnecessary, based on bad assumptions and fraught with the potential to cause new problems.

Finally, after a three-handed debate, the group backing genetic augmentation with a bunch of Texas cougars won the day. But that wasn't the end of it, because of course once the scientists had reached a consensus, then the bureaucrats started second-guessing everything.

Meanwhile, the extinction clock was still ticking closer and closer to zero.

The US Fish and Wildlife Service had a particularly hard time saying yes. This would be the first time ever that the feds had attempted to save an animal from extinction by breeding it with a close relative. Rare is the bureaucrat who wants to be first, especially with a closely watched project that could easily go awry.

Finally the delay passed from the realm of annoying to dangerous. In April 1994, nine scientists wrote to Secretary of the Interior Bruce Babbitt and to US Fish and Wildlife Service director Mollie Beattie. They said there was a plan that could save the panther, yet some higher-ups in the agency had "conspired to frustrate this objective." Their letter spelled out who would be at fault if panthers disappeared. That finally ended the foot-dragging.

Two years after Seal's group proposed it, the Fish and Wildlife Service produced a two-page memo that officially approved the experiment. Genetic augmentation—or as it was now being called, "genetic restoration"—would be all right so long as state biologists exercised careful scientific control to guarantee that the kittens "most closely resemble the species as listed."

In January 1995, all the bureaucrats involved gave Roy McBride the green light to go capture eight female cougars from Texas and turn them loose in South Florida.

That month was a big one for the government trying to revive big predators. Just as McBride got his approval, a truck carried fourteen Canadian wolves into Yellowstone National Park, which had been completely wolf-less since the last one was killed off in the 1920s. Within seven years there were more than one hundred of them.

Although McBride and Maehr didn't see eye to eye on some things, they agreed on genetic augmentation, or genetic restoration, or (as some journalists were now calling it) "outbreeding," which made it sound like the polar opposite of inbreeding.

No matter the name, "I wasn't particularly fond of the idea," McBride told me.

But because he's a professional, McBride agreed to carry out the assignment anyway. After all, it kept him busy doing the thing he loved, hunting pumas.

He headed to Texas to do what he'd been hired to do, in the place he knew better than anyone else. His only instructions were to be sure the cougars were all young, healthy females, from places far enough apart to ensure they weren't closely related to each other. The game commission wanted females because males would roam around more, making them harder to track, McBride explained to me years later. Females would be more likely to stay put near where they were released, he said.

If this were a movie, we would now see a montage featuring the most visually striking imagery of the story. The movie would leave behind the murk of the swamp, the dampness and the dark shadows of the Fak and the Big Cypress. Instead the camera would pan across a classic Western vista, a bright sun washing across the rocky land, a big sky overhead, not a sign of a house or a car at this place hundreds of miles from civilization.

We zoom in on a solitary figure. A tall and lanky hunter rides through this vast and trackless desert, the rugged mountains forming a picturesque backdrop. His battered Stetson is angled to keep the morning sun out of his eyes. There's a grim set to his jaw.

But wait, there's something wrong here. Our cowboy hero isn't riding a noble steed, a Thoroughbred that comes when he whistles, a twin to the Lone Ranger's Silver. No, he's astride something smaller, less dignified.

It's a mule. McBride picked that as his mount because of the need for a sure-footed ride in this rough terrain.

Our rider has no backup. There's no capture team to trail along behind him now. No burly guys in uniform ready to climb a tree. No veterinarian toting a big pack full of medical equipment. He didn't even bring his sons along this time. It's just McBride and his dogs, searching for signs and scents amid the mesquite brush and prickly pear cactus. He likes it this way— just him against nature.

Unlike in Florida, where the panther hunters weren't allowed onto private lands, here McBride is welcomed by every rancher he meets. They know him and his reputation. They are delighted to see him. They don't like the cougars, which frequently prey on their sheep. They know he's here to take some of them away.

"They were *very* eager!" McBride told me.

There were other differences from Florida too. When his dogs caught a scent and began to chase a cougar, the cat didn't run up a tree. There weren't enough trees for that. Instead it would scramble atop a boulder or slip inside a cave.

That meant that, unlike in Florida, McBride couldn't just fire a tranquilizer dart at the cornered cat. Instead he would have to maneuver his mule around to flush it out—quite a trick, given how skittish the mule was about getting close to a cougar.

"The mules don't like 'em," he explained. "I blindfolded him so he couldn't kick me."

So there he was, all alone, riding a blindfolded mule, his quarry in a hiding place nearly inaccessible to a humans, the fate of the panthers back in Florida riding on his rare abilities. No pressure.

But McBride performed the usual McBride miracle. In just a matter of months, he caught between fifteen and twenty cats, he told me.

Many of them were unsuitable for the job. They were male, for instance. Or they were too old. Or they didn't seem healthy enough. Those he turned loose again.

Whenever he caught one that seemed like a keeper, he'd shoot it with the tranquilizer dart containing a drug called ketamine. Once it was asleep, he'd hoist the drugged cat onto the back of the still-blindfolded mule and lead it back to where he had left his truck. Then he'd hitch the mule to the truck and load the cat into the front seat, as if it were some drunk uncle he'd picked up passed out in a bar. McBride would then climb behind the wheel and start making the long drive home with the mule trotting along behind and the snoozing cougar slumped down next to him.

He kept the cougars in the front seat, he explained, so he could monitor how comatose the cat was. The ketamine that knocked them out didn't always last for the whole trip. If he had put the cat in the back of the truck, it might have awakened and jumped out. Keeping the cougar in the truck cab, while risky, seemed preferable to losing one.

"If it began to recover, I'd give it a little more ketamine," he said.

At home McBride had built a pen to keep the cougars quarantined, both from other cougars in the wild and from each other. They had to be penned up for thirty days, as requested by Florida officials. A veterinarian stopped by to take blood samples and check for any obvious health problems.

"The hardest thing was feeding them," McBride told me. "They ate a lot. I'd feed them javelinas and road-killed deer. Gosh, they ate those things real quick!"

Texas parks officials brought him dead animals, and gave their blessing to removing the cougars from the state. It's not as if they were endangered in Texas.

Once he had eight female cougars that had passed all the

health tests, it was time to haul them back to Florida. That turned out to be even trickier than catching them.

McBride looked up a number for an airline at the nearest airport, which was two hundred miles away, and called to ask advice on how to transport such a cargo. The man on the other end of the line spelled it out for him. He couldn't just stuff them into regular pet carriers, as if they were somebody's Pomeranians. He'd have to buy or construct special cages for each cougar. The airline employee told him the dimensions would have to be this, the air holes would have to be that, the handles would need to look like so. There would have to be a way to water the cougars during the flight without opening the door. That's the only way they would be allowed onto the plane. He even sent McBride the blueprints.

McBride took careful notes on everything, looked over the blueprints, then got some wood and started sawing and hammering. Before long he'd built all eight cages. He thought they were pretty luxurious compared to the standard pet carrier.

Being McBride, he of course figured out how to persuade the cougars to climb in with a minimum of fuss. Then he loaded each crate into a trailer and, two months after his initial phone call, hauled them to the airport.

That's where things went sour.

The airline employees on duty took one look at McBride and his traveling cat troupe and said no way. No giant apex predators with sharp teeth would be allowed on board.

"They had a fit," McBride told me. "They said, 'You are not going to put those animals on an airplane.'"

McBride was flabbergasted. He had followed the instructions to the letter. He was all set to fly these cats to Florida. Now it was looking like he'd have to figure out how to truck them across most of Texas, through the coastal part of Louisiana, Mississippi and Alabama and then down the spine of Florida to the southern tip. Even the idea of hauling them two hundred miles back to his home was daunting.

Fortunately, just as he was about to turn around in defeat, the employee he had talked to on the phone showed up.

Just like that, everything changed. This guy gave McBride a big smile and a thumbs-up to load the cats. They were cleared to fly to Florida, making the trip in hours instead of days. It turned out that this particular airline employee had a vivid memory of his conversation with McBride about the cougars.

"He'd been waiting to see 'em!" McBride said, laughing.

In Florida, the biologists decided to release the female cougars in pairs. Two would be turned loose in the Fak, two in the Big Cypress and so on.

The first pair were taken to the Fak. There, near the end of an unpaved road ten miles from the nearest house, McBride put them into a chain-link enclosure. The release plan called for keeping them penned up there for two weeks. They'd be fed deer meat and allowed to acclimate to the sights and smells and sounds of the swamp that was to be their new home.

At the end of March 1995, state officials planned to turn them loose with the appropriate pomp and ceremony. They invited fifty dignitaries and reporters from around the state to serve as witnesses for this momentous event.

When everyone showed up, though, they discovered something surprising: only one cat remained in the pen. It was an eighty-pounder that crouched beneath a tall oak, panting in the heat and snarling at anyone who dared to stare at it through the slits in the burlap screen.

Where was the second one? It had already escaped.

One of the reporters who covered the release party wrote that the seventy-pound female cougar had "initiated her own early-release program by repeatedly hurling her body at full speed into the chain-link fence until she loosened the metal clips holding it to a corner pole—and out she went."

Fortunately the biologists had already attached radio collars to both cougars, so they knew precisely where the escapee had gone. Once they turned the remaining captive loose, they could track both of them from the air, following their progress as they accustomed themselves to their new home and—everyone hoped—mated with whatever remaining males could still produce viable sperm.

The other releases proceeded with less drama. Every few days, someone from the capture team would take to the air and buzz around checking on the cougars' locations, tracking where they ended up, marking how close they were to any males.

Seven months passed like that.

Then, in October 1995, game commission officials were ready to hand out cigars. A miracle had happened. Their Hail Mary pass had landed just right to become a touchdown.

One of the Texas females had given birth to two kittens, a male and a female. They appeared to be free of all genetic defects. No kinked tail. No cowlick. No heart murmur. No problems with their reproductive system. The cougars McBride had selected had succeeded where nearly everyone expected yet another failure.

Three of the females didn't get to play their part, McBride told me. One Texas cougar was run over on a highway. Another was shot dead, no one knows why or by whom. One more died under somewhat cloudy circumstances, he said. That one had been pregnant at the time.

But the other five performed like champions. They adapted well to their new surroundings and produced litter after litter of defect-free kittens sired by male panthers.

Their offspring freshened up the gene pool, boosting the panthers' dwindling population, and raising the state animal's chances for surviving into the twenty-first century. The turnaround seemed as dramatic as any miracle from biblical times: "Lo, the Lone Star cougars went forth and multiplied…"

By the time all this happened, of course, the woman who started the process, Roelke, was long gone. She was off in Africa, chasing a different kind of cat.

Also gone was her nemesis, Dave Maehr. He had left the game commission job he loved so much, quitting under pressure.

Unlike Roelke, though, he didn't go far.

CHAPTER FOURTEEN

"FLORIDA WILL BE DEVELOPED"

There was something about the Big Cypress that kept draw-ing him back, over and over. For some reason, Dave Maehr couldn't leave it alone, even after his boss told him to back off.

What was it that drove him to violate the order about leaving it alone? Was it because Deb Jansen was there? A woman with more experience than he had, one who wanted to run her own separate panther capture program with help from McBride and the Texan's two now-grown sons? After all, she was someone with the credentials to challenge his claim to being the supreme authority on the subject of Florida's state animal.

Or perhaps what drew him back was the fact that panthers

kept turning up in the Big Cypress even though it was, according to him, "terrible panther habitat." When the capture team did find panthers there, Maehr contended they were "essentially the 'living dead' of the population." But there sure seemed to be a lot of the living dead walking around.

Whatever the reason, he continued leading his team onto the federal preserve without giving Jansen a heads-up.

In April 1993, he did it again—and then, in July, he hand-delivered a videotape to the park service staff at Big Cypress. What was on the tape? When I talked to Jansen about it sixteen years later, she said she didn't recall. Maehr's personnel file doesn't say, except to note that he had delivered it "in violation of a direct order of your supervisor." Apparently the supervisor was concerned the tape would further damage relations with the Big Cypress staff.

I talked to Maehr's supervisor, the guy who made such a big deal about the tape. He said he couldn't remember what was on it or why he was so angry about it. But he also said the fact that he couldn't recall was a sign of how many other things Maehr did that broke the rules. This one just blended in.

Whatever was on the tape, it became the last straw. When Maehr's boss found out about it in August, he opened a formal investigation. That led to Maehr being notified just before Christmas that he was being suspended without pay for ten days. His offenses: insubordination and conduct unbecoming a state employee.

There was a worse punishment in store. Maehr's boss said he would be postponing the start of the 1994 capture season by two weeks. When it did start, instead of Maehr running the show, the leader would be Walt McCown. Also, the boss decreed, Jansen would be working closely with the team—as a colleague, not an antagonist.

Maehr fought back. He demanded a hearing. He contended he was blameless in everything.

At the hearing, he argued that Roelke had caused him stress. He accused Jansen of not doing proper research. He said that the reason the panther program had had three supervisors in thirteen years was because his boss was a bad boss. He wound up this remarkable speech by saying that while he was optimistic about the panther's future, he didn't feel the same way about his own.

"Unfortunately it is not clear to me if the commission is interested in having me continue to document the biology of a secretive, endangered carnivore that is the center of daunting political and sociological obstacles," he told the hearing board. "Regrettably the panther project has become a blueprint for personal tragedy..."

He both won and lost the fight. The head of the game commission reviewed his case and decided he didn't merit a ten-day unpaid suspension. It would be three days, period. But shortly afterward, Maehr's boss let him know that he wouldn't be allowed to go out in the field with the capture team anymore. Ever. He also wouldn't be supervising anyone.

Instead, Maehr's boss told him, his new assignment would be working on preserving panther habitat on private lands. After all, didn't he keep harping on how important habitat was to the future of the subspecies? Time for him to show what he could do to fix that.

His job would be to go out and meet with the ranchers and other major landowners and convince them to keep their property as pristine as possible. He would study maps and identify important habitat that was worth preserving and try to make that happen.

Maehr could still do his bear research, the boss said. He could still do aerial monitoring of both the panthers and the bears too. But, mindful of the time that Maehr had faked some data about a capture on Seminole Indian property, the boss told him he would not be allowed to crunch the numbers. He could not even input the data he personally collected: "Panther data are to be provided to Darrell Land, to whom the responsibility for management of panther data is being assigned."

For Maehr, who thrived on publishing every little bit of data he came up with, this was too much. Without the data, without being in charge of the capture team, he couldn't claim to be Mr. Panther anymore.

Maehr quit. Rather than submit to this humiliating punishment, he gave up the job that was paying him $71,000 a year. In his resignation letter, he wrote that "events over the last two months have hastened a decision on my part to pursue other avenues of professional fulfillment and development."

But Maehr wasn't done with panthers—or with battling his boss.

On his last day on the job, in February 1994, Maehr showed up at a public hearing in Fort Myers. At the nighttime hearing, landowners were complaining about what they saw as heavy-handed government efforts to force them to maintain their property to suit panthers rather than allowing them to maximize their own profit. Reporters for the Fort Lauderdale paper were there to cover that, and so Maehr gave them a scoop.

"Florida Panther Researcher Resigns, Citing Poor Plans, Cutbacks," said the headline.

Maehr told them that the game commission was doing such a poor job of saving the state animal that he couldn't stomach it anymore. He said he had decided he could do more good as a private consultant. He also warned, "If we don't take serious steps to addressing the [land] issues, all the treatments of symptoms we have done over the years will have been no good."

It was a classic bit of PR razzle-dazzle from Mr. Panther. The reporters who wrote the story had no time to pull Maehr's personnel file that night and see the real reason he had quit. His boss, who was also at the meeting, could not give the real reason either. State rules said he couldn't talk about personnel issues beyond verifying that Maehr had resigned. Thus the reporters could either take Maehr's word for why he was leaving or else hold on to their scoop and risk having some other reporter beat them to it. They went with Maehr's version of the story.

Maehr, in the interview, made no mention of the panther's genetic problems or the failure of captive breeding. He pinned everything afflicting the big cats on the loss of habitat. Everything else was just a "symptom," not the cause of their woes.

When the meeting was over and he was done talking to the reporters, Maehr walked out of the Lee County Courthouse and was, seemingly, done.

Two weeks later, though, he turned up again, this time in Florida's northeastern metropolis of Jacksonville. He was meeting with officials from the US Fish and Wildlife Service and the US Army Corps of Engineers. Now he was a private consultant, the job he said would allow him to do more for panthers than anything the game commission would allow.

And what was he doing as a private consultant? Maehr was there representing a developer called Corkscrew Enterprises. Corkscrew was seeking a federal permit for filling in wetlands in panther habitat in order to build a big subdivision.

Just as he had done in Ohio, Maehr had flipped sides.

When I saw the name of the development Maehr was pushing, one that would wind up destroying not only wetlands but also panther habitat, all I could do was laugh.

It was called The Habitat.

Why did Maehr, the great defender of panther habitat, go to work for guys who wanted to pave it? I wish I could have asked him. Unfortunately, before I had the chance to do an in-depth interview with him, he died in a plane crash while doing bear research. So all we can do is speculate.

The human mind has an almost infinite capacity for self-justification. Nobody wakes up in the morning and thinks, "Today I will betray all my ideals in exchange for money."

People do what they do for reasons that they think justify their actions—to feed their family, to change the system from the inside, to get back at people who wronged them. I suspect all of these came into play for Maehr.

I looked for clues to Maehr's reasoning in his 1997 book *The Florida Panther: Life and Death of a Vanishing Carnivore*. He talked a little about The Habitat. He described how, while he was working for the game commission, he judged that piece of land to be good habitat for panthers. Shortly afterward one of the radio-collared panthers wandered across it, proving his point. Despite his recommendation, he noted, his bosses chose not to block the development.

However, he wrote, by the time the project won its wetlands-destruction permit from the feds, its design had been "transformed to minimize impacts on wetlands and wildlife including panthers. The permit...would require the developer to leave significant areas of forest on the property that would adjoin neighboring conservation property."

This is the "I worked with them to make it a better project" excuse. Of course, the panthers probably would have preferred the land stay the way it was, with no development at all. That was Maehr's original position too, but then he changed.

Maehr didn't mention in the book that he had been employed by that developer, helping to get that crucial federal permit. Somehow the subject of his consulting work for developers never comes up in the book at all, even though it continued for more than a decade after he quit the game commission. It's not even included in the "About the Author" section, suggesting Maehr knew how that would look to readers. All his back-cover biography talked about was how he had led the capture team, earned his doctorate and landed a job as an assistant professor at the University of Kentucky.

Before Maehr died, a graduate student named Nathan Gove working on a thesis about panthers sat down with him for a

lengthy interview. Gove carefully led up to a question about
Maehr's consulting work, but Maehr wasn't fooled. He had
heard the whispers of people questioning who was paying him.
He insisted he was no Dr. Jukebox, ready to play any song you
wanted if you put a quarter in the slot. The identity of the people who paid him didn't matter, he contended.

"What does that have to do with anything?" he replied.
"What that suggests is that my work is influenced by who pays
me... And I would argue that my position as an academic, as
someone who now is completely independent in terms of any
income that I might get that demands a certain way of looking
at things, then I'm probably less biased than anybody out there."

Clearly, though, the criticism got under his skin.

"That's the thing that's so troubling, is what's being offered is
that, you know, 'Dave Maehr has suddenly turned to the Dark
Side, and he did it for money,'" he told Gove. "And it's like,
'No, I worked on this thing for ten years at a pauper's salary.'"

Rather than pursue that train of thought to the end, Maehr
veered off on a tangent, and the grad student never quite got
him back on track.

When Maehr was sitting on the developers' side of the table,
pushing for a permit for The Habitat, there was a biologist from
the US Fish and Wildlife Service sitting on the other side whom
you could call "the anti-Maehr." His name: Andy Eller.

A reporter once described Eller as "an introvert with a tendency to speak in a barely audible monotone." He had dark
hair, glasses, a mustache and, generally, a sheepish look. That
look could fool you, because under that nebbishy exterior was
a will of solid steel.

When Eller was growing up in Norfolk, Virginia, his closest friend was a kid who liked catching snakes and turtles, so
Eller joined in.

"We kept them for pets," Eller told me, "depending on how tolerant our mothers were."

Some of his natural encounters were more unusual. He was fishing at a lake once and took a break to pee.

"I was standing there, urinating in the lake," Eller told me, "and I looked up into the eyes of a grackle." Rather than freaking out, he said, "I was struck by how yellow its eyes were."

He became so enamored of nature that he collected first editions of classics of environmental literature, such as Rachel Carson's *Silent Spring*. He wound up studying forestry at Clemson University. After graduating he got a job at a national wildlife refuge working with red-cockaded woodpeckers, which are listed as an endangered species. He did such a good job he was transferred to the regional office in Atlanta and put in charge of acquiring land for all the wildlife refuges in the Southeast.

Then came 1991, and the turning point in his life.

Because of his real estate experience, Eller's bosses assigned him to work with the chief of the Florida Panther National Wildlife Refuge in drawing up a map of panther habitat that needed to be saved. Together they examined the suitability of more than a million acres of privately owned land across nine Florida counties, with an eye toward recommending the government buy some to expand the refuge.

Once they were done, Eller's bosses in Atlanta assigned him the job of implementing the plan. Veteran biologists warned him not to get his hopes up. But for five years he attended development meetings and got to know all the landowners, chatting up local government planners about various projects. Somehow, nothing happened but a lot of talk.

"It turned out to be mostly a public relations job," Eller said.

He cobbled together a proposal for a brand-new wildlife refuge and pushed and prodded the bureaucracy until it landed in Washington.

"It never got funding," he said. "That was a huge disappoint-

ment to me. I thought that helping one of the most endangered
animals in the country would rank pretty high." He never even
got a straight answer about why his plan got shot down, he said.

Eller's habitat work is what landed him in the meeting about
The Habitat, where he met Maehr the consultant.

"My initial and lasting impression of him was that he was in-
telligent and witty," Eller told me. "My experience with him
was mostly positive."

But then came one of the biggest, thorniest developments to
ever tear up a place where panthers lived.

Eller's maps showed exactly what Maehr had been saying all
along: a lot of Pantherland wasn't public property. It belonged
to private landowners—cattle ranchers, mostly.

While most people think of Florida as being nothing but
beaches and theme parks, ranchers own more than four million
acres of pasture and range across the central and southern part
of the state. Some of the ranchers can trace their family's cattle
holdings back to before the Civil War. As late as the 1890s, at a
time when the West had stopped being so wild, Florida's ranchers
were still getting into range wars and hanging cattle rustlers from
the nearest tree branch. The open range era lasted until 1949.

Some of the state's remaining eighteen thousand or so ranchers have been careful to maintain their property as a good habitat for wildlife. Some, on the other hand, cannot wait to cash in
by selling their land to developers or paving over it themselves.
Some are not real ranchers, just real estate investors who have
parked a few cows on their future development site to claim
an agricultural exemption on their property taxes until they're
ready to cover it with concrete.

One of the ranchers ready to cash in was Ben Hill Griffin
III. A beefy, bullet-headed businessman, Griffin was the only
son and namesake of Florida citrus and cattle baron Ben Hill
Griffin Jr., whose name is also on the University of Florida's

football stadium, aka "The Swamp." Under the younger Griffin, the companies the family owned had begun to diversify beyond orange trees and cows, taking on everything from mining to sod-growing to real estate development. The Griffin family businesses controlled hundreds of thousands of acres, and more than a few politicians. To say the Griffin family is influential is like saying that Superman can lift heavy things.

In the early 1990s, the Legislature decided to build a new university—the state's tenth—near Fort Myers. The lawmakers left it to the state Board of Regents to pick the site from three finalists culled from a list of twenty-two properties. One of the three finalists was, from an environmental standpoint, the worst possible choice. More than half of the land was swamp. It lay in a district zoned for conservation, to aid in recharging the underground aquifer. And it was designated as prime panther habitat. But it was owned by Ben Hill Griffin III, who had offered to donate it to the state at no charge.

Can you guess which one the Regents chose?

To Griffin, his land was ideal for the new campus: "It had the greatest access to I-75. It had a mile frontage on a 775-acre lake." (Actually the "lake" was a rock quarry that had filled up with water, but somehow that never was mentioned.)

Griffin scoffed at the idea that panthers might live on his property. Weren't they nearly extinct?

"The panther ain't never been there, ain't comin' back," he drawled. "You look close enough, you may find a dinosaur track out there, but I don't think the dinosaur is coming back again."

Griffin's reasons for donating his land to the state were anything but altruistic. He owned all the property around the potential college campus, and he expected the new university to spark a major development boom in an area he had already envisioned as a new town. In other words, the Regents building the campus in that spot would destroy more than just six hundred forty acres of panther habitat. It would lead to the destruction of thousands of acres of habitat all around it too.

Whatever Griffin wanted in Florida, he usually got. Thus the state agencies that had to approve permits for the work did so, overriding the objections of their own staff biologists. But to get permission to build the college on such a soggy site, the Regents needed a wetlands destruction permit from the US Army Corps of Engineers. And to get that permit required approval of Eller's agency for any potential impact on endangered species—panthers, for instance.

Corps officials were initially inclined to say no. The wetlands impact was too big and the reasoning behind it made no sense. After all, there were other, drier places to build the campus that would produce a smaller impact.

But then the calls began coming in from Griffin's friends in the federal government. The colonel in charge of the Corps's office in Jacksonville was out on an airboat in the Everglades one day when his cell phone rang. When he answered, his ear got blistered, but good, by Florida's Republican senator, a Fort Myers banker named Connie Mack. The senator was cussing him out for not giving Griffin what he wanted right away.

Meanwhile, the Fish and Wildlife Service was having some heartburn about the impact on panthers. In addition to the campus itself, the first permit they had to consider included a new road at its entrance that was expected to draw nearly one thousand cars a day. When the agency expressed its concerns, the Board of Regents wrote back describing the new college's environmental education program. To them, teaching college kids about nature would make up for bulldozing places where the state animal lived.

Contrary to Griffin's comments, panthers did indeed live there. A draft report by the Fish and Wildlife Service noted all the panther signs around Griffin's property—tracks and scrapes and radio telemetry readings, not to mention the occasional roadkill. Each one was a strike against approving the permit there, according to David Ferrell, the Fish and Wildlife Service biologist who was then in charge of the agency's regional office in the Atlantic Coast town of Vero Beach.

"We had seen a female migrating back and forth across there," Ferrell told me when I finally tracked him down for an interview. He and his wife had both worked for the agency in Florida, and both had left the agency and the state with a bitter taste in their mouths. They had moved to where they were not easy to find and even switched careers.

Ferrell, a California native, had a background as a fisheries biologist, working in Alaska for another federal agency and then in Washington for a congressional committee before moving to Florida to oversee a dozen people in the Vero Beach office. A big part of their job was reviewing development plans to see what impact a project might have on various endangered species. The Corps of Engineers was supposed to consult with them on every wetlands destruction permit that affected panthers, manatees, Key deer and other protected wildlife. The permit for what state officials called "The Tenth University" was the first really big one he dealt with.

Ferrell wanted to be sure his staff didn't screw this one up. He said he made several visits to the site in 1993, accompanied by the state game commission's top panther expert—Maehr, who was on shaky ground but had not yet been forced out.

Griffin's land, Ferrell told me, was "all soggy," making him wonder how the Corps could possibly approve it. When he and Maehr sloshed around the property, Maehr called it "very good habitat," according to Ferrell. In fact, Maehr said he'd thought he had found a spot where a panther had slept, further proof that panthers were using Griffin's property. Plus, there appeared to be a female panther repeatedly crossing the property from a nearby Audubon Society preserve known as Corkscrew Swamp. (Maehr's team had picked up a dead panther immediately north of the property about a year before, which Darrell Land later called "a physical presence that's hard to deny.")

Ferrell was mindful, too, of all the spinoff development from putting a college in that spot, and what that would mean for the panthers' habitat. It would be a seed just like the old Everglades jetport, ready to sprout destruction all around.

"If they developed that area it would not be just the footprint of the campus but also all the apartments and the shopping malls and so forth," he said. Wiping out so much habitat all at once would do more than just displace a few cats: "It would have an impact on breeding."

When the Fish and Wildlife Service provides the Corps with a report on a project needing a wetlands permit, the report is known as a "biological opinion." If the agency decided the development would not put the future of any endangered animals in jeopardy, then it was called a "no jeopardy" opinion. But if the wildlife service reviewed the site and the science and concluded that this particular shopping mall or subdivision *could* jeopardize the future of an endangered critter, then it was called a "jeopardy" opinion.

In May 1994, Ferrell and his staff concluded that building the new university on Ben Hill Griffin III's land would definitely jeopardize the future of panthers—and at a time when their future seemed particularly precarious. Captive breeding had failed and McBride had not yet gotten approval to bring in any Texas cougars, so there were no more than about thirty of the cats remaining. The idea of destroying hundreds of acres of their habitat seemed like folly.

"This is a direct and permanent loss of habitat that would be a fairly significant loss of panther habitat," Ferrell told me. "We'd lose reproduction, we'd lose habitat. The population could begin to spiral downward."

If a biological opinion turned out to be a "no jeopardy," then Ferrell could sign it on his own. If it was a "jeopardy" opinion, then he had to send it to his boss. This was a clear "jeopardy" opinion, so he sent it along to his boss in Atlanta, and held his breath.

Someone shared the draft with Griffin's paid consultants, who showed it to him. He made a few phone calls. One of them went to Florida's senior US senator, Robert "Bob" Graham, a Democrat.

Graham was a wonkish, Harvard-educated lawyer whose family had made a fortune developing the Miami Lakes community in South Florida. His father is credited with being the first to plant sugar cane in South Florida. Yet the pudgy politician had convinced the voting public he was just a regular guy by creating what he called "Work Days" in which he would show up to work for one day a month at a regular-guy job: teacher, firefighter, sheriff's deputy and so forth. Those made him popular enough to be elected to two terms as governor from 1979 to 1987, and then got him elected to a US Senate seat. In office, he cultivated a reputation as a leader on environmental causes. He was among the first Florida politicians to push for restoring the Everglades, and he cofounded the Save the Manatee Club with singer Jimmy Buffett. Some people claimed he was the model for the character of Skink, the wily ex-governor turned eco-terrorist in Carl Hiaasen's wacky Florida crime novels, although Graham wouldn't be caught dead wandering the state's highways clad in a loin cloth and a shower cap. He was also, incidentally, the governor who signed into law the declaration that the panther was the official state animal.

Yet now Graham was being asked by a major campaign donor for help in getting permission to wipe out a bunch of panther habitat. Without publicly endorsing the project, the senator agreed to provide some back-door assistance.

On September 26, 1994—a date which will, for panther fans, live in infamy—Ferrell's bosses in Atlanta convened a meeting there. They did so at Graham's request. Neither Ferrell nor his

Vero Beach staff were invited. Neither were any of the state game commission's panther experts. Instead, the attendees included Ben Hill Griffin's attorney, two officials from Lee County (which was eager to see the university and its surrounding development get built) and—representing Griffin's development consultants—Dave Maehr.

If anyone took notes at that meeting, they were never made public. Years later, when a reporter asked Griffin what occurred that day, his response echoed the lyrics of an old Charlie Rich country hit: "Who knows what goes on behind closed doors?"

But the upshot of the meeting was clear as crystal: the "jeopardy" opinion would be changed to a "no jeopardy" opinion, clearing the way for construction to begin.

All they did was change one word. They didn't tinker with all the scientific arguments leading up to the conclusion. Ferrell told me his bosses just inserted the word "no" before "jeopardy."

As Griffin put it in his interview, "They finally saw the light. Maybe they considered that this was some $50 million gift to the people of the state of Florida. But how many times do you have the opportunity to help found a new university?"

Ferrell got wind of what was happening up in Atlanta and called his boss.

"He said we weren't at the jeopardy threshold yet," Ferrell said, still sounding disgusted twenty years later.

Horrified to see politics override science, Ferrell and the federal agency's chief panther expert wrote a lengthy memo to the top agency official in Atlanta, protesting the decision: "We are disappointed we were not afforded the opportunity to brief you prior to a no jeopardy decision being reached." Building a college and its entrance road in that spot would clearly jeopardize the panther's future, they contended. The cumulative impact would be enormous.

The Atlanta official rifled the memo back the same day he received it. It was now covered in handwritten notes responding to their arguments. "There is no biology here," said one, and "Not biological," said another, and, most damning, "Florida will be developed."

That last one rocked Ferrell's faith in his own agency.

"It changed the way we looked at the panther," he said. When I asked why, he said, "Because we had no support... My agency had buckled." Not long after this, Ferrell was transferred into a position that did not involve reviewing development in panther habitat.

What was best for panthers lost out against what was best for "big, influential people," Darrell Land told a reporter in 1994. "They won out. Wildlife is kind of an afterthought."

Years later, in an oral history for the wildlife agency, one of the Atlanta bosses responsible for rejecting Ferrell's recommendation talked in general about how politics influences endangered species decisions: "Somebody once said, in dealing in the Endangered Species Program, you have to walk down the line. You have people that want you to protect everything and do everything there on one side and have other people saying don't even worry about this, they're going to die off anyhow. So as long as people are chewing on both sides of your derriere as you walk down that fine line, you were doing a good job." In this case, though, Griffin and his prodevelopment friends had no derriere-chewing plans, because they got exactly what they wanted.

Thus construction began, both on the campus of what was now called Florida Gulf Coast University and on the entrance road, which was named for Griffin. But when the students first arrived and tried walking around the still swampy grounds, they came up with a different name for the place: "Mildew U." In less than ten years, the university would be fined three times for illegally pumping water off the campus, trying to dry the place out. More than one person wondered if Griffin had donated that property to the state because he would have had a hard time selling any houses he built there.

What happened with the FGCU jeopardy opinion set the template for all future Fish and Wildlife Service decisions, according to Craig Johnson, who followed Ferrell in supervising the agency's South Florida office from 1995 to 1998.

"That really was the first step," he told me. In his three years in charge, he and his staff tried thirty times to have development projects classified as putting the panthers in jeopardy, "and they were all overturned" by Atlanta, just like with FGCU, he said. "The answer was always: the panthers aren't there yet."

When I asked Johnson what it would have taken to get the Atlanta office to agree that a developer was going to put panthers in jeopardy, he said, "Probably their extinction."

Johnson, who was in a New York street gang in his youth, said he got just as sick as Ferrell with the political arm-twisting that allowed development to routinely wipe out panther habitat.

"I worked in some pretty rough places," he said. "Turned out none of them was harder than Florida."

Maehr, in his interview with the grad student years later, defended his work on creating a college where panthers once roamed. He claimed that he had never believed that the campus was good panther habitat, and that his sole contribution to the project was to try in vain to get the buildings clustered together rather than let them sprawl all over the campus.

"I never lobbied to build the university," he said. But then, apparently in reference to panther advocates who tried to fight it, he added: "One of the things that I said was, 'Let the university go, because you're going to get incredible mitigation out of this. You're going to get land you can protect elsewhere, and it's going to be valuable habitat for the panther, and not this marginal...crap that is not going to be very beneficial to [the] panther population."

A year after he helped get FGCU approved, Maehr set himself up as the ultimate expert on what was and was not panther habitat. He became the most influential scientist in Florida for determining the pattern of development all across the region—but he did it by cutting corners, just the way he'd done before.

CHAPTER FIFTEEN

MR. INFLUENTIAL

In October 1995, Maehr published not one but two new scientific papers in a well-respected journal called *Conservation Biology*.

One of them, titled "Demographics and Genetic Introgression in the Florida Panther," argued that bringing cougars to Florida from Texas—a task that McBride had just completed—"should be reconsidered." The reason: Maehr said that he had seen no signs that panthers were having trouble reproducing, and in fact he thought the population was already rebounding before the Texas cats got involved.

He was, of course, pretty much alone in making that argument, and that paper drew little attention.

The other paper, though, would become the most influential scientific paper ever written about Florida's state animal.

Titled "Landscape Features and Panthers in Florida," the piece said that a review of the state game commission's large collection of radio telemetry readings showed that panthers preferred large forests over every other kind of habitat. The data also showed they wouldn't cross more than three hundred feet of nonforested land, Maehr's paper said.

The conclusion was obvious: if you wanted to save panthers, you had to save large forest patches that were less than three hundred feet apart. Any other kind of habitat didn't matter, even if you found a panther's paw print in the middle of it. Go ahead and pave that stuff over!

To produce this paper, Maehr teamed up with another scientist named James A. Cox from the Tall Timbers Research Station, located near the state capital in Tallahassee. Cox knew about birds, not mammals. He was one of the state's leading experts on red-cockaded woodpeckers, but he had never seen a panther, much less studied their habitat. Maehr needed him as a coauthor because he was an expert on mapping wildlife, showing where they lived and bred, and what terrain they preferred.

Maehr had an interest in Florida's birds—in fact, he had co-written a bird book in his spare time. As a result, he and Cox sort of knew each other. But it was Cox's own curiosity about panthers that got them working together, Cox told me.

"It was a classic example of people coming together," he explained.

Cox was curious about whether the panthers' habitat could be mapped so it could be protected. And Maehr "had all this data," he said.

Technically it wasn't Maehr's own personal data. It was data that had been gathered by perhaps a dozen state employees—Maehr himself, but also Chris Belden, Deb Jansen, Darrell Land, even Walt McCown, who hated to fly. They had all gone up in little planes with their H-shaped antennas and their headphones, checking for the radio signals from collared panthers roaming around down below. Because they were government employees tracking signals from government equipment, the data they collected was owned by the taxpaying public. That meant anyone—even Maehr, who had been forced out of his state job a year before while under a cloud—could request access to it, and then use it for any purpose they pleased.

Cox wasn't all that familiar with how telemetry worked, but he knew how to use Geographic Information Systems software to analyze what Maehr told him the data showed. He could then turn it into a map, and link it to the types of landscape present in South Florida. Maehr brought him a lot of data to work with—14,500 locations from forty-one radio-collared panthers dating back to the first one Belden tracked from a pickup truck.

When Cox asked Maehr questions about how the telemetry readings were collected, he found some things that troubled him. One involved the time when the readings were taken.

"These were daytime recordings—places where panthers were bedding down," Cox told me.

Panthers generally sleep during the day. They're creatures of the night. That's when they move around, hunt for prey, mate. The telemetry data reflected none of that.

"I asked Dave about that and he said, 'It's the best we've got,'" Cox said. "He didn't appreciate how this might bias the picture."

Cox soon discovered they had another potential problem, this time involving how the telemetry readings were collected.

"I figured that with telemetry readings there's going to be some error," Cox told me. "I assumed it would be a random error. In reality Dave and the others who were plotting out the telemetry readings, when they got a reading they would plot it in the nearest forest cover they found. They did that based on where they thought the panthers should be."

Because they expected the panthers to be found in forests, that's where they put the readings—even if it wasn't really where the panthers were sleeping. They could be in a palmetto thicket or an orange grove, and the biologists would say they were in a forest if there was one nearby.

Yet that wasn't the worst thing Cox found. That one involved Maehr and Maehr alone.

"He threw out all the stuff that was in the Everglades," Cox said. He threw out whatever data came from Big Cypress too.

When Cox asked Maehr why, "he said he thought it was an anomaly. Dave had strong opinions. He wasn't quite objective. It was based on his professional opinion."

Maehr didn't trust telemetry readings that didn't match his theories, and his theories said those areas were poor habitat. Even though the readings for the Everglades and Big Cypress showed, very clearly, that panthers were there, and were hopscotching among the tree islands and swimming across the strands, he didn't buy it.

Cox told me he tried to convince Maehr that what he was doing was wrong, but he failed. Maehr could win any argument by reminding Cox of his greater expertise.

"I couldn't be forceful with him," the ornithologist said. "He was the panther person."

In scientific circles, journals like *Conservation Biology* act as the gatekeepers of knowledge. The journals don't publish every paper that's submitted to them. Instead, each article has to undergo a rigorous process called "peer review." The peer review process is supposed to screen out slipshod work and block crackpots and flimflam artists from getting their stuff into print. Only the best, most authentic scientific work merits publication.

At least, that's the theory.

Peer review works like this: a scientist submits a paper for publication. The editor contacts other scientists in the same or similar fields—the author's peers—to read it. If the peers reviewing the paper find problems, then the editor sends it back to the author with suggestions on how to fix it. If the peers find too many flaws, then the paper might even be rejected.

Any paper that survives the peer-review process and makes it into print is generally held by scientists to be, if not the gospel truth, then pretty close to it. But there are flaws in the peer-review process, big ones that scientists seldom discuss. The biggest one is this: the peer reviewers generally don't see the raw data. They see only the completed paper.

Maehr, in the completed paper, didn't mention he had tossed out a bunch of data on the Everglades and Big Cypress, so the reviewers had no idea he had done so. They also didn't know that Maehr was extrapolating all panther habitat use, both night and day, from readings that only covered where they slept when the sun was up. They definitely did not suspect that the telemetry readings were based on where the biologists flying overhead had expected the panthers to be, not on where they actually were.

The editor of *Conservation Biology* at the time was a professor from the University of Central Florida named Reed Noss. Tall and slender with a bushy mustache, Noss was a rarity among Ph.D.'s. In addition to his many academic awards and honors, Noss had also earned a seventh-degree black belt in karate. He counted Dave Maehr as a friend, not to mention the nation's top panther expert, so he didn't think twice about running the Maehr-Cox paper once it passed peer review.

According to Noss, the peer-review process is based on trust. If someone abuses that trust, he or she can flip the whole system over on its back and pin it to the mat.

"Peer reviewers have to rely on what the authors report in their paper," Noss explained. "Ultimately the onus is on the authors to use all the available data or explain why certain data were excluded from the analysis."

People who knew the panther data already—people like Deb Jansen or Chris Belden—would have immediately spotted that Maehr had left things out. But one of the rules of peer-review is that the people closest to the situation are strictly forbidden to be the ones reviewing the paper, Noss said.

"It's kind of a catch-22," he admitted.

To review the paper, Noss chose puma experts from other parts of the country. They read it over and, he said, they made "very favorable" comments about it. They found no obvious flaws in either the form or the conclusions.

Besides, Maehr had published dozens of other papers on the subject of panthers. He had years of fieldwork in his background. Surely he knew what he was doing. According to Cox, one of the reviewers of the Maehr-Cox paper told them, "This looks great!"

Looks, of course, can be deceiving.

To Cox, the biggest problem with the paper he wrote with Maehr is what happened after it was published.

"Some people tried to get the results worked into the regulatory arena, which was a huge, huge mistake," he said.

The person who did the most to use the 1995 paper to justify developers' plans was none other than his coauthor. Maehr was on the verge of completing his Ph.D., and he'd landed a professor's position at the University of Kentucky, but he continued hiring himself out for thousands of dollars in consulting fees.

Rather than content himself with his academic and writing work, he continued aiding builders and developers and mining companies that wanted to run a steamroller over state and federal regulatory agencies. It's impossible to say how much money he was paid by all the people who wanted to wipe out panther habitat, but one contract—to help get a highway built—was paid for by the taxpayers of Lee County. That means it's a matter of public record. The amount he was paid for that one job: $60,000.

That case is particularly instructive in demonstrating just how panthers lost thousands of acres of habitat even as its population numbers were growing.

Lee County—named for Robert E. Lee, even though the Confederate general never set foot there—is on Florida's Gulf Coast, with beaches on one side and cattle ranches on the other, and developers eager to build on both. The county seat is Fort Myers, where local politicos found the notion of building FGCU in panther habitat to be no problem at all.

In 1997, the Lee County Commission voted to extend a highway called Daniels Parkway by three miles to accommodate what they expected to be lots of future development. The new highway would cut through wetlands, which meant it needed a Corps of Engineers permit. It also sliced straight through what everyone, even Maehr, recognized as panther habitat, which meant the Fish and Wildlife Service had to get involved too.

Neither agency was particularly keen on saying yes to such a destructive project. But both of them had a way to make things look copacetic on paper, whether it worked out in real life or not. The way to do it was with something called "mitigation." That meant finding a way to make up for the damage—say, restoring old wetlands or creating new ones to make up for dumping fill dirt in other wetlands for development.

However, that system doesn't really work with endangered species. Creating new panther habitat is nearly impossible. A religious man might say that only God can create a pristine wilderness, and He hasn't done that in quite a while. Restoring lost habitat is tricky too. To do it means tearing down the houses and stores built there, and hardly anyone ever wants to do that.

Instead, the agency counts land that will be preserved from development as if it were newly created habitat. That way, what's preserved can, on paper, make up for what's lost, even if in reality it does not. It's like having a dollar and spending half of it on candy, then claiming the 50 cents you saved totally makes up for the 50 cents you blew on sweets.

A biologist working for the Fish and Wildlife Service reviewed the Daniels Parkway project and concluded it would destroy 1,540 acres where panthers roamed. She decided that the only way the agency could say yes to that would be for Lee County to spend more than a million dollars buying 262 acres of panther habitat somewhere else to preserve it from development.

Lee County officials didn't like that price tag for the mitigation. They also didn't like how slowly the Corps was moving on their permit. They recalled Ben Hill Griffin III's use of his political clout to push FGCU through. Lee County had no such automatic clout. But the county commissioners figured out that such clout can be purchased, and for a lot less than a million dollars.

They spent $317,000 to hire a Washington lobbying firm called Dawson & Associates, headed up by a former top official in the Corps. The contract called for the company to "advise and assist" the county in "obtaining more timely resolution and significantly more reasonable terms in the federal permit."

They also hired Maehr. He then worked with one of Dawson's paid experts to produce a tool for figuring out how much panther habitat would be affected by any development project. The tool, based on the findings of the Maehr and Cox paper, was called the Panther Habitat Evaluation Model, or PHEM for short.

Maehr's PHEM could be used to calculate "functionally equivalent panther habitat units based on weighted scores for six habitat factors." The PHEM focused on forests to the exclusion of everything else, including cattle pastures and orange groves. Even if panthers had been recorded using those areas more than a few times, PHEM didn't care. They could be bulldozed with no impact on the panther's habitat.

Then the Dawson expert took Maehr along to show off PHEM to the top federal wildlife agency officials in Florida.

First the Dawson man met alone with Jay Slack, a rotund bureaucrat from North Carolina who had recently replaced Craig Johnson as the guy in charge of the US Fish and Wildlife Service in South Florida. They spent an hour alone in Slack's Vero Beach office, during which, according to a report to Lee County from Dawson & Associates, the Dawson man explained "the realities" that Slack "needs to appreciate." By "realities" he meant: our lobbyists have more muscle than the Hulk. They're tight with both the Corps and Congress. They can even influence Florida politics. He claimed they helped then-Governor Jeb Bush pick the latest executive director of the state water agency in charge of restoring the Everglades.

Once the Dawson guy had finished throwing a scare into Slack, he wrote in his report to Lee County, Slack was "very receptive and indicated a strong willingness to work with us to get this problem solved."

Then it was Maehr's turn in the spotlight. He and the Dawson man met with Slack and two other Fish and Wildlife Service supervisors for three solid hours, according to the Dawson report. Maehr went into some detail about how his new PHEM system worked. They all "listened very intently," the Dawson report said. Because none of the federal agency people were panther biologists, they didn't spot its flaws.

As a capper, the Dawson man then handed out free copies of Maehr's panther book to each of the federal officials. According to his report, "there was a bit of glee as everyone got Dave to autograph their new books."

Once the wildlife agency's permit reviewer on Daniels Parkway looked over PHEM, though, she immediately spotted flaws in it. But the Dawson lobbyists made sure her hands were tied.

Dawson's lobbyists persuaded a Republican senator from the state of Washington with the Snidely Whiplash-type name of Slade Gorton to help out Lee County. He inserted a few carefully crafted lines into the federal budget bill that kneecapped any attempt by the Fish and Wildlife Service to reject Maehr's PHEM. The lines said that the agency must "ensure that measures designed to minimize the impacts on the Florida panther related to the Daniels Parkway extension are reasonable and conceived properly."

Slack told me the message was clear: "Congress is saying, 'Do this.'"

So the wildlife agency gave in and did what Maehr told them to do. Instead of requiring Lee County to buy and preserve 252 acres of panther habitat, the agency used PHEM and concluded it would need to buy just 94 acres. Once the wildlife agency surrendered, so did the Corps. Lee County got its permit to build the road in December 1999, and Maehr got his money.

Over and over, this pattern was repeated.

The Fish and Wildlife Service okayed development that wiped out swamps, pastures, even smaller patches of forest, because Maehr's calculation tool said panthers would not use those areas. Thus the agency also did not require developers to make up for paving over all those areas. Between 1999 and 2005, the agency gave a green light to permits for thirty-five development projects that affected 38,484 acres.

Anytime someone thought about writing a jeopardy opinion, Slack shot them down, according to David Ferrell's wife, Linda, who worked under Slack.

"We were told in no uncertain terms, jeopardy opinions would not be tolerated and we would not do jeopardy opinions," she said. "We were told that, politically, it would be a disaster."

When I asked Slack how he could justify saying yes to so many projects, to writing so many no-jeopardy opinions, he gave me a reason so ironic that it beggared belief.

"The number of panthers has been steadily on the rise," he said, failing to mention that that was solely the result of the desperate move to bring in Texas cougars. "It just didn't add up to a risk of extinction."

If a developer thought the agency was moving too slowly in saying yes, Florida's congressmen and senators were quick to intervene on their behalf, no matter which party they were in. Graham, for instance, helped out with getting permits for a destructive rock mine and more than one subdivision built where panthers had once roamed.

To get Graham to talk about why he did this, I showed up at an event in Tampa where he was plugging one of his books. This was several years after he retired from politics, but he was just as evasive as any active-duty politician. After several tries at talking to him out in the open, I had to trail him into the men's room, where he couldn't get away. Even then, he wouldn't take responsibility for pushing the wildlife service to bow to developers. A letter from Florida's senior senator wouldn't make that much of a difference to a federal agency, he contended.

"I think the agencies are experienced in what that means— not to change a decision, but to request them to review it in a timely and professional manner," he said.

The people who were the target of those letters knew better.

"Elected officials always say they just want to facilitate a dialogue, but rest assured, a threat is implied," explained Andy Eller.

By 1998, Eller had joined the ranks of permit reviewers cranking out no-jeopardy opinions on projects in panther habitat. At first Eller just did the job and kept his head down, but soon he too began questioning the science being used.

The main trick, he said, was that of ignoring the sheer number of projects that were flattening panther habitat like a big steamroller. If the wildlife service had considered the cumulative effect of all of that development, the loss would be so staggering that no one could deny that it jeopardized the panthers' future.

But he was told to just take them one by one.

"No single project would ever jeopardize the Florida panther," Eller explained.

David Ferrell told me that every time his staff tried to bring up cumulative impact, the bosses in Atlanta "just shot the biologists down. Management made the decision that it wasn't an issue."

I interviewed one of the Atlanta bosses, a guy named Sam Hamilton (more on him later). He contended that ignoring the cumulative impact was the right thing to do.

"You have to look at the project itself," rather than lumping it in with all the others, he insisted.

Yet in one of several legal challenges that environmental groups filed against the Fish and Wildlife Service, a federal judge said the law required just the opposite. US District Judge James Robertson tossed out a permit for a six-thousand-acre mine because the wildlife agency failed to consider the cumulative impact on panthers of that project and all the others it had approved.

Meanwhile, even as the wildlife agency was slinking along doing whatever developers wanted, its leaders were also assembling a team that would be charged with deciding which panther habitat needed to be saved from them.

The picks for the panel members were like a panther biologist version of the Avengers superhero team, the best of the best. The members included Roy McBride, Deb Jansen and Andy Eller.

And also Dave Maehr.

CHAPTER SIXTEEN

THE SHOWDOWN

Roy McBride was in bad shape.

On this afternoon in 1998, when McBride stopped by a biologist's office at Everglades National Park to chat, he bumped into Jane Comiskey, a painfully shy biologist and computer modeler from the University of Tennessee. Comiskey is a slender woman with dark hair and a distinct Tennessee twang to her soft voice. She was visiting Florida to work on some Everglades data. She and McBride had met once before, briefly. Looking at him now, she couldn't believe how haggard he looked.

"I had never seen anyone look that tired," she recalled. "He started telling me about his wife. She had PSP—it's like Lou Gehrig's disease. He had nurses there with her in the day but he would take care of her at night. She had a call bell and she would wake him up all hours of the night. He was basically living on coffee."

Normally a field biologist like McBride would have little to say to a computer modeler like Comiskey. The two are from different tribes, speaking different languages, and each displays little regard for the other. But this pair quickly bonded because Comiskey had a relative who was also suffering from PSP—progressive supranuclear palsy, a brain disorder that affects everything from walking to speech, mood and behavior. She had seen its ravages firsthand.

"It's tough to watch the mental and physical deterioration of someone you love," she said.

She understood about the hell of that bell too, a ting-a-ling tone that sounded in the deep night and the early morning and into the twilight hours until you began to question your sanity. Her ailing mother-in-law had had one of those too.

Plus, Comiskey wasn't your typical computer modeler.

"I had done a lot of fieldwork in botany," she said. "I did a lot of work with my husband... Several years of intensive fieldwork." They did so much field research together, she said, that he ended up producing a thesis that was more than seven hundred pages long.

She and McBride had a lot of differences—for instance, he loved listening to right-wing pundit Rush Limbaugh on the radio, while she couldn't stand the guy's voice or politics. But they became friends nonetheless, with a bond so tight that Comiskey would frequently type up his reports for him and have long conversations with him on the phone, especially after his wife died.

Then they teamed up to challenge Dave Maehr.

The Everglades was in bad shape.

The River of Grass had been dying for decades, its flow choked to nearly nothing, its water quality degraded by pollution. Half of it had been paved over and turned into subdivisions or drained to become sugar and vegetable farms. The other half, thanks to Corps of Engineers flood control structures, had become—as the *Washington Post* put it—"a shrunken, fragmented, convoluted mess, sucked dry when it needs water and flooded when it doesn't."

It had become more like a Trickle of Grass.

In the late 1990s, state and federal officials cobbled together a plan for reviving the Everglades. It didn't call for ripping out all the concrete, the levees, the pumps, the canals, and the farms and turning loose the old flow. Because the Corps was involved, the solution required building even *more* artificial structures to redirect the water.

And because a Florida water management agency controlled by then-Governor Jeb Bush was involved, the purpose of the project was only partly to save the state's best-known natural resource. The other purpose was to double the water supply for future development in South Florida. That's how it won the support of both the Florida Legislature and Congress.

As usual with a multibillion-dollar government project, there were acronyms galore. The whole thing was known as CERP—the "Comprehensive Everglades Restoration Program." Part of the management team over CERP would be a group to oversee how the Everglades plan would help the wildlife that lived there. That big group was called the "Multi-Species Ecosystem Recovery Implementation Team," or MERIT for short.

The very first assembly of experts under MERIT would be the one to study the effects on the panther. Thus it was called the "Panther MERIT Subteam." For some reason nobody ever called it by the obvious acronym: PMS.

The Panther MERIT Subteam was supposed to set the standard for all the other subteams to come. Each subteam studying all the other species affected by CERP—the Key deer, the

Cape Sable seaside sparrow, the manatee and so on—would be modeled on the panther one.

The approach the US Fish and Wildlife Service took seemed like a good plan, one that would be easy to duplicate: gather the top experts on the Florida panther. Put them together with experts on maps and computer models. Ask them to figure out how much land panthers need to avoid extinction and where it was located. Then the US Fish and Wildlife Service would use the results to regulate development in panther habitat and keep panthers from going extinct.

The federal biologist who assembled this panel in late 1999 sent an email to a colleague explaining its purpose: "This region is losing an incredible amount of habitat to development, and we need to know how much habitat loss the panther can sustain before the population is no longer viable; if it is truly viable now."

The first person she invited to join was, of course, Maehr. He was Mr. Panther, after all, the man who had literally written the book about the subject. He was also the author of the most influential scientific paper, as well as the author or coauthor on plenty more. The choice was strategic as well. The woman assembling the panel said she would rather have Maehr on the inside, working with the team, than on the outside, firing off salvos of withering criticism about its work.

Her second invitation went to Comiskey. The Tennessean had been running computer models of the future fate of deer and panthers in the Everglades over the next three decades. The results didn't look good.

"In preliminary model runs," she told me, "my panthers were consistently going extinct before the thirty-one-year simulation period ended. To get a panther population that would persist even thirty-one years, the model had to be given parameter values that were more optimistic than those observed in field monitoring."

Comiskey recommended the next invitation go to McBride.

The wildlife agency biologist expressed surprise. She said she had been told McBride wanted to stay in the background. He wasn't likely to want to be involved in a bunch of meetings where he'd have to speak up. Comiskey knew better. She convinced the biologist in charge to give McBride a call anyway. Sure enough, he said yes.

The other team members included Jansen; Andy Eller; Tom Hoctor, director of the Center for Landscape Conservation Planning at the University of Florida; and mapping expert Randy Kautz of what used to be the game commission but now was being called the Florida Fish and Wildlife Conservation Commission.

With the exception of McBride, Jansen and Eller, Comiskey said, the rest had no prior experience with panthers. If they knew anything about the big cats, they had learned it from reading Maehr's writings.

What happened with the Panther MERIT Subteam over the next two years is "a pretty sordid story," Hoctor told me later. The whole saga is "a great case study in the mixture of science, politics, and the Endangered Species Act."

In December 1999 the Panther MERIT Subteam met for the first time at the Fish and Wildlife Service's South Florida headquarters in Vero Beach. Vero is nearly two hundred miles away from where panthers live. From such a distance, the cats could seem less real, more like an abstraction, just numbers on papers you push around.

The Vero offices are in a pair of boxy gray buildings sitting side by side near downtown, across the street from a Japanese-Thai restaurant and the headquarters of the Florida Irish American Society. You'd never know from the dull exterior that the people inside are busy wrestling with decisions that could affect the fate of the state animal.

At the start of that first two-day meeting, the Subteam members went around the room and introduced themselves, as people do at such professional gatherings. They talked a bit about what they did and how it could relate to the panthers. They also went over the ground rules, including the rule that said all the Sub-team members were supposed to keep all their discussions private until they had a report that they could release to the public.

Then Jay Slack—the rotund bureaucrat so intimidated by lobbyists during the Daniels Parkway permitting—addressed the gathering.

According to the minutes of the meeting, Slack "discussed what the Fish and Wildlife Service needs in terms of a conservation strategy for the panther in South Florida that will include both recovery and regulatory recommendations." He warned them to limit their scope to just the state's nineteen southernmost counties, but promised whatever they came up with "will have implications for the overall recovery plan for the panther statewide."

More importantly, Slack said that whatever the Subteam produced would also be used for "regulatory recommendations." In other words, the plan would guide the wildlife agency in reviewing permits for would-be developers of panther habitat. It could finally give federal biologists the justification to block rampant development.

At least, that was the plan.

After Slack left, the group brainstormed about their "vision" for what it would take to declare the endangered panther no longer endangered: "The primary components of this vision are (1) how many panthers do we need in South Florida? (2) how much habitat is needed to support a viable population in this region?, and (3) what is the configuration of the habitat needed?"

What doesn't show up in the minutes is that Comiskey and McBride were already convinced that Maehr was blowing smoke.

Comiskey and McBride had heard Maehr speak at a conference in Gainesville earlier that year about a new scientific paper he was working on. She said Maehr told the crowd that in his new paper, he estimated there were thirty breeding female Florida panthers whose kittens had an 80% survival rate—*before* McBride brought in the Texas cougars. That would mean there had been no need for the whole genetic restoration program, just as Maehr had been contending right from the start.

Comiskey knew that didn't match any of the data she'd seen, which showed fewer than a third of all panther kittens survived. McBride had a more practical objection: If there really were that many panthers, what were they eating? Because there sure weren't enough deer and hogs to fill up that many cats. McBride knew there were other serious problems in Maehr's science, but he couldn't pinpoint just what, Comiskey said.

But Maehr dismissed their objections. He regarded McBride as "just a redneck with hounds," Comiskey said. "And I was just a data person, and what did I know?"

This made for some ripples of underlying tension among the Subteam members, right from the start.

The Subteam met in Vero Beach again in February, where, according to the minutes, there "was a lot of discussion about what comprises panther 'habitat.'" Despite their differences, the group plugged away, slowly making progress. Kautz had even begun to cobble together some preliminary maps.

Then, in May 2000, everything started to unravel.

Consultants from a South Florida engineering and development company called WilsonMiller, Inc. contacted Kautz to demand copies of his preliminary maps. When the stunned Kautz failed to respond, they contacted Eller, repeating their demand.

Eller was floored. How did these guys find out what the Subteam was working on? How did they know what to ask for and when?

Eller emailed a colleague that he didn't know how to deal with the request. He explained that WilsonMiller "represents some of the largest and wealthiest developers in the area and the information, in its current form, could be misinterpreted and used against us."

The colleague told him that they had no choice. Under the Freedom of Information Act, they couldn't refuse to hand over the documents. They were a matter of public record.

But the question no one could answer was: Who tipped off the developers?

The WilsonMiller map demand came about the same time Roy McBride dropped a bomb on Dave Maehr.

Of all the Subteam members, McBride was by far the most qualified to go after Maehr. He'd been hunting big cats long before Maehr came along. He'd not only seen more Florida panthers than Maehr, he'd seen pumas and cougars and mountain lions on more than one continent. And yet in Maehr's book, he's described as nothing but "the houndsman." Readers would never know he had an advanced degree.

At the February 2000 meeting, McBride was asked to "provide a current map of where the panthers are and the current population estimate." He turned in a written report ahead of their May 2000 meeting. The title was "Current Panther Distribution and Habitat Use: A Review of Field Notes: Fall 1999 to Winter 2000," but it should have been, "Everything Dave Maehr Ever Said Is Wrong."

The report was typed up and edited by Comiskey. She was so shy that she almost couldn't bring herself to speak in the meetings, but she was happy to help McBride. McBride's report started off by pointing out that the capture season that had just concluded was the twentieth one so far, and most successful one ever. His current population estimate of sixty-two adult panthers was "the highest that I have been able to verify thus far."

The reason for this was simple, McBride said: those Texas cougars were doing what everyone had hoped and prayed they would do. They were breeding with male panthers and producing healthy kittens. Those kittens survived, unlike the purebred panther kittens.

"Clearly," he wrote, "the population is beginning to expand and is filling in unoccupied habitat within the existing range." Such a boom should have occurred a lot sooner, he wrote, if what Maehr had said about the population bouncing back before the Texas cougars showed up was true.

In fact, he wrote, "the estimate of seventy-four pure Florida panthers offered by Maehr...is not defensible, especially since he characterizes the area south of I-75 as being unable to support a breeding population of panthers." That many panthers could not possibly be crammed into the area that was left, he said.

Then, in the section marked "Discussion," McBride really went after Maehr's science. All of Maehr's arguments, he wrote, were refuted by one thing: the success of the cougars in breeding with the panthers.

"Events of the past two years have contradicted published theories and predictions about panther ecology in South Florida," he wrote. His first example: Maehr labeling Big Cypress "terrible panther habitat," where the only survivors were "the living dead."

"However," McBride wrote, "the greatest population expansion over the past two years has taken place in this area."

Over and over, McBride wrote, Maehr had called the Caloosahatchee River near Fort Myers a barrier that kept panthers from going north into Central Florida. Yet when the Texas cougar-fueled population boom occurred, three panthers swam across that river to find new territory.

That meant Maehr's arguments against the need for bringing in Texas cougars to refresh the gene pool were wrong as well, McBride wrote. McBride had also been opposed to the breeding program. With its success, he was willing to admit he was wrong, something Maehr could never do.

Twelve cats from the first generation of cross-bred panthers, McBride noted, "are not only occupying habitat that has been characterized by Maehr as poor habitat, but they are raising healthy kittens in it. These kittens are robust, seem wilder, more alert, and display greater vigor and stamina when trying to elude the hounds."

McBride reminded the readers that Maehr had issued dire warnings about how the cougar genes would wind up swamping the purebred panther genes. That, McBride noted, had not happened.

McBride then made the point that as the population expanded, the new cats would need more habitat—not less, which is what they were currently getting from developers and the Fish and Wildlife Service. His conclusion also took yet another swipe at the guy who helped make the Daniels Parkway extension possible.

"The future of the panther depends on whether the agencies and the public want them badly enough to preserve wild Florida and all that goes with it," McBride wrote. "No one really knows what constitutes a minimum viable population of panthers, and likewise no one knows how large an area is needed to support them. Yet, just as beavers cut down big trees with little bites, so goes what's left of Florida's wildness. A Daniels [Parkway] here, a Daniels [Parkway] there, and pretty soon it's gone forever."

Although some of the federal biologists who had been forced to use the PHEM had questioned the accuracy of Maehr's work, this marked the first time anyone had challenged his work in any written report.

Years later, McBride said he wasn't trying to be malicious toward Maehr. He was merely reporting what he'd seen.

"The evidence was just mounting," he told me. "You couldn't deny it."

The response to this bombshell was less than overwhelming, Comiskey said. No one seemed to pay much attention to it—

after all, Maehr was considered Mr. Panther, so how could he get everything wrong? And who was this McBride guy? Had he published any papers?

The exception to this lack of a response, of course, was Maehr himself, who waved away the report as the work of a misguided ex-colleague who held a longstanding grudge against him. He contended McBride had never forgiven him for violating protocol on their first capture together, when Maehr fired the tranquilizer dart at the treed panther instead of waiting for McBride to do it.

When I asked McBride about this supposed grudge, he was baffled. He said he not only held no grudge, but he couldn't even remember who shot the gun on Maehr's first capture. After all, while that panther pursuit was special to Maehr, for McBride it was just one out of thousands across his lengthy career.

He also pointed out that despite such supposed animosity, years later Maehr hired him to come trap some grizzlies for his students in Kentucky. If he and Maehr had been such bitter enemies, he said, why would they ever work together again?

In the end, McBride took his stand simply because it was, as he put it, "the right thing." But he wasn't surprised at the reaction it received. Comiskey recalled that before he turned it in, he already knew what the Subteam's reaction would be.

"You know, I doubt if the rest of the Subteam even reads it," he told Comiskey. "And if they read it, they won't understand it. But Dave will read it, and he will understand it."

In other words, he'd know they were onto him. While Maehr may not have realized it then, McBride's report marked a turning point for Mr. Panther's career and reputation.

As brutally honest as McBride's report was, Comiskey was working on something even more damaging. She was redoing the analysis from the Maehr and Cox paper, using all of the same radio telemetry readings.

That was the tricky thing about Maehr using publicly available data: other people could get access to it too.

As Comiskey worked, she was stunned at the results she was seeing.

"I started on a Saturday and finished at three in the morning because I just couldn't believe it," she told me. As she worked, "sometimes I redid analyses a dozen times before I could accept that published analyses were really as wrong as they seemed at first."

Slowly, she uncovered each of the things that Maehr did wrong. The most astonishing, to her, was that he'd left out data that didn't fit his theories about where panthers lived, then tried to hide the omission. What was worse, she found, was that Maehr hadn't just tossed out a few telemetry readings here and there.

He had left out 40 percent of all the data. Four out of every ten radio collar readings didn't make it into his report.

Comiskey's computer model wouldn't leave out anything. Her findings indicated that there were about two million acres of habitat available for adult panthers with established home ranges in South Florida—roughly double what Maehr had reported. And it consisted of more than just large forest patches, because panthers clearly used farms, pastures and other types of land.

To explain all this to the Subteam was tough for the tongue-tied Comiskey.

"I've suffered most of my life from speech phobia," she told me. Whenever she tried to speak at the Subteam meetings, "I would break out in a rash. I would lose my voice. My mind would go blank." She found out that if she took beta-blockers, she could steady her nerves just enough to talk to this small group.

When Comiskey shared her findings with the rest of the Subteam, it drove an even deeper wedge between the members. Every time the Subteam gathered for a meeting, Maehr would make some comment about his published findings, only to run into open resistance from McBride and Comiskey, as well as Deb Jansen, who had seen enough to take their side. Maehr would snap back, accusing them of personal attacks, scoffing that their observations were mere speculation, questioning their standing to make such claims.

Maehr's authority was backed up by lots of peer-reviewed studies. None of his critics could point to anything like that. Each time the argument came up, the other members of the Subteam sided with Maehr, but the repeated arguments took their toll on the group's progress.

After a few such arguments, Maehr joked to a federal biologist that he was starting to feel like he should wear a bulletproof vest to the meetings.

Southwest Florida was in bad shape.

Development ran rampant through the areas set aside for recharging the region's water supply, providing habitat for endangered wildlife, cleaning pollution from stormwater runoff. Some developers didn't bother to get permits before they started clearing land because the fines they incurred cost them less than delaying their project. Money flowed everywhere, sometimes legally, sometimes not. Three Collier County commissioners, the county manager and several developers were arrested in a corruption scandal.

The colonel in charge of the Corps of Engineers in Florida at the time later told the *Washington Post*, "We were approving projects all over the place; we had no idea what we were doing."

Around the time the Subteam began meeting, the National Wildlife Federation and its Florida subsidiary filed a lawsuit against the Corps of Engineers, the Fish and Wildlife Service and the Environmental Protection Agency, contending they weren't obeying the laws on protecting wetlands and endangered species. The suit took aim at some of the biggest projects in the region, not just golf courses and country clubs but mining too, all of them seeking permits for wiping out swamps and eliminating panther habitat.

Those permit applicants then jumped into the suit too. One of them took the step of presenting an affidavit from a panther expert who testified that the Florida Wildlife Federation's objections were baseless.

Their paid expert? Maehr.

The Florida Wildlife Federation promptly countered with their own experts: McBride, Comiskey and Jansen. Each one said Maehr had everything wrong. Jansen's affidavit, for instance, said Maehr's "depiction of the status of panthers and the habitat suitability for panthers in Big Cypress is inaccurate... This mischaracterization of panther habitat suitability in Big Cypress may have implications in panther habitat evaluations in other parts of its range and result in the further loss of panther habitat."

The bottom line, McBride said, was that "what we were seeing in the field didn't match up to what was in his papers." The cat hunter also officially complained to the wildlife service that Maehr was concocting phony citations in his papers, claiming "personal communications" with McBride that never occurred.

"Dave has never contacted me to verify a personal communication," he wrote. "My experience does not support Dave's statements in any way, and in fact directly contradicts them."

In response, Maehr was defiant, warning that his opponents were worse than merely mistaken.

"They will go far in making a mockery of MERIT, 20 years of panther research, and the scientific method in panther conservation," Maehr grumbled in an email to the federal biologist who set up the Subteam. In another email, he told her, "I am sure that the perpetrators of such foolishness are too wrapped up in personal vendettas to realize the harm that they are doing. It is sad that I have been and continue to be virtually the only person doing science on the panther."

The lawsuit fizzled out over a legal glitch. But the Florida Wildlife Federation had noticed Maehr's name attached to several of the permits they were protesting, including the one for The Habitat. Clearly, even though he was now a professor of conservation biology in another state, Maehr was still getting paid by Florida developers to give his blessing to projects built in panther habitat—and paid rather handsomely. His own affidavit said that one client was paying him a "$4,500 per month retainer"—in other words, $54,000 a year on top of his professor's salary and any royalties from his book. And that was just one of his clients. Who knew how many more developers were paying him?

Yet he was also serving on an influential committee for determining where panthers would be allowed to live in the future. To the environmental activists, that seemed like a clear conflict of interest. And if there was one person with a conflict, there might be others.

The Florida Wildlife Federation wrote to the Fish and Wildlife Service with a simple request: please require everyone on the Panther MERIT Subteam to disclose who's paying their bills. To illustrate the need for such a move, the letter went into some detail on Maehr's paid consulting work—work which had never been disclosed to the other members of the Subteam.

Of course, the Fish and Wildlife Service officials who got the letter realized this put them in a bind. They had been making permitting decisions based on Maehr's scientific work. To raise questions about his expertise and ethics now would call into question everything they had been doing.

Thus, the federal agency's response to the letter was to ask the Subteam members if they believed that their work was somehow being compromised. That was it.

Slack told the Florida Wildlife Federation he would not require any disclosures. McBride, Jansen and Comiskey each wrote to Slack, urging him to reconsider, but he refused. Instead, he ordered the closed-door Subteam meetings to be thrown open to anyone who wanted to attend, so critics could see what was going on.

The wildlife federation dispatched one of its advocates to sit in on the Subteam meetings. WilsonMiller sent a pair of its employees too. The WilsonMiller delegates didn't just sit on the sidelines and watch, either. They repeatedly objected to what the Subteam was doing. They claimed that the Subteam was trying to include too much of their clients' property in the maps of protected panther habitat. They "were adamant the zones should be more reduced," Hoctor of the University of Florida told me.

Feeling the heat from all this new scrutiny, Maehr protested that his approach—no matter who was paying him—remained the same throughout his career: "open, scientific, and objective." He would continue decrying what he called personal attacks, but from then on, he would do it via email.

He quit showing up for the Subteam meetings. In the face of the barrage of criticism from McBride, Jansen and Comiskey, he had retreated rather than continue trying to justify what he'd done.

While Maehr's departure didn't stop the Subteam from fighting, it did cut down on the conflict enough that the group could at last make some real progress. They agreed to divide panther habitat into three categories:

1. The Primary Zone, the 3,548 square miles currently occupied by panthers. Keeping it intact was crucial to the species, they agreed.

2. The Secondary Zone, made up of 1,200 square miles adjacent to the Primary Zone. It wasn't occupied by panthers yet, but most likely would be eventually as the panther population continued expanding. Thus it, too, needed to be saved from development; and finally

3. The Dispersal Zone, a forty-three-square-mile corridor that

averaged just three miles wide, which if preserved would allow panthers in Southwest Florida to move northward on their own into Central Florida to find new areas to occupy.

When Slack's staff briefed him about the Primary-Secondary-Dispersal breakdown, he was not happy at all. The official notes from his briefing say: "Are all of the lands identified as primary, dispersal, and secondary zones essential for the long-term persistence of cats in south Florida? Address concerns that delineation of primary, dispersal, and secondary zones appear to cover more area than is necessary for panther conservation."

In other words, he had the same concerns as WilsonMiller, the developers' consultants. He was in favor of saving the panthers, but only if doing so didn't cut into the ongoing development of Florida.

In the meantime, Comiskey, McBride and several like-minded scientists joined forces to publish their own peer-reviewed paper on Comiskey's computer modeling, the modeling that showed Maehr was wrong about panther habitat. Now Maehr couldn't say that his opponents hadn't gotten a peer-reviewed paper published the way he had.

Maehr, while absent from the meetings, had nevertheless been thinking about all the work the Subteam had been doing. He sent Kautz, the mapmaker, a new paper he was proposing to publish in a scientific journal.

When Kautz saw it, he freaked out.

"As written, it is an unmitigated rip-off of all of the work that has been accomplished to date by the panther Subteam," he protested to Maehr. "The methods are nothing more than an overly simplistic copy of the team's work. Moreover, the manuscript glosses over many issues of data quality and accuracy that the team has wrestled with for the last two years."

Maehr didn't care. He published the paper anyway.

As if that wasn't enough, WilsonMiller proposed its own new methodology for deciding what was panther habitat and what wasn't. They called it the "Florida Panther Habitat Assessment Methodology," and under "science" it cited one main source: the Maehr-Cox paper from 1995 that Comiskey had just discredited.

In spite of all of this controversy, by April 2002, the Subteam was all but done. They had produced a 191-page report, complete with detailed maps, that showed what land the Corps and the Fish and Wildlife Service had to protect in order ensure panthers would continue to exist. The report included twenty-five pages of detailed recommendations on how to preserve enough land to guarantee the panther's future.

Hoctor told me they were all pretty pleased with the result: "All these people who don't agree on some things agreed on what should be done."

To Kautz, what the Subteam had produced was a landmark document: "We actually drew lines on a map and said, 'This is the habitat that needs to be protected.'"

What they wanted to protect wasn't just a few big forest patches, either. The Primary Zone covered a variety of landscapes, including forests, swamps, pastures, citrus groves and other areas that weren't covered by Maehr's discredited theories.

If they had confined their work to only the remaining wilderness forests in Southwest Florida, the result would have been "a Swiss cheese map," Hoctor explained. The group agreed "that the Swiss cheese map was not enough to identify what we need to protect them." The reason: panthers are "extremely sensitive to human activity and...apparently sensitive to roads." That meant the group needed to include plenty of buffers around their habitat, he said.

They also included recommendations on how to protect all that land. One recommendation: declare all three zones to be "critical habitat." That was a step the wildlife agency had avoided taking for thirty years. Such a designation would likely make it harder to turn the places where panthers live into mines and subdivisions.

Now that the Subteam's work was done, all that was left was for the paper to be peer-reviewed by other scientists and then published in a scientific journal. That would mean it could be officially accepted by the Fish and Wildlife Service as a guide to approving or rejecting new development permits where panthers live.

A December 2002 briefing memo from agency officials in Florida to their bosses in Washington said the report was "undergoing internal review" at the Florida level, then would go to the regional office in Atlanta and finally to Washington. Then it could be made public for comment.

But it never made it to that last step.

Every time someone from the Subteam checked on what was happening, Comiskey said, they were told it was still being reviewed "and there was always a target release time, sometimes a specific date, sometimes just a month or season. When a given deadline passed, a new time frame was set."

It was as if the Subteam report were the Ark of the Covenant from *Raiders of the Lost Ark*: it was an artifact with powers far too dangerous to use, and thus consigned to a box in some massive warehouse.

A year passed. Then two. The Subteam members kept sending each other emails about the lack of action. In one, Jansen wrote that because of "continued rampant growth in south Florida, the agencies have only a short time frame to make this document a worthwhile effort." But nothing happened.

As Jansen feared, instead of using the Subteam's recommendations to guide permitting decisions, the Corps and the Fish and Wildlife Service kept approving development in the zones that the experts said was crucial to the panther's future.

"It's frustrating," Jansen told me. "We've identified what

these animals need. It's frustrating to see this habitat is going to be broken up by homes now."

Not only was the report never published, but the proposal to start other MERIT Subteams as part of the Everglades restoration program never happened either. Instead of a template, the panther Subteam became a dead end. The one thing the Fish and Wildlife Service learned from the panther Subteam was that it shouldn't start any other Subteams because of how they might unmask the way the agency kowtowed to developers.

Kautz and the other members of the Subteam grew so frustrated they decided to get a report published themselves in a peer-reviewed scientific journal. But no journal had room for the whole report. It was too much, with its maps and its long list of recommendations.

They whittled it down to a sixteen-page version that was published in the February 2006 edition of *Conservation Biology*. The *Readers' Digest* version lacked many of the details of the original, including the twenty-five pages of recommendations on how to protect the three zones. It left the authors unsatisfied, and left the door open for the permits to keep on flowing.

After seven years with no publication of the full Subteam report, I tracked down Jay Slack to ask him what happened. Despite the debacle with Maehr and the Subteam—or perhaps because of it—he'd been promoted to a job in another state, one that had nothing to do with regulation.

Slack told me he couldn't remember the specifics of those discussions from so long ago. Nor could he recall what became of the Subteam's original report after it disappeared into the bureaucracy.

"I don't know how it all transpired at the end," he said. "My understanding was, it evolved."

In the end, the one lasting legacy of the Panther MERIT Subteam wasn't a map or a document. It wasn't a move to block new development in panther habitat. No, the Subteam's legacy was that it led to the event that finally destroyed Dave Maehr's stranglehold on panther science.

CHAPTER SEVENTEEN

THE VERDICT

Andy Eller missed out on a lot of the Subteam drama. After the first few meetings, his bosses told him he had to drop out. He had way too many development permits to approve. If he spent his time helping the Subteam figure out how to save the panther, he'd inconvenience some congressman's campaign contributor. That just wouldn't do. It didn't help that Dave Maehr had complained about there being too many federal employees in the meetings—namely Eller and Jansen.

While working on permits, Eller's idealism rapidly eroded. He was starting to realize that the Vero Beach office of the Fish and Wildlife Service was a place known for what he called "drive-by permitting." Nobody had time to do an in-depth review of each project, especially if that review might result in a jeopardy finding.

To make sure no development ever got a red light, Eller explained to me, he was told to use phony numbers. For instance, on one project involving the Lee County Port Authority, his bosses made him write that not only was there no shortage of panthers now, but that there was a *surplus* of twenty-eight panthers. Imagine that! Too many panthers!

"This was an example of blatant misrepresentation of scientific information to make the panther appear less endangered than it was," Eller would write later.

At a Vero staff meeting in 2001, Jay Slack told Eller and all the other permit reviewers that the agency's official policy, coming straight from the top in Washington, was to never ever write another jeopardy opinion. This was shortly after former Texas Governor George W. Bush had been sworn in as president. Bush had chosen as his Secretary of the Interior a silver-haired Colorado lawyer named Gale Norton. While serving as Colorado's attorney general, Norton had argued to the US Supreme Court that the Endangered Species Act was unconstitutional. With Norton in charge of their agency, Eller and his coworkers believed Slack was telling them the truth.

Except maybe he wasn't.

"There was no such policy," Craig Manson, Norton's assistant secretary for fish, wildlife and parks told me. Instead, he said, the only policy was that the final decision on a jeopardy opinion was left to the regional directors.

"Regional directors had a fairly large amount of discretion in how they reviewed these," Manson said. "For example, some RDs merely rubber-stamped them; others would say, 'Let's see if we can make this work.'"

The regional director in Atlanta who oversaw the Vero Beach Fish and Wildlife Service office was not the rubber-stamp kind. And he had a personal reason for not liking endangered species issues.

Sam Hamilton hailed from Mississippi. He parted his hair

down the middle and wore Teddy Roosevelt glasses that made him seem a bit owlish. He also had a gunslinger mustache that gave him the look of an old street cop who's been moved to a desk job but still scores well at the pistol range.

Hamilton, the son of a World War II fighter pilot and a Red Cross nurse, started working for the wildlife agency right after graduating from Mississippi State University. When he became the agency's first statewide director in Texas, he ran into a buzz saw of opposition over an endangered species—an experience that affected his judgment for the rest of his career.

In 1994, word got around among the state's ranchers that Hamilton intended to classify land in dozens of counties as "critical habitat" for the endangered golden-cheeked warbler, the only bird to breed nowhere but Texas. Such a designation would mean that any alteration of those areas would get heightened scrutiny from the agency.

Actually nothing of the sort was going on. The whole thing was a misunderstanding. That didn't stop the ranchers from marching on the state capital and holding rallies where they complained that their property rights were being stolen.

Even the state's chief executive complained about Hamilton and his federal agency.

"Texans can run Texas. We do not need to be told how to protect our land or the critters that live on it, whether it's a blind bug or a gold-throat warbler," said then-Governor George W. Bush.

The ranchers' anger toward Hamilton took on violent personal overtones. Someone sent Hamilton death threats concerning his children. Shortly thereafter, the agency transferred Hamilton to the Atlanta regional office. With him gone, the controversy faded.

Critical habitat was a problem for panthers too. Back when panthers were put on the original endangered list, the agency wasn't required to designate any critical habitat for the cats. That was a later change in the law, and thus animals on the original list, including panthers, didn't qualify for automatic habitat protection. As a result, every no-jeopardy opinion cited the lack of critical habitat for panthers as a justification for saying yes to developers.

To ask Hamilton about this, I showed up at a 2010 conference where he was a speaker. We chatted in a hotel hallway during a fire alarm that emptied the ballroom where he had been speaking. When I questioned him, Hamilton explained that after the furor in Texas, he opposed designating critical habitat for any endangered species or subspecies, no matter how deserving.

"In my experience, it inflames public opinion," he said.

He contended that the agency got what he called "a better bang for the buck" by cutting deals with willing landowners— although he could not explain how that could persuade unwilling landowners to help the government enforce the Endangered Species Act.

I asked Hamilton if he had told his underlings he would never approve a jeopardy opinion on anything, not even panthers. I saw his eyes go wide and his face turn red. The question infuriated him.

"That's not true!" he shouted at me, jabbing the air with his finger. Then he added, "I *love* cats! Cougars, pumas—they're my number one!"

He denied ever rejecting a request to sign a jeopardy opinion. But when I pressed him further, he conceded that if the staff in Vero Beach were too scared to send one to him, then he would never get the chance to say no.

The crucial thing about jeopardy opinions for endangered critters like the panther, Hamilton told me, was this: "They've got to be based on facts and sound science."

But as Comiskey's analysis proved, and as Eller's "surplus panthers" biological opinion demonstrated, the science that was being used to approve all that development wasn't sound at all.

★ ★ ★

Unlike Eller, John Kasbohm didn't miss a single Subteam meeting.

He wasn't a member of the Subteam, although he probably should have been. Tall and balding, with a sandy beard and glasses that gave him a studious look even in outdoor photos, Kasbohm had a Ph.D. and an interest in bears and other big mammals. He'd worked as a federal refuge manager, and he chaired the federal committee in charge of saving the Florida panther, the one that was supposed to make sure the official recovery plan was being carried out.

By sitting in on the meetings, Kasbohm had a ringside seat to all the wrangling over Maehr's science. He listened closely, but did not comment on what he heard.

Then came the fateful day that the members of the Subteam got a helicopter tour of Big Cypress. They were supposed to go in groups of two, and Kasbohm decided to tag along. During the forty-five-minute ride from Naples to the copter landing site in Big Cypress, he shared a car with Comiskey.

She saw her opportunity.

"I made the case as strongly as I could that the responsibility rested on him...to resolve disputes about panther science," Comiskey told me. "We all had a role to play—things that fell within our purview and that we could not shirk responsibility for. My role as data expert on the Subteam was to assess the validity of the papers that formed the underpinnings of FWS's habitat conservation activities—were assumptions warranted, were methods sound, were analyses performed correctly, was data integrity respected, did conclusions follow from analyses. Roy's role was to ground-truth conclusions about habitat use and viability in that body of literature in light of his extensive field experience. Kasbohm's obligation was to resolve discrepancies between Maehr's work and findings in our work...to assure that the science used by recovery agencies was sound."

Kasbohm agreed with Comiskey that there was a problem with the science. He had an idea for a solution: convene a panel of independent experts to review every single one of the peer-reviewed papers on panthers and determine what was right and what wasn't.

"The idea, as I remember, was to take an impartial second look at panther science with the hope that everyone involved with panthers could agree on basic data and its interpretation," he told me. That way perhaps they could "put to rest ongoing concerns related to the quality and interpretation of panther data."

Convening such a group is about as common as seeing a black swan riding a black panther at high noon on Leap Day. Seldom do scientists feel compelled to search for flaws in an entire field this way. Yet Kasbohm managed to persuade not one but two normally stodgy bureaucracies—the state and federal wildlife agencies—to go along with this plan. Fortunately, the battling Subteam helped make his point: something had to be done to end the disputes.

Kasbohm set about assembling the panel that would become known as the Science Review Team, or SRT for short. He put together a group of four scientists. They weren't exactly a diverse group: all white, all male, all gray-haired, all Ph.D.'s, but all from states other than Florida.

One had studied Siberian tigers in Russia, pandas in China and jaguars in Brazil. Another was considered the world's premier expert on creating wildlife corridors for endangered animals to move through the landscape. A third was known for leading research on bears, deer, tigers and sea turtles (oh, my!). Those three were Howard Quigley, Paul Beier and Michael R. Vaughan.

The fourth was Mike Conroy, whom I met at a conference. He was a pudgy guy with glasses and a bristly mustache. At the time the SRT convened, he worked as a population ecologist for the US Geological Survey, which means he was an expert on the dynamics of species populations and how they interact with their environment.

The four doctors had no idea how to go about doing the review that Kasbohm wanted. They had never done anything like this before. They had no template to follow, and no guidance from Kasbohm or anyone else.

"I think we pretty much winged it without a recipe," Conroy said told me.

They didn't even know what they were getting into. According to a report that they issued after their work was done, "the SRT members did not have a glimmer as to what the points of contention might be."

When they asked Kasbohm and Darrell Land point-blank what sort of controversies led to the convening of their panel, the pair "both responded that it would be better for us to glean answers from the literature rather than having anyone lay out their perceptions of the issues. They assured us that the areas of contention would be obvious once we delved into the literature."

They were right.

The SRT convened for the first time in Naples in April 2002, quickly discovering that they were all fairly compatible with each other if not exactly chummy. Soon thereafter they began to dig into more than three thousand pages of scientific literature that had been published over the previous twenty years. They were checking for errors, lapses in logic, data gaps, messed-up methodology and any other obvious problems.

The job wasn't quite as onerous as it sounds, Conroy told me.

"A lot of it was overlapping," he told me. "It was a lot of the same reports in different form. There weren't that many that were unique."

They also got a helicopter tour of panther habitat, courtesy of Deb Jansen. It nearly went awry. Conroy showed up nauseous from a case of food poisoning.

"I waited miserably in the hot office while the first half of our group went up, and when they returned I decided to ride as it surely couldn't be worse than being sick in the office bathroom in ninety-degree heat," Conroy told me. "To my pleasant surprise the moment we got airborne, I immediately felt better from the cool rush of air...and had a great time seeing habitats."

Then McBride took them out to show them what panther habitat looked like on the ground. Despite McBride's long history of studying pumas, Conroy regarded him as "fairly typical of field-knowledgeable good ole boy types. I would certainly rely on his natural history expertise, less so on his opinions regarding panther recovery."

When it came to actually looking at all that literature, they started off working separately, each one poring over the documents to see if there was anything that sounded a little off.

"It took a surprisingly short time for us to concur on all the major points—less than a week, as I recall," Conroy said. He said it probably helped that 75 percent of all panther-related science literature was by an author or coauthor named Maehr.

In November of 2002, seven months after their first meeting, they all got together to compare notes. Each one of the four had come to the exact same conclusion. Just as Comiskey, McBride and Jansen had been saying all along, they found that Maehr's papers were as full of holes as a Zurich cheese shop.

Their next step was to quiz the panther experts. They gathered in Athens, Georgia, at the University of Georgia's Center for Continuing Education. They called in Comiskey, Land, Kasbohm and some others to ask questions about what they'd found, behaving something like a grand jury questioning witnesses behind closed doors.

"The interview was in a fairly small room—I remember it more as a classroom than a conference room," Comiskey told me. "The panel sat in a row at one end of the room, probably behind a rectangular table, and I sat facing them at another table... The atmosphere was neither friendly nor unfriendly, a bit formal. I probably talked too much, too fast."

To the four men sitting in judgment, their sole female witness came across as shrill and vindictive.

"Jane seemed on a mission to trash everything Dave did," Conroy told me. "She found some legitimate errors, as did we, but I think she painted Dave with too broad a brush."

Comiskey urged them to consider not just what had gone wrong with Maehr's science, but also the tremendous impact his work had had on erasing so much panther habitat.

They were unconvinced.

"One member said—somewhat dismissively, with a degree of exasperation—something to the effect that 'with all due respect, you can't really expect us to believe that,'" Comiskey told me.

Comiskey explained to them about the Daniels Parkway extension. She told them how Maehr's Panther Habitat Evaluation Model had given Lee County and its powerful lobbyists the cover to claim that the highway wouldn't be as bad for panthers as the Fish and Wildlife Service biologists believed.

"I said I realized it was hard to believe, that I and others had had the same reaction," she said. "If it had been one or two errors marginally affecting one or two issues in panther science, the process of explaining it to people and ultimately correcting it would have been far easier. The fact that we were facing a network of interlocking errors in a body of peer-reviewed papers touching all aspects of panther science, with the potential to derail panther recovery, made it seem so much less likely to be true."

They eventually sat down with Maehr that day and questioned him too. As Conroy recalls it, "Dave was initially defensive and later seemingly chagrined about his errors, to the extent he made them. No, he didn't attempt to justify everything. Yes, it was awkward, but I think he handled it well, and we left on good terms."

There are no notes from this showdown, but I picture the four Ph.D.'s facing the fifth across the table. At first he's not worried. After all, he's not just Mr. Panther anymore, he's Dr. Panther now, thank you! He knew a couple of his inquisitors a little, because they had served as reviewers on a couple of his minor papers. I picture Maehr smiling and nodding at the opening questions, but quickly realizing what was going on when the tone of the inquiry changed, and they zeroed in on the flaws in his work.

As the questioning continued, I wonder if he could tell what was going to happen, what damage this report would do to his reputation. I wonder if he could see it the way a man about to drive off a cliff sees it coming and knows it's too late to stop. In this case, the time to hit the brakes was way back before he even cranked up the car.

As an indicator of what Maehr was thinking, consider this. Around the time the SRT was winding up its inquiry, Maehr called his old friend Reed Noss, the professor who had edited *Conservation Biology* in 1995 when that journal published his paper with Cox. Their conversation did not go well.

"He called me and he wanted me to come to his defense," Noss said. "I told him, 'I can't. You've got to step up and admit that you were wrong.' He got very upset. He wouldn't do it… When he faced criticism, he just dug in his heels and fought back, which was not the right thing to do."

Noss told me he and Maehr never spoke to each other again.

In 2003, the SRT released a report containing its verdict. As you might guess, it ripped apart Maehr's work, piece by piece, and yes, they called him out by name. They didn't label him a fraud, but they made it clear that Dr. Panther had done some pretty shady things.

Because they were scientists, they didn't scream out their findings in impassioned prose. They were cool and calm—but there was no mistaking what they were saying.

"The conclusions that panthers prefer large forest patches and are reluctant to travel from forests are unreliable because the analyses excluded (without mention or rationale) a large fraction of the available data, ignored errors inherent in telemetry data, and did not rigorously compare used habitats to habitats available to the radio-tagged panthers," they wrote in their final report. "The conclusion that Everglades National Park and most of Big Cypress National Preserve are poor habitat for panthers is not scientifically supported."

Naturally, they zeroed in on the 1995 paper that Maehr had written with Cox, the one that had become the basis for so many permitting decisions, not to mention subsequent Maehr papers. The notion that panthers wouldn't cross an area of more than three hundred feet between forests despite data showing they crossed miles and miles of territory was, as one SRT member said later, "a very improbable conclusion."

Making it worse, of course, was that Maehr had dumped so much data that didn't jibe with his own theory, and didn't disclose that in the paper.

"They excluded animals that were out in the swampland and then came to the conclusion that panthers only used forest," an SRT member explained to a reporter later.

At the time its report was released, the SRT's findings seemed to hit like Thor's hammer. This was an unprecedented slam against the author of most of the literature in a single scientific field. It was also a vindication for the little band of biologists who had been pointing out his deliberate errors.

But the dent this hammer made turned out to be a somewhat shallow one.

Despite what the SRT said about him, Maehr didn't get charged with fraud or even get a traffic ticket. He wasn't punished by his university. He faced no suspension, no reprimand, nothing. He didn't have to give back all the money he'd raked in. He continued publishing scientific papers too. The only real changes were that he shifted his focus more to bears than panthers, and his publications tended to be in smaller, less prestigious journals.

To McBride, that hardly seemed like an appropriate penalty for what Maehr did.

"What offends me is he's still publishing," McBride told me over lunch in 2007. "Science never punishes its own."

Conservation Biology never retracted the 1995 paper. It's still available online just as it appeared originally. There's no cautionary note warning readers not to rely on its findings. Reed Noss said the amount of time that passed between publication and the SRT verdict—eight years—made it difficult to correct or retract.

I talked to Ivan Oransky about that and heard a different opinion. In 2010, Oransky, an award-winning health reporter and a journalism teacher at New York University, cofounded an online publication called *Retraction Watch*. The blog documents and sometimes criticizes the retractions and corrections run by scientific journals, looking into instances of plagiarism, incompetence and outright fraud, not to mention identifying repeat offenders.

"Retractions are reserved for extreme cases," he said. "If journals retracted every paper that turned out to be wrong, they'd be retracting a million papers a year."

The key to whether a retraction is warranted, Oransky said, is summed up in one word: fraud. If someone deliberately tried to mislead the journal's readers, that's something that merits retracting.

Even in cases of fraud, though, journal editors shrink from running a retraction, he said. One way they avoid it is by citing the amount of time that's passed since publication, as Noss did. Some editors won't do anything about a paper that's more than six years old, while others will run a retraction on papers twenty years old or older.

"It's a hell of a convenient excuse, when really what it means is, 'I didn't want to deal with it,'" Oransky said. "Journals can do what they want to do—they're not regulated. But I think [refusing to retract the paper] is an abdication of responsibility."

Oransky was hesitant to give an opinion on whether the Maehr and Cox paper deserved a retraction, "but it sounds like the journal ought to do *something*," he said.

For a paper so flawed, he suggested, *Conservation Biology* could post something on the paper called "An Expression of Concern" saying that its findings were debunked, and attach it so that no one could access the paper without first seeing the note about it.

"That's the least they could do," he said.

Maehr may have seemed chagrined when talking to the SRT, but after the report came out he resumed his usual defiant stance.

He told a reporter for a publication called *Endangered Species and Wetlands Report* that the SRT had made a mountain out of a molehill. He claimed that any habitat lost because of development permits based on his work was "in peripheral areas of debatable use."

He then wrote a twenty-page defense of his work addressed to the state and federal officials on the panther recovery team. In it, he repeatedly bashed Comiskey and complained about what he called "a negative spin" that had been put on his own studies.

As for that flawed 1995 paper with Cox, he wrote, "As the SRT has repeatedly pointed out, I cannot claim perfection in explaining the details of methodology, especially in Maehr and Cox (1995)—we are talking about a sampling of writing and analyses that were done a decade or more ago. There was no intent to mislead or be vague.... Hindsight is 20-20, of course, and I would like nothing better than to go back in time and correct some of the deficiencies in a few of my papers. Nonetheless, I stand by what I have written, and the SRT itself has confirmed the importance of these contributions."

Somehow, in writing his defense, he never got around to explaining why he tossed out 40 percent of the data.

The author of a 2005 story on the SRT noted that Maehr "admits that mistakes were made in data analysis, but defends his conclusions." He conceded that he had used daytime data for a nighttime creature, but he contended that he'd seen no evidence to indicate that panthers prowling at night abandoned the places they occupied during the day.

"The bottom line is that those data do reflect a 24-hour cycle of activity and habitat use," Maehr argued, as if the SRT had never existed. He cited no evidence for his claim, either.

By 2009, when the grad student interviewed him, Maehr went even further. He called the SRT "a witch hunt."

Then he went on the attack. He contended that "there was ample evidence to show Jane Comiskey was routinely communicating with the SRT… I mean, she was *lobbying* them." (Documents provided to me by Land show that Comiskey and Maehr had an equal amount of contact with the SRT's members.)

Maehr even argued that any problems with the 1995 paper were not really his fault. He blamed Cox, his coauthor, for being "fairly new" to the use of the mapping technology known as Geographic Information Software. "We were blindly wading through an evolving technology. We just kind of muddled our way through. And, I mean, it made it through the review process, it got in *Conservation Biology*, and it's not like we were trying to pull the wool over anybody's eyes."

Of course, not mentioning in your paper that you left out so much data might seem pretty wool-like in terms of eye covering.

In 2008, when Maehr died in a plane crash while doing bear research, his obituaries were almost uniformly glowing. The

SRT rated a mention in only one of them. For the rest, it was as if that brutal SRT report had been nothing but a bad dream.

In the end, the person whose life was most affected by the SRT and its verdict wasn't Maehr. It was Andy Eller.

CHAPTER EIGHTEEN

THE WHISTLEBLOWER

Nothing could stop the development permits from rolling off the regulators' assembly line. Nothing.

Even as the Subteam was arguing over Maehr's errors, panther habitat continued being paved over with the blessing of the US Fish and Wildlife Service and the Army Corps of Engineers. Even as Comiskey's review of the data exposed the flaws in Maehr's studies, the two agencies kept saying yes to developers. Even as the Science Review Team was writing its scathing report on Maehr, the wildlife service kept on basing the decisions on Maehr's papers.

Andy Eller's mistake was that he tried to put on the brakes.

In 2002, Comiskey sent emails to the wildlife agency describing the flaws she'd found in Maehr's work and requesting that the agency take action. Eller included her concerns in a draft of a biological opinion he was writing for a project called Winding Cypress, a 1,928-acre development near Naples that would convert a somewhat soggy landscape into 2,300 homes and a golf course.

Eller was already in trouble with his bosses over that project. He had discovered that the Corps's staff—which often skipped visiting development sites, preferring to take the developer's word for what was there—had misclassified three hundred seventy acres of wetlands as uplands. Classifying those acres correctly would likely cost the developer more money to make up for the damage done. When Eller pointed out the error, the developer complained to his bosses.

"I was ordered to back off," he said.

When he tried to include Comiskey's questions about Maehr, things got worse. Rather than being applauded for his thoroughness, Eller was told to rewrite his opinion and make it sound positive. He refused. His bosses rewrote the opinion for him, thus clearing the way for the development to wipe out another big chunk of panther habitat.

The pressure to produce more permits, regardless of what the science said, began to get to Eller. When a *Washington Post* reporter came calling, asking how the federal government could work to restore a famous marsh called the Everglades on one side of the state while paving over the swamps and marshes on the other side, Eller didn't play the happy camper. He didn't mutter, "No comment!" and run for cover. Instead, he said, flat out, that the way the Corps and the Fish and Wildlife Service were handling all those permit requests was wrong.

"It's a heinous process, and it's getting worse," Eller told the reporter, on the record. "Southwest Florida can wear a biologist down."

Up until that story hit the papers, Eller had avoided getting into serious trouble with his bosses. They shot down all his attempts at writing an honest biological opinion, but he continued receiving good job reviews. Suddenly, after reading his two-sentence condemnation of the whole permitting process, his bosses decided he was now a bad employee, a slacker, a guy who dawdled over his work too long.

About a week after the *Post* story, Jay Slack called him in for a meeting that, according to Eller, was short but not at all sweet: "He stated that I needed to find another job, that our relationship was not working, and that it was time for me to 'hit the bricks.'"

But Eller stuck to his job and to his guns. He continued trying to put real science into the biological opinions, and he continued getting his hand slapped.

In the same month that the Science Review Team issued its final report, his bosses hand-delivered a letter to him that said he would be suspended for two weeks without pay and that Slack intended to remove him from federal service.

Instead of falling into line, Eller felt compelled to take an even bolder stance.

A month after serving his suspension, he informed Slack's deputy, Allen Webb, that he had coauthored a scientific paper with Comiskey. He said the study had been peer-reviewed and would be published in the journal *Southeastern Naturalist*. The paper openly criticized Maehr's Panther Habitat Evaluation Model— the PHEM, the same model that the agency was still using in permitting decisions, despite what the SRT said.

Webb was a burly, slow-moving Florida native. Before joining the Fish and Wildlife Service he had worked in construction management for one of Florida's biggest development companies. He was convinced that panthers belonged in a zoo. They might as well be in one now, he contended, because their wild population needed constant care and attention from biologists. He was not happy to hear Eller's news about a new attack on Maehr, and he made that clear.

Other wildlife agency biologists who published scientific papers won commendations from their bosses, Eller said. They were praised for their initiative and perception. Not him, though, not in this instance. Instead, he said, Webb told him "that I would probably be terminated for my participation, although I had worked on the paper on my own time, received no remuneration, and did not criticize the agency."

Before his bosses could put his career on the chopping block, Eller struck the first blow.

He filed a whistleblower suit under a law called the Data Quality Act.

You've probably never heard of the Data Quality Act. I sure hadn't, not until Eller sued.

It's only two paragraphs long, and was slipped through Congress in 2000 as a provision buried deep in a massive budget bill. But holy cow, does it pack a punch.

The act is particularly concerned about the Internet, that modern invention which gives the average citizen far greater access to government resources than at any previous time in history. What if the government was giving out bad info? The Data Quality Act requires federal agencies to ensure that the information they use meets certain standards for accuracy. That includes "influential scientific, financial or statistical information."

The law's main beneficiaries have been businesses seeking a leg up on government regulations. Logging companies have used it to challenge regulations, as have the makers of herbicides. But Eller could see that Maehr's PHEM definitely met the act's definition of "influential scientific…information" that fell short of being accurate.

"The unsound science used and disseminated by the USFWS has compromised panther recovery policy [and] population management," Eller's suit said. "Interrelated errors in concepts and findings are found throughout most panther recovery documents."

Maehr's scientific papers, Eller's lawsuit contended, are "a work of intellectual dishonesty, formulated as a result of political pressure demeaning all biologists working in public service."

Eller didn't file the lawsuit by himself, either. He joined forces with a group called Public Employees for Environmental Responsibility, a national nonprofit that represents government bureaucrats, biologists and law enforcement employees trying to expose wrongdoing in their own agencies. Its motto is, "Protecting Employees Who Protect Our Environment."

Over the years, PEER exposed a plan to build a port on the largest undeveloped island on the eastern seaboard; saved an Arizona river from excessive groundwater withdrawals; and spent eight years battling to win the chief of the US park police her job back after she was fired for talking to a newspaper. The organization was cofounded in 1997 by a US Forest Service whistleblower and a former director of the Government Accountability Project, which represents whistleblowers, so you can understand their focus.

PEER's involvement meant that Eller's lawsuit would make a splash far beyond Florida's borders. The organization blasted out press releases to news organizations around the country about Eller's charges against his bosses. Other organizations joined in to back Eller, such as the Union of Concerned Scientists and the Mountain Lion Foundation. A US senator from Connecticut, Joe Lieberman, began sending letters to the Fish and Wildlife Service asking for details about the permits that it was issuing in panther habitat.

Nothing makes a bureaucracy angrier than seeing its dirty linen aired in public, and Eller had just strung up a clothesline full of it. On the day after George W. Bush was reelected as president, the Fish and Wildlife Service fired Eller. The stated reason: he was too slow in getting development permits approved. His dismissal letter contained not one word about his legal challenge. A spokesman for the agency—with a straight face—told a reporter for the Fort Myers paper that the timing was just a coincidence.

Eller was escorted out of the Vero Beach building carrying a pile of papers, a sweater and several framed postcards of paintings by the renowned Everglades landscape artist A.E. "Beanie" Backus.

Of course, getting fired just made Eller an even hotter commodity for the press and the public. He was no longer just a whistleblower. Now he was a martyr.

At an annual gathering of Florida environmental groups known as the Everglades Coalition, he was hailed as a hero and given an award. PEER released a statement by other Fish and Wildlife Service employees supporting him and noting, "If Andy Eller can be fired for simply doing his job, any other ethical and hard-working employee can be too."

The *Washington Post* ran a story about him headlined, "Panther Advocate Fights to Get Job Back." The *Post* reporter didn't just phone it in, either. The newspaper sent him to visit Eller's sparsely furnished apartment in Vero Beach, where he noted that a visitor had to choose between sitting on the floor and waiting for Eller to go get a fold-up camping chair out of his truck. Because Eller had no wife or children, the *Post* reporter pointed out, he also had nothing to lose in taking on his own agency.

But that wasn't quite right. With no income, Eller had to sell off two of his three off-road motorcycles, and half of his 2,100 books, including the first editions of nature books he treasured so much. He stopped dating or going to the movies. He also lost something less tangible.

"I'm looking at the world a lot differently than I used to," he told a reporter from the *Palm Beach Post*. "I can't believe that at 46 I actually had any innocence to lose, but I feel like I've lost a lot."

Eller joked that he'd become hooked on the therapeutic experience of unburdening himself to random reporters.

"I think I found a new drug—the novelty of the media buzz," he said.

The Fish and Wildlife Service, meanwhile, had suffered a serious blow in court. A federal judge ruled that the development permit for a new six-thousand-acre Florida Rock mine along Corkscrew Road in Lee County was invalid because the biological opinion saying it wouldn't jeopardize panthers was "arbitrary and capricious." The judge said it also failed to take into account the cumulative effect of all the lost habitat from all the other projects that had gotten permits. Recall that Florida Rock's consultant on the project was none other than Maehr.

This was not exactly good publicity for an agency that Eller had said was "already known for drive-through permitting." (A year later, the state's largest newspaper, the *St. Petersburg Times*, got hold of an email sent out by one of Eller's former coworkers that damaged the agency's image even further. The email sent to developers and other permit applicants said the wildlife agency's biologists were way too busy to write biological opinions themselves. In other words, everyone was having trouble meeting deadlines, the very thing Eller had been accused of doing. The email said the agency had come up with a solution to the problem: have the developers and their contractors write the biological opinions for the permit reviewers, instead of making the reviewers do it. The agency would provide a template full of boilerplate language and the developer could just insert a few words to fill it out. Approval would quickly follow.)

Two weeks after the judge's ruling, in March 2005, the agency announced that it now agreed with Eller that it was using faulty science—Maehr's science—in approving permits. You would think the SRT report would have been enough, but no, it took Eller's suit to force the agency to acknowledge that it was doing things wrong.

Agency officials said they would go back and revise a number of biological opinions. But there were a couple of catches.

One was that despite any revisions, the opinions would still reach the exact same conclusion, namely that the development project would not put panthers in jeopardy. The second: Eller was still fired.

Eller had little time to relish even this partial victory, because he was gearing up for the appeal of his firing to a civil service board. That meant sitting through depositions of his former coworkers and hearing them saying, under oath, exactly what their bosses wanted them to say about him for fear they too would be fired.

Eller and his agency were playing chicken. Ultimately, the agency was the one that swerved away.

On the eve of Eller's trial, the Fish and Wildlife Service finally agreed to rehire him—with two conditions. One was that he could no longer work anyplace where Florida panthers existed. After eighteen years, that bridge had been burned. The second condition: the agency would not have to admit that it was wrong to fire him in the first place.

PEER called the deal "a message that there's hope" for government whistleblowers. The conditions were fine by Eller, who despite enjoying his celebrity was now weary of battling developers and politics and bureaucrats. He wanted to work somewhere where he could avoid those headaches. By this time Eller had given up his Vero Beach apartment. He moved to a friend's home in the Carolinas where he could live rent-free and contemplate the way his quiet life had been turned upside down.

Eller's sacrifice resulted in his agency changing the content of just four biological opinions—one of them the one for Florida Rock's mine, the one that a judge had already ruled was wrong. But the agency's changes didn't alter the finding of those biological opinions. They were still written in such a way as to make it sound like it was okay to wipe out panther habitat.

Jay Slack, who had been overseeing the office that produced those flawed opinions, did not get punished. Instead he was promoted to run the National Conservation Training Center in West Virginia. His salary there made him one of the twenty highest paid employees of the agency.

Recall what Slack said when I asked him about why he never approved any requests to write a jeopardy opinion: "The number of panthers was going up. It just didn't add up to a risk of extinction."

In other words, because the Texas cougars sparked a baby boom among the endangered Florida panther population, that made it okay to wipe out thousands of acres of panther habitat with development and mines—thus destroying land that the expanding population needed.

The regional director who had overseen Slack's performance, Sam Hamilton, also didn't get punished. Instead, he got an even bigger boost. In 2009, President Barack Obama nominated him to be director of the whole agency. Most environmental groups disregarded his background and backed his nomination.

Not PEER, though.

"In order to justify his agency's approvals of waves of development, Hamilton enabled FWS managers to skew science, terrorize scientists and drive out whistleblowers," PEER charged in a press release.

For his promotion to be final, Hamilton needed approval from the US Senate. At a forty-five-minute confirmation hearing in front of a Senate committee, Hamilton was praised by two senators who opposed the Endangered Species Act—quite the turnaround from his Texas days. Only one senator, Barbara Boxer of California, brought up Maehr and the Science Review Team mess. Hamilton gave a nonanswer that never mentioned Eller or his lawsuit, and Boxer asked no follow-up questions.

Hamilton's nomination drew unanimous support from the committee, a sign he would face no opposition from the full Senate. But afterward, a reporter asked him a far more pointed question about the twenty-eight surplus panthers that Eller had been forced to include in the airport opinion. How could he justify doing that?

Hamilton shrugged it off as a typo. He said the staff had simply "transposed numbers... Didn't make a whole lot of difference in the end."

CHAPTER NINETEEN

THE SKUNK APE'S SCAPEGOAT

On the same day the US Fish and Wildlife Service rehired and reassigned Andy Eller, the agency issued one more "no jeopardy" opinion on a project that would be built smack-dab in the middle of panther habitat.

But this was no mere subdivision they were approving. This was an entire city—a city of God, you could say.

At least, that was the intention of its founder, Tom Monaghan, a man who made his millions off America's love of guaranteed quick delivery of hot pizza. In 1960, Monaghan and his brother Jim spent $500 to buy a pizza joint in Ypsilanti, Michigan, that was called DomiNick's. Five years later Tom Monaghan re-named it Domino's. Within fifty years, there were more than five thousand of them. Starting in 1979, Domino's pledged that customers would get delivery of their order within thirty minutes or their pie would be free. It sounded like a great gimmick, but the company ended the guarantee in 1993 after people who had been injured by speeding delivery drivers won a series of million-dollar jury verdicts against the company.

In 1998 Monaghan sold his controlling stake in the company for $1 billion. He then turned his attention to starting a small Catholic college in Michigan that he called Ave Maria. He wanted to create a law school too, and turn Ave Maria into the premier Catholic university in the world. But town officials in Ann Arbor balked at his proposal for a 250-foot-tall crucifix, and so Monaghan began searching for a new place to build his dream city with its ginormous cross.

Monaghan had spent some time vacationing in Florida, so that's where he began scouting locations. In Collier County, the Barron Collier Company made him an irresistible offer: one thousand acres of land for free, in exchange for the right to develop the property and split the profits. It was another version of the FGCU plan: drop a college in the middle of an undeveloped area, and wait for that seed to sprout into massive, sprawling growth all around it.

With such a large canvas on which to paint, Monaghan's dream grew larger. Instead of just building a university and a law school, he decided to build a whole town and give it the name of Ave Maria too. He sank $100 million into carving his personal city out of farms, swamps and forests nine miles from the nearest town. It would have the largest crucifix in the world as well as the church with the largest seating capacity in the nation. The church's facade would feature a thirty-foot-tall sculpture of the Annunciation, depicting the Archangel Gabriel greeting the Virgin Mary with the words "Ave Maria"—or in English, "Hail Mary" (not to be confused with the football play of that name).

And his city! His city wouldn't be like any other city in Florida. It would be, Monaghan said, a place where such heathen practices as birth control and pornography wouldn't be allowed.

Ave Maria would spark a Catholic revival in America. It would be "a saint factory" that would "change the world," he boasted.

His own law school faculty warned him that in America, the land of the free, he couldn't run the lives of Ave Maria residents like a feudal lord, but he ignored them.

The plans for the town and college of Ave Maria called for paving over more than two thousand acres of the area identified by the MERIT Subteam as part of the "Primary Zone" for panther habitat, and nearly three thousand acres of what the Subteam had called the "Secondary Zone." Remember, that's the acreage the Subteam said had to be preserved.

To the Fish and Wildlife Service, though, that was no problem, because Monaghan and Barron Collier said they would make up for the lost acreage. How? By preserving seven thousand acres of panther habitat elsewhere from ever being paved over, and building an underpass on a local road so panthers could avoid being run down.

On paper, this sounded like a great deal to the federal agency. In real life, though, the math doesn't work. The developer was taking twelve thousand acres of land that panthers used or were likely to use, paving over five thousand acres, then claiming that the seven thousand that was left made up for the loss. Again, it's the whole "I spent fifty cents but I saved fifty cents and that means I've still got a dollar" fantasy.

Ave Maria was officially founded in 2005. One warm afternoon about four years later, I drove out to look at the place. It was like a ghost town. There was no traffic on the main drag, and only a handful of cars in the driveways of the few Spanish-style homes that had been built. I stopped in at the Publix grocery store that had opened there. Publix is the most popular grocery chain in Florida, but this was the emptiest Publix parking lot I have ever seen at a store that wasn't closed.

Turns out the demand for homes in the middle of a swamp

where you aren't supposed to look at porn or use birth control was not quite as high as Monaghan had expected.

Monaghan tried to strong-arm students and faculty from his Michigan college into moving down to his new Florida town, thus filling those empty homes and driveways. But that didn't work either. According to the *Miami New Times*, this "led to scores of firings, a federal investigation, $259,000 in revoked financial aid, and a half-dozen lawsuits totaling roughly $2 million." He even got into a fight with the Catholic diocese over who would pastor his enormous chapel because Monaghan wanted to name his own priest. As a result, the doors stayed locked except on special occasions.

But by the time it was clear that this new town was unnecessary, it was too late. The panther habitat was gone and would not ever come back. To Jansen, watching the habitat that the Subteam had singled out as necessary be paved over was nothing short of maddening.

"It's frustrating to see this habitat is going to be broken up by homes now," Jansen told me. "And we aren't moving forward with finding other areas."

But as the habitat disappeared, the panthers became more visible than before.

While the Fish and Wildlife Service was bending the rules to accommodate Florida developers' desire to build in panther habitat, the panthers themselves were expanding into new territory. A clash was inevitable.

Thanks to the Texas cougars' fresh genetic material, panthers experienced a baby boom of healthy cats. As the young kittens grew bigger, they needed some turf to call their own. They squeezed into areas that hadn't had panthers in decades, or they settled in spots where no panther had ever been recorded.

But there was no longer as much undeveloped land as there used to be. Places that once held ideal habitat were now covered in paved roads and mass-produced houses and sodded lawns and manicured golf courses. All that new development not only supplanted the places panthers would live, but it also drove out the deer and the hogs they would normally catch and eat.

And so, in the freshly built suburbs where newcomers to Florida had bought cookie-cutter homes, the new residents slowly realized that the panthers still regarded this as their place to live. Any wandering pets allowed to stay outdoors could wind up as the panthers' dinner.

In 2001, a panther ate someone's house cat. The details are unknown, although it was probably FP96, which lived in the Florida Panther National Wildlife Refuge but went outside the refuge boundaries to forage. The consequences turned out to be dire.

The cat it had eaten was infected with feline leukemia, and so 96 had been exposed. The disease is fatal to panthers. Soon the virus spread to other panthers, affecting two panthers in the Big Cypress, one on the Seminole Indian Reservation and six more in the Okaloacoochee Slough. Ultimately five of them died.

Wildlife commission biologists finally contained the outbreak but only through an extraordinary effort. The capture team went out and caught every panther they could find and inoculated every single one of them against the virus. Doing that took four years.

Then, in 2002, one of the original Texas cougars killed some pet goats at a home in the Golden Gate Estates neighborhood. Golden Gate Estates is a massive subdivision that had been carved out of the Big Cypress by 1960s con men out to make a fast buck, not build an actual suburb (they left out schools, parks and utility lines). Soon panthers were taking Chihuahuas, chickens, goats and anything else they caught out in the open. (Especially goats. They love goats the way *Sesame Street*'s Cookie Monster loves chocolate chip cookies.)

Reports of panther sightings, once a rare and amazing surprise, became somewhat more common. Some took on a darker tone. An ornithologist listening for bird calls in the Florida Panther National Wildlife Refuge encountered a panther that later appeared to be following him. The ornithologist, his adrenaline pumping, walked backward through the underbrush, keeping an eye on the panther, until he got to a clearing where he could finally jump on his all-terrain vehicle and ride away. He said later that he probably wasn't really in danger.

"I think it was just trying to figure out what I was doing out there," he told me. "Once I started to think about it, they're essentially ambush hunters. You wouldn't see them until they jumped on your back. I think it was a fairly innocent encounter."

Not everyone was so sanguine about seeing the state animal. The calls coming into the wildlife commission's Naples office tended to be from people who were irate about what the panthers were doing. How dare panthers show up in their backyard and eat their labradoodle!

"Folks are generally kind of upset," Land said. "They don't really know—should they be scared? Should they be worried? We try to calm them down."

I interviewed some of the people who were having problems with panthers. About 10 a.m. one summer day, a thirteen-year-old named Roberto Zambrano went into his uncle's backyard near Naples to feed the family's goats. For some reason they didn't come when he called.

Suddenly he was staring right at a panther. The panther fled. The goats were dead.

"I said, 'Oh my God!' and I ran back to get my brothers," Roberto said.

A motion-sensor camera planted by state biologists clicked pictures of a female panther teaching its two kittens how to hunt by tracking down and killing the goats.

Mark Poole had an even more electrifying encounter. One evening he was walking the fence line at his house near Naples, trying to find the hole that he figured his missing goats must have used to escape. At the back of his property, three hundred feet from his house, he saw a dark shape. When he got within twelve feet, it made a sound in its throat that sounded something like a growl.

The something was a panther. It was eating one of his chickens, and it was not going to let go, not even when confronted by a human.

Poole backed up fast, until his backyard motion-sensor light popped on. That's when the panther skedaddled, leaping the four-foot fence with ease. After that, Poole started carrying a shotgun when he went into the backyard, and worrying about his kids catching their school bus down the street.

"It wasn't afraid of me," he said, "and I'm a lot bigger than a fourth-grader."

Afterward, he put barbed wire atop his fence, and hooked up his motion-sensors to a radio that blares loud rap music to scare away intruders. Of course, Poole told me, "Maybe it thought I was the intruder."

The most extensive series of attacks occurred over a three-week period in 2004 at a campground in Ochopee. What made it worse is what the campground managers did in response.

This is where I have to explain to you about the Skunk Ape.

You have probably heard about Bigfoot, the big, hairy humanoid that allegedly runs around the woods out West like a super-hirsute version of Homer Simpson. You may have heard that Bigfoot (assuming Bigfoot exists, which is a big assumption) is related to other fabled beasts such as the Yeti, Sasquatch and Abominable Snowman.

What you may not know is that Bigfoot has a couple of cousins that supposedly live in Florida. Yes, that's right—Florida is such a weird state that it's got not one but two pseudo-Bigfoots.

One is the Bardin Booger, which supposedly skulks around

the pine flatwoods and swamps of Putnam County in North Florida. The first reported sighting was in the 1940s in the unincorporated area known as Bardin (hence the name). There have been plenty more sightings reported since then.

However, that area is in the heart of Florida black bear country, making it likely that whatever creature people saw, it was either a bear or a humbug. The one sighting that everyone agrees was legit happened in 2006, when the *St. Augustine Record* reported that the Booger appeared at Palatka's Azalea Festival, carrying an American flag and a bouquet of azaleas.

The better-known hairy hominid is the South Florida version known as the Skunk Ape, which as far as I can tell is the only legendary creature that has a stench that's as famous as the creature itself. The Skunk Ape allegedly lurks in the Everglades and the Big Cypress, and like all Bigfoot relatives exists primarily in a series of blurry and inconclusive photos and video clips.

Yet somehow, the Skunk Ape has gained a level of tongue-in-cheek acceptance among longtime Floridians that has eluded the Bardin Booger.

I suspect his cachet is due to the thing that gives the creature its name—namely its scent, which has been described as resembling rotten eggs and methane gas, or wet dogs mixed with skunk. It stinks like crazy is what I am saying.

How Florida-famous is the Skunk Ape? In 1977, a state representative from Fort Myers sponsored a bill that would make it a misdemeanor to possess, harm or molest one. Sadly, the bill did not pass. The legislator blamed the ape's own political apathy, telling reporters, "They're very important, but I can't get them to the polls."

The world's leading expert on the Skunk Ape is a guy named Dave Shealy, who by a strange coincidence also runs the Skunk Ape Research Headquarters in the tiny South Florida town of Ochopee. (Ochopee is also famous for being the home of the smallest post office in the nation—it's just big enough for the stamps to fit inside). The Skunk Ape Research Headquarters does not resemble a science lab or a base camp for adventurers as much as it does a classic Florida roadside attraction full of kitschy tchotchkes for tourists.

The building stands on the Tamiami Trail, aka US 41, and what you notice first about it are selfie-ready statues of a gorilla-looking creature out front. The only Skunk Apes you're ever likely to see.

Adjacent to the campy HQ is an actual camp, and also a petting zoo. Both were run by Shealy's brother Jack. The petting zoo boasted quite an impressive menagerie—and only a low fence to keep the animals in and any intruders out.

Thus, over a series of nights, a panther with a taste for the exotic killed sixteen goats, four emus, three turkeys, five ducks and a chicken.

"He wiped me out," David Shealy told a reporter. He blamed the state's biologists for letting it happen because of course that's who manufactured all those hungry panthers without making sure they had enough deer to eat.

"Nobody approached us about compensating us for our animals," he grumbled to a reporter. "I've got photographs of the cat killing my animals. It shouldn't be my problem. It's their experiment."

State biologists held off intervening because they hoped the panther would eventually back off. Instead it kept coming back for more.

"We couldn't seem to break him of staring at this food that had been pretty much offered up to him on a buffet table," Darrell Land told a reporter, with more than a trace of sarcasm.

The panther attacking the petting zoo turned out to be an eight-year-old male. State biologists figured it had probably been pushed out of its own turf by a younger male. Like many other Florida retirees, he was now heading to the buffet line for the early bird special, and the buffet line happened to be at the Skunk Ape HQ. And it featured actual birds.

Fed up, Jack Shealy consulted with a couple of his friends and decided to do something drastic. They set up a video camera in a separate enclosure, and put a goat into it. They staked the goat within the enclosure with a rope around its neck, not un-like the goat intended to tempt a dinosaur into the open in the original *Jurassic Park* movie.

If this were the Old Testament, you'd say they had put out a scapegoat.

Then they waited. Sure enough, the panther jumped the fence and attacked the goat, and they got it on video. But the pan-ther didn't make it a quick kill. It chomped and tore at the goat, but left it standing. One of the trio was monitoring the cam-era's video feed, and so he leaned out of the trailer where he was watching the attack and banged on its metal side, scaring the panther away.

Somehow the goat survived the attack. The guy who shot the video posted something about it on a website, contending it showed that panthers were vicious killers who didn't deserve to be protected by the law. He blamed "enviro-socialists" in government agencies for forcing dangerous animals on people simply trying to protect their property.

"There is something profoundly wrong in America when bureau-scientists can quarter large-bodied predators on citizens' lands," he wrote. "We fought King George for merely quar-tering troops, not predatory animals on our ancestors' lands."

But the video backfired. An animal rights group promptly complained to the authorities about it. Prosecutors charged the three men with conspiracy to commit animal cruelty. Turns out it's against the law to put out live bait for wild animals. By tethering the goat out for the panther to eat, the trio weren't just torturing the goat—they were also changing the behavior of the panther by making it too easy to catch prey.

Shealy and a second man pleaded no contest. The third insisted on a trial. The jury found him guilty after deliberating just twenty minutes.

As for the panther, the state biologists laid a trap for him: a big wired-up box with a chunk of venison inside. The cat went right for the bait. When they examined what they had caught, they discovered it was hardly the ruthless killer that the Skunk Ape guys had claimed. The cat turned out to be a scrawny thing, with patchy fur and a missing canine tooth.

It was Florida Panther 60, which had survived being hit by a car. The collision left it with nerve damage that prevented the injured cat from pursuing wild prey the way it should have. Suddenly the repeat attacks on the petting zoo made a lot more sense. This wasn't a male panther past his prime. This was a handicapped panther unable to follow his wild instincts to hunt. He had to eat, and so he went after captive prey. The biologists hauled the injured panther up to White Oak to try to nurse it back to health.

Then, two years later, the same thing happened all over again. This time the marauding panther was no invalid. He was something of a celebrity.

Florida Panther 79 was one of the first cats born of the Texas cougar–Florida panther cross-breeding. To say he'd helped the population rebound would be like saying cheerleaders sometimes jump around at football games. FP79 was better known among panther biologists as "Don Juan," because he'd fathered about thirty kittens with nine different females. He was the father of virtually every litter produced in the Big Cypress south of Alligator Alley.

Don Juan had once been the dominant male in Big Cypress, the lion king over a six-hundred-square-mile fiefdom, but no more. Panthers in the wild can live to be twelve years old. Don Juan was a grizzled oldster of ten, and instead of enjoying his golden years, he really *had* been pushed out of his turf by a younger male—perhaps one of his own descendants.

At the Skunk Ape petting zoo, Don Juan gobbled up a turkey. Down the road he grabbed chickens and even a cat. When one homeowner's dogs tried to fight him, he left them torn to shreds.

Deb Jansen and one of McBride's sons showed up with a pack of dogs. They tracked Don Juan down, shot him with a tranquilizer dart and hauled him far away from where he'd been feeding. Two days later, while driving to the Big Cypress Preserve's headquarters, Jansen got the kind of bad feeling that is common in the *Star Wars* movies. She pulled over to check Don Juan's radio collar transmissions. Sure enough, Don Juan was back.

They nabbed him again, and this time they took a step they had been reluctant to take. They took Don Juan away from the wild. He would live the rest of his life in captivity.

His first new home was at the Busch Gardens theme park in Tampa, in a small compound in the shadow of a roller coaster. Later he was moved to Ellie Schiller Homosassa Springs Wildlife State Park, a four-hour drive north of his former kingdom. At the park he was part of a menagerie on display for tourists that included manatees, red wolves, whooping cranes and even a hippo named Lucifer that had been officially declared a citizen of Florida by a former governor. The cat that had attacked a zoo became part of a zoo himself.

Score it as Civilization 1, Wilderness 0.

The attacks at the Skunk Ape HQ marked the start of a new phase of human-panther relations, one that echoed the pioneer days. People who had never seen a panther before now found it frightening to spot one.

Take what happened with FP124. No other case better illustrates the complexity of panther management and the uncertainty of the cats' relationship with humans. In 2006, out of the population's fourteen to seventeen reproducing females, FP124 had given birth to litters in each of the previous two years, a rare accomplishment. She had become a significant contributor to the future of the endangered cats.

But that year 124 and her most recent kittens kept showing up near the Ochopee reservation of the Miccosukee Tribe of Indians, freaking out the tribe's leaders.

The tribe wasn't rolling in dough like the Seminoles, but the Miccosukees did have their own gambling casino, and the steady cash flow that that entailed. That provided them enough revenue to keep on retainer the former US attorney of South Florida as their corporate counsel. His wife was a South Florida congresswoman, giving the tribe additional political influence.

The tribe persuaded wildlife officials to remove one of FP124's kittens after it was seen near the site of their ceremonial Green Corn Dance, which was about one hundred yards from several Miccosukee homes. Over the objections of environmental groups, the capture team went out and darted the kitten, then eleven months old. They carried it in a truck about sixty miles to the north and turned it loose in a forested area. Five months later it was dead, killed by a larger male panther that was defending its turf from this interloper.

A year later, when 124 was spotted chasing a deer near the tribe's environmental education center, the tribe's leaders began lobbying for her removal as well. Biologists and environmental groups fought back, arguing that 124 had yet to do anything that appeared threatening.

Tempers flared. Anecdotes became weaponized. A United Parcel Service driver spotted the cat and kittens, and stories circulated that the sight had scared him so badly that he refused to deliver packages to the area anymore. When Jansen talked to him, though, she got a different take.

"He's our deliverer here at Big Cypress," she said. "He also delivers at my house."

When he delivered a package to the Big Cypress preserve office, Jansen said, he started talking about the panther he'd seen, and Jansen jotted down some notes.

He kept saying "what a wonderful experience he had had," Jansen told me. "It was right at dusk when he saw this female panther. He slowed the van down so the door wouldn't rattle. He kept talking about what a wonderful experience it was."

The people pushing the hardest for 124's removal weren't Miccosukee at all. The loudest complaints came from one of the tribe's advisers, a former park ranger whose wife ran the environmental education center where the panthers were seen the most. The ex-ranger contended that the panthers weren't even real panthers anymore. Despite how closely related the panthers and cougars were to start with, he contended that the cougar's DNA was somehow "taking over" that of the panther.

"Bottom line: these ain't panthers anymore," he told a reporter. "They're predominantly Texas cougars and they're behaving as cougars do: reproducing more quickly, stalking people. That's the bottom line here."

That story began spreading among others who didn't trust the government to get anything right, or who considered the Endangered Species Act to be an affront to private property rights. The stories claimed there were now hundreds of super-aggressive cougar-like panthers roaming in the woods, getting ready to pounce on children waiting at bus stops. This was usually followed by the suggestion that it was time to open a hunting season on them.

Roy McBride, who has seen more types of puma than anyone else in Florida, dismissed this as nonsense. If panthers seemed more aggressive now, it was because they were healthy cats. The ones he hunted before the genetic restoration were generally weak and skittish. They were suffering from holes in their hearts or other defects. There weren't very many of them, either, so seeing one was a rare occurrence, whereas now the population was growing and active. Hence the apparent contrast in behavior between 1995 panthers and 2005 panthers. The 2005 panthers were behaving more like a normal cat would, whether a panther, a puma or a cougar.

And as for the idea that there were hundreds more panthers roaming around than what the government would admit, Mc-Bride said, that theory lacked one key supporting element: Where were the thousands of deer and hogs that those panthers would need to eat? They didn't exist, and neither did that mysterious army of super-panthers. (The conspiracy theorists weren't fazed by this objection. One went so far as to suggest on Facebook that McBride and his sons, Rocky and Rowdy, were nothing but a bunch of liars-for-hire, willing to say anything to protect their government contract.)

The wildlife commission came up with a compromise solution to the Miccosukee complaints. Instead of removing 124, the state set up an automated twenty-four-hour phone line that allowed callers to check on the panther's location at all times.

In the meantime, Darrell Land and the rest of the capture team developed a protocol for responding to such reports of human-panther encounters. They decided to begin treating them as if they were 911 emergency calls. They also began documenting what they called "panther predations"—instances in which the big cats would chow down on goats, sheep, chickens, dogs and miniature horses. Once the biologists began really looking into some of the cases, though, checking the ground for panther tracks, it turned out that the killer wasn't always a panther. Sometimes it turned out to be a bobcat, or a bear, a coyote or even a pack of feral dogs.

But things got worse. Cattle ranchers began grumbling about their calves disappearing, and blaming panthers for cutting into their expected profits. Quite a few of them also subscribed to the theory about hundreds of vicious super-cougars stalking their ranchland. Some were so antigovernment that when the

US Fish and Wildlife Service offered to compensate them for their losses, they refused to take the money.

"We don't like the Florida panther, and we don't like the Florida panther preservation program," one rancher told federal officials.

One of the ranchers who complained the loudest about panthers taking cattle was a woman named Liesa Priddy of Immokalee, who said that over a two-year period her JB Ranch lost ten calves to panthers. She estimated each calf cost her $1,000. (Later, then-Gov. Rick Scott appointed her to a seat on the state wildlife commission, where she tried to single-handedly rewrite the state's policy on dealing with panthers without bothering to consult with the agency's own panther biologists.)

Amid all the wild rumors and antipanther rhetoric, dead panthers began turning up.

In February 2009, Land and his colleagues discovered a dead panther in Collier County that, for once, had not been run over by a car or killed by another panther. You didn't need the Florida Museum of Natural History's metal detector to see that it had been shot dead.

Because killing an endangered animal is a federal crime, the law enforcement arm of the US Fish and Wildlife Service took over investigating what had happened. Nine years later, they have not yet solved the case. They have also refused to release any further details about what happened, including where the panther was killed and how.

In April 2009, the biologists discovered a second victim, a female panther shot dead in rural Hendry County, just outside the boundary of the Big Cypress National Preserve. At two years old, the dead panther had been just about ready to breed for the first time.

Once again the Fish and Wildlife Service law enforcement arm swooped in to take charge of the investigation. Once again, they refused to release any information about the circumstances of the death. Just as with the first panther shooting, this one remains unsolved.

Then, in October 2009, a third panther was found shot dead—this one with an arrow. This time, the investigators nailed their man. His name was "Scuttlebutt."

From atop his tree stand, Todd "Scuttlebutt" Benfield could see the tawny fur of a Florida panther prowling through the underbrush. Benfield, a bow hunter looking for deer, knew that panthers eat deer.

So he loaded a three-bladed Muzzy Broadhead arrow in his Matthews Solocam Switchback XT bow, aimed it at the panther and let fly. The arrow found its mark, killing the cat. Benfield later explained that he did this "because I thought the Florida panther was competing and interfering with my hunting."

Benfield knew he could get in trouble for what he'd done. He came back to the site the next day with a buddy and dragged the panther's carcass fifty feet into the woods, trying to hide his crime. He even dismantled his tree stand.

Even as he took the stand apart, though, a state wildlife commission employee was uncovering the panther's body from its hiding place. It had clearly been shot with an arrow. Scuttlebutt was a well-known bow hunter whose stand was in this area. He also had a record of violating game laws. He was the obvious suspect.

Two days later, a Fish and Wildlife Service investigator questioned Benfield. He denied shooting the panther, but he made it clear he felt no love for Florida's state animal.

"I don't like those damn things," he told the investigator, noting that he'd heard stories about them killing calves and "they are going to hurt someone."

The investigator came back about a month later with a search warrant to go through his house and car, and then came back with another warrant allowing the authorities to collect his

DNA. Despite the clumsiness of Benfield's cover-up, closing the case took three more years (and no, federal officials have never explained why).

Scuttlebutt ultimately pleaded guilty in federal court and was sentenced to pay a fine of $5,000, pay another $5,000 to the National Fish and Wildlife Foundation, publish an apology in the *Naples Daily News,* and put in two hundred hours of community service. A judge ordered him to spend three years on probation, during which he was banned from hunting. In his apology, he wrote that one reason he was sorry for what he did was because of "the negative publicity that it may have brought to hunting."

Meanwhile, squeezed out of their home territory and shot at by poachers, the rejuvenated panther population began doing some hunting too—for a new place to live, one they had called home long, long ago.

CHAPTER TWENTY
THE WANDERERS

The panther crouched in the dark near the river's edge, hidden from the lights of the nearby campground. He had avoided this small outpost of civilization for a week, hiding in the woods during the eighty-degree days, emerging in the cool of the evening to continue his search.

Now he was ready to take the plunge.

Every few seconds the red bulb of a navigational marker flashed above the rippling waves, then blinked out, leaving only the full moon to show the way. He picked his way down the sloping bank, brushing by holly bushes, crunching across seashells.

With a splash, Florida Panther 62 slipped into the chilly current of the Caloosahatchee River and paddled toward the northern shore.

★ ★ ★

Thanks to the Texas cougars there were more panthers than ever before. Thanks to the Fish and Wildlife Service (and local and state government officials) approving so much development, the cats were trying to live and eat and mate in a much smaller area than ever before. Something had to give.

Historically, the dwindling population of panthers had spent the past four decades hemmed into the state's southern tip, kept in place by the Caloosahatchee River. The river rolls along for sixty-seven miles, connecting Lake Okeechobee with San Carlos Bay at Sanibel Island. For much of its length, it's too wide for an animal to easily cross. For instance, as drivers on Interstate 75 reach Fort Myers, they traverse the river on one of a pair of two-lane bridges that are each forty feet wide from curb to curb.

Thus, young male panthers in search of turf to call their own would bump up against the river and, finding no way across, would usually turn back. They would end up someplace where an older panther was already in control, and the two would fight, often to the death. Maehr declared the Caloosahatchee to be a barrier that no panther could penetrate.

But then, three years after the Texas cougars were turned loose, Florida Panther 62 proved the river was a barrier that was far from impregnable, and changed the notion of what constitutes "panther habitat."

FP62 was one of a litter of three male kittens born in rural Collier County. When he and his siblings were just balls of spotted fur, a biologist snapped the only picture of 62. Later the trio were captured, fitted with radio collars so biologists could track them and released back into the wild.

When FP62 was old enough to split from his mother, he headed north to stake out his own territory and became what biologists call "a wanderer." Over time, as I followed his travels he became, to me, "*The* Wanderer."

In April 1998, he was five months shy of his second birthday when he reached the Ortona Lock and Dam on the Caloosa-hatchee. There's a campground there where snowbirds park their RVs. The campers' major activity is watching million-dollar yachts cruise through the locks from Fort Myers and Naples, heading east, bound for Palm Beach, or occasionally aimed back toward the Gulf Coast.

About one thousand feet west of the campground is a spot where the old Atlantic Coast Line trestle once carried freight trains across the river. The trestle and rails were torn out years ago. Darrell Land told me 62 followed the overgrown railroad grade straight to where the old trestle stood. The river there narrows to about 150 yards across, and the slope of the banks is gentler, making it the ideal spot to cross.

"He hit the river and spent a few days looking for a land bridge," Land said. "When he didn't find one he just said, 'What the hell!' and swam across."

Over the next two years, 62 ricocheted around the state like a pinball, crossing highways, dodging bulldozers and demonstrating that all of Florida could be used as panther habitat.

Even the outskirts of Disney World.

The big cat emerged from the water and shook himself. He made his way up the bank, the intermittent flash of red light illuminating his way. He skirted the scattered stucco homes on the north side of the river and turned west into palmetto-fringed ranch land, where he could feast on feral hogs.

Soon he was prowling the wet prairies of Fisheating Creek, in roughly the same area where Roy McBride found that first panther when he was working for the World Wildlife Fund. Though 62 could dine on an abundance of deer there, something did not suit him. He kept moving.

As spring turned to summer, he angled north and began paralleling US 27 as it climbs the spine of the state. Near Sebring he spent one warm day beneath a billboard, in a patch of woods by a mobile home park.

High above him a Cessna 172 circled, its engine whining like a riding mower. Land and other state biologists used the plane to go out three times a week and follow The Wanderer's radio signals. They chuckled when they saw his latest refuge. Mobile home park residents think of that woodsy patch as their nature trail, Land told me.

"Imagine," he said, "if one of those residents was taking his poodle for a walk and had that cat step out on them!"

To some people, the travels of Florida Panther 62 showed that, despite all the development going on throughout the state, there was a hidden pathway for a wide-ranging predator like the panther that would allow travel from south to north through Florida.

The big flaw in this notion of contiguous wilderness is a cross-hatch of highways. Dozens of South Florida panthers have fallen to four-wheeled predators. Somehow 62 scampered across US 27 and several state roads unscathed.

As he closed in on Orlando's thicket of busy highways, the odds rose that his journey would end under the tires of an eighteen-wheeler. As Land put it, "I fully expected some Saturday morning I would get a call that he was lying by a road somewhere."

Remember the official panther recovery plan? The one that Belden put together so many years ago? It called for establishing three colonies of panthers. The existing one in South Florida wasn't supposed to be the only one. There were supposed to be two more. That requirement remained a part of every iteration of the plan—the 1981 original, the 1987 revision and the 1995 version.

This was no radical notion, but rather the height of scientific practicality. What if some deadly illness—say, feline leukemia—or a hurricane or a major wildfire were to sweep through and kill all the panthers in Southwest Florida? Having more than one colony would guarantee there would be a remnant outside that region.

But the Fish and Wildlife Service had never tried to open up any new territory for panthers. All it did was say yes to wiping out more and more of the original territory.

In 2009, a trio of scientists from Tennessee examined potential places in other states where Florida panthers could find habitat similar to what they were losing at home. The study identified nine locations. They were in Arkansas, Alabama and Georgia, as well as North Florida. Officials in Arkansas, Alabama and Georgia were quick to say they did not want any panthers in their states. They could see what a controversial creature it could be.

That meant the one place they might still be welcome would be Florida—north of the Caloosahatchee.

For months The Wanderer had been on the move—dodging cars, avoiding people, traveling only in the deep velvet night. Near dawn on a July morning, he found a place to stop, a place as different as could be from where he grew up.

He stalked across ridges of white sand, their pale desolation brightened by yellow button flowers and catclaw briars. He came to a dried-out wetland, thick with ferns and stiff saw palmetto. Shaded by bay trees, he holed up there as day broke, sleeping for hours.

Over the next few months he spent his nights exploring this new domain. In the early morning mists he would melt back into the swamp, back to the place he was fast making his home.

Florida Panther 62 had settled into a little-known slice of scrub called Catfish Creek State Preserve. Old-timers dubbed it the Tub Hills because of its sink-like ponds, clear and cool. It sits on some five thousand acres of ancient sand dunes bordering Lake Pierce in Polk County, an hour east of Tampa.

The sole state employee at Catfish Creek at that time was a

park ranger named Pat Mitchell. He lived in the shadow of a fire tower with his wife and three children. More than once, tracks or radio signals showed that The Wanderer had crept within a few hundred yards of their home.

Mitchell only saw his neighbor once. The ranger was tooling along in his truck when a deer leaped in front of him. As Mitchell slammed on the brakes, he saw a flash of tawny fur, nothing more. He got out of his truck and found a fresh panther track—the reason the deer was in such a hurry it nearly became roadkill.

After 62 set up housekeeping at Catfish Creek, biologists would fly to Polk County three times a week to check his location using the radio signals. Through the changing seasons, even when the winter winds sent the temperature tumbling to well below freezing, 62 stuck to Catfish Creek.

Still The Wanderer wandered a bit. He roamed over to nearby Lake Kissimmee State Park, the Tiger Creek Nature Preserve, even the Disney Wilderness Preserve that's part of Disney's Animal Kingdom theme park in Central Florida. Invariably, he returned to Catfish Creek.

In fact, 62 stuck around Catfish Creek for so long that some biologists wondered if he was launching his own panther colony. There were unconfirmed reports of a female panther with kittens. But the McBride boys and their dogs scoured the area and found no sign of a second cat.

Some environmental advocates suggested that the state play matchmaker: transplant a South Florida female to Catfish Creek, so The Wanderer would wander no more. But feds would have to clear such a move, and they were reluctant to take such a dramatic step. They remembered all too well the hostile reception that transplanted pumas received when Chris Belden was overseeing the North Florida experiment.

While holed up at Catfish Creek, 62 turned three years old,

the age at which young males reach sexual maturity. Suddenly, he had places to go.

One morning in early March 2000, Land flew up from South Florida on a regular tracking run for Florida Panther 62 and found him far north of his usual hangout. The cat had somehow crossed Interstate 4—widely known as the most dangerous highway in America, with more deaths per mile than any other road. Then he had gone to ground near an old theme park for baseball fans called "Boardwalk and Baseball," later to become part of Legoland.

He was in a small swamp that offered the only natural cover for miles. He clearly was looking for love in all the wrong places.

"The whole area was being bulldozed for some kind of housing development," Land said. "He was completely surrounded by bulldozers."

Somehow The Wanderer made it out of there and back to Catfish Creek. But then, one night in May, 62 roared out of Catfish Creek like a teenager late to pick up his prom date.

He started northeast, then veered southward, cutting across Florida's Turnpike. Over the next two months he went on what Land called "a rocket run," covering some two hundred miles. He zoomed from the shores of Lake Hell 'n' Blazes, at the headwaters of the St. Johns River, to Lake Washington, a few miles outside Melbourne, before looping south again. He crossed back over Florida's Turnpike and even swam the Kissimmee River.

Eventually his path took him back to the Caloosahatchee, nearly twenty miles west of where he had crossed. The biologists tailing him wondered if he was trying to rejoin the main population of panthers and find a mate.

They also wondered how much longer they could follow him. Time was running out.

The last batch of batteries that biologists had put in the panthers' radio collars had turned out to be defective. They had spent the spring recapturing the panthers whose collars were about to conk out and replacing the batteries. FP62 had one of the collars with bad batteries. The capture team had been about to go after him in Catfish Creek when the big cat bolted.

"We were planning a preemptive strike, but I think through ESP he picked up on what we were planning," Land said. "Lord knows what put the burr under his butt. Without the Vulcan mind meld, I don't think we can know."

Land, in his airplane, kept tracking him, waiting for him to settle down again. Eventually The Wanderer decided to linger a while in the Telegraph Swamp in Charlotte County. It was late June and the temperature was much warmer than usual for capture season. Land's boss decided to delay the capture for fear the heat and stress might kill 62.

After a couple of weeks, The Wanderer was on the move again. He rambled north through the flat green ranch land of eastern Charlotte. By July he was crossing the DeSoto County line in rural Central Florida. That's where the signals stopped.

"Lord knows where he is now," Land said. Personally, I'm hoping he wound up at the governor's mansion in Tallahassee, or maybe he's skulking around the R.A. Gray Building where FP3 stands stiffly on display.

While 62 was the first panther with a radio collar to cross the Caloosahatchee, he would be far from the last.

In May 1999, a second young male panther swam the Caloosahatchee near the Ortona Lock. Four months later he was killed by a car as he tried to cross US 27. In April 2000, a third radio-collared male swam the river. A few days later, biologists found his body near Fisheating Creek. They never could figure out what killed him.

Although they didn't make it far, the crossings by those other panthers showed that 62's crossing of the Caloosahatchee was no anomaly. The Wanderer became viewed as a trailblazer, suggesting there could someday be a second panther colony in Central Florida.

Not all panthers had radio collars, which led to some surprises. In July 1999, while 62 was at Catfish Creek, someone found a large feline track on a preserve next to Myakka River State Park in Sarasota County. Experts confirmed they were left by a Florida panther, one apparently without a radio collar.

More and more panthers showed up north of the river. One wound up just outside Tampa, some two hundred miles north of the river. Its journey ended just past the centerline of Interstate 4, not far from where it crosses Interstate 75. As the panther crossed the asphalt between a recreational vehicle dealership and a furniture warehouse, a westbound car or truck ran it over, crushing its skull. The driver kept going.

The death marked the first confirmed panther sighting in that area in thirty years. It was also the first panther I ever saw, its body limp and lifeless, the light gone from its eyes.

Another panther made it all the way across the state line into Georgia before it was gunned down by a panicky deer hunter. The hunter pleaded guilty to violating the Endangered Species Act and was sentenced to two years of probation, during which he could not hunt anywhere, and fined $2,000. That was apparently the first and last time a panther showed up in Georgia, at least since the Endangered Species Act was passed.

Like FP62, all of these wanderers were males. Not one female had crossed the river, and the feds kept insisting they would not allow one to be transplanted. If it happened, it had to happen naturally. That way, no one could criticize the government for the appearance of a new panther colony in the center of the state. If it was anyone's fault, it would be God's.

While The Wanderer and his followers were wandering around the state looking for a place to settle down, some people were trying one more time to save what was left of the place he came from by getting it declared "critical habitat."

In 1993, Congress changed the rules for the animals and plants protected by the Endangered Species Act to require each new endangered species listing to designate where its critical habitat existed.

But because panthers were put on the list before 1993, the Fish and Wildlife Service had never designated any land as its critical habitat. They were not legally required to do so, and thus they—and in particular Sam Hamilton—chose not to. The agency could have looked at the rapid spread of urban sprawl and tried to slow it down with a critical habitat designation, but of course that might have upset all the developers with political connections.

In 2003, an environmental group petitioned the agency to declare that a big chunk of Southwest Florida was critical habitat. Five years passed. Finally agency officials announced their answer: no. Jay Slack's successor as head of the agency's Vero Beach office said he feared limiting development in panther habitat might "cause unintended harm by inducing negative public sentiment" toward the animal. Much better to pave over their habitat and keep everyone feeling well-disposed toward the cats.

Then, on the same day in 2009 that Barack Obama was sworn in as president, several environmental and civic groups— including the Sierra Club and Public Employees for Environmental Responsibility—filed a similar petition. This time the petitioners had science on their side. They specifically asked the wildlife service to declare as crucial habitat the entire 3,548-square-mile Primary Zone that the Subteam said was essential for the panthers' future survival. Backing up that request was a letter to Obama signed by five of Florida's Democratic congressional representatives urging him to take action quickly because another "new town" like Ave Maria, this one a nine-thousand-home development ironically named "Big Cypress," had been proposed for construction on more than three thousand acres of the Primary Zone.

The answer, delivered a year later, was once again a resounding "no." (The congressional representatives could have sponsored a bill to require the wildlife agency to declare critical habitat, but for some reason they failed to follow up on their letter with any action.)

So a coalition of environment and civic groups—the Sierra Club, the Center for Biological Diversity, the Conservancy of Southwest Florida and the Council of Neighborhood Civic Associations—sued the Fish and Wildlife Service to force it to declare critical habitat for the panther. That didn't work either. A federal judge threw out the suit, saying that the way the law was written left the decision entirely up to the agency, regardless of what science said.

What the agency wanted was not to dictate anything to the big landowners. Instead, agency officials said they liked a "cooperative" approach. They liked how three environmental groups, Audubon of Florida, Defenders of Wildlife and the Florida Wildlife Federation, were working with the developer of Big Cypress to create enhanced protection for some panther habitat on that property while still allowing development in the rest.

Defenders of Wildlife has been working on panther-related issues for a long time. When I asked the Florida chapter chief, Laurie Macdonald, to explain how her organization could go from a hardline fighter to a dealmaker, she said the answer was simple.

"This all started when Defenders issued a notice of intent to sue over Ave Maria," said Macdonald, a slender woman with long, dark hair and a wide knowledge of Florida's big mammals. "Then...the president of the Barron Collier Company called me and said, 'Hey, you want to talk? Maybe we can do this in a way that's a win-win-win—for conservation, for the landowners and for panthers.'"

She decided to try negotiating because pushing the Fish and Wildlife Service to do its job just wasn't working, she explained. The recognition that federal employees would never do their jobs was the turning point. Better to save some habitat than none, she contended.

It was hard to argue with her viewpoint about the agency. In 2010, I analyzed the Fish and Wildlife Service's response to permit applications for projects in panther habitat and found it had allowed development to wipe out forty-two thousand acres of habitat. Although in some cases the wildlife agency required developers to make up for the loss by preserving panther habitat elsewhere, sometimes it didn't require that at all. As a result, during that same time period, the agency made developers save only thirty thousand acres—which means twelve thousand acres were wiped out with no requirement at all for making that up.

In the meantime, as more and more of the habitat was destroyed, more wanderers were hitting the road, leaving South Florida behind—and another set of environmental activists was rising up to help them.

CAT CAM BINGO

If you knew Carlton Ward Jr. only by his family background, you'd expect him to be a politician or a lawyer or a banker, someone who worked in a plush, beautifully paneled office on the top floor of a Tampa office building. His great-grandfather was governor of Florida and the founder of one of the state's big law firms. He's an eighth-generation Florida native who grew up in the state's most densely populated county.

But his mother made sure to instill in him a sense of wonder about the natural world. So while he's tall and square-jawed, thoughtful and fairly eloquent, Ward makes his living not as a mouthpiece in a three-piece suit but as a nature photographer. His work primarily focuses on the parts of Florida that lie far inland from the state's better-known coastal areas.

"We have an amazing, wild interior that is the source of almost all of our drinking water," Ward explained to a reporter once. "It's the source of our $100-billion agriculture economy. It's where all of our wildlife in any significant scale can still survive, but it's hiding in plain sight."

Over the years, Ward has befriended several wildlife biologists to learn the best places to set up his camera. One of them, bear expert Joe Guthrie, looks something like Ward's shaggier younger brother. He grew up hunting in the woods and hollows of rural Kentucky. He began tracking Florida bears with radio collars as a grad student, part of a University of Kentucky project led by none other than Dave Maehr.

Guthrie and Ward were chatting one day about how bears and panthers need a lot of territory for roaming around. Fortunately, Guthrie said, a lot of Florida's wild places had connections that allowed such wide-ranging predators to travel for miles on end. He told Ward about one bear that traveled five hundred miles in two months. That one comment planted a seed in Ward's mind.

When Maehr died, some of his students and friends gathered at a remote Central Florida wildlife research lab, the Archbold Biological Station, to pay tribute. Guthrie and Ward were there. So was one-time MERIT Subteam member Tom Hoctor. Hoctor gave a talk about "critical linkages" in Florida's landscape and how large mammals like bears and panthers could use those linkages to travel up the spine of the state. The idea of tying together Florida's remaining wild places into a single, long unit is one that's been discussed since the 1970s, but getting any government agency to take action on it has proven, at best, difficult.

Hoctor's talk and Guthrie's anecdote combined to give Ward an idea for a photo project: set out on a journey along the path of those linkages and document what it looks like, "to build a story around the science, make it more appealing to the public," he told me. Working with Guthrie, Ward plotted a route, commissioned a map, raised money and recruited a few other voyagers—including a documentary filmmaker—to join what they called the Florida Wildlife Corridor Expedition.

Their goal: a one-hundred-day, one-thousand-mile journey that would trace the best remaining natural path from Everglades National Park at Florida's southern tip to the Okefenokee Swamp at the Florida-Georgia border. The photos and documentary would show people that a statewide corridor existed and could, with the public's help, still be saved.

They started off in the spring of 2012 paddling kayaks through Florida Bay at the state's southern end. At that point, Ward said, they hadn't quite grasped the magnitude of their undertaking.

"We trekked for twenty-one straight days and were still on public land," Ward said. "We left it and were on ranches. We camped on twenty-nine different cattle ranches during our trek." He found that the ranchers were all very supportive of what they were doing too, he said.

By crossing Florida on foot, in kayaks, mounted on horses, or riding mountain bikes, they saw the landscape in a new way—a way that a panther might see it. When they got to the Florida Panther National Wildlife Refuge, Darrell Land joined them for a little bit. Because they were traveling in the daytime, they didn't see any panthers, but they saw signs that a panther had passed by.

"Darrell pointed out a fresh scat with deer hair in it," Ward said.

The trip convinced Ward that the panthers can make the same sojourn. Squeezed out of their longtime home south of the Caloosahatchee, they can make their way to a new home, just like 62 did. Inspired, Ward started working on a new project called "Path of the Panther."

"I'm trying to capture the essence of what it's like to be a Florida panther living in the Florida woods," he explained. "I'm trying to find evocative imagery that can help people emotionally connect with a panther."

He's hopeful the story will have a happy ending, but he knows that's out of his hands.

"The biggest variable is human tolerance," he said. "If we can coexist with panthers, then panthers will survive."

But there's a big problem with the dream of the wandering panthers creating a new home turf. How could they start a new colony if the only ones swimming across the river are male?

Male panthers have a range of two hundred square miles. The females don't go that far—just seventy-five miles. They tend to stay close to their mothers, so the chances of one crossing the river seemed remote. Federal officials refused to move one north, insisting a female would make it without human help someday. Yet year after year passed, and the closest any female got to the Caloosahatchee was three miles south of its banks.

As everyone waited to see whether any female panthers would ever go wandering, the first generation of panther chasers began heading for the exit.

Melody Roelke was back in the United States. She collaborated with Stephen O'Brien and other scientists on a paper that said the genetic restoration project had been a big success. Were he still alive, it would be hard for even Maehr to argue otherwise, with an estimated two hundred panthers now crowding into every available open space in Southwest Florida.

Roelke was still keeping an eye on the many blood and semen samples she had collected from panthers before she left Florida. Theoretically, she said, someone could use them someday to build a new panther from scratch—although first they'd have to figure out how to get rid of the genetic defects.

But Roelke wasn't working with cats of any kind anymore. No more panthers. No more cheetahs.

She was now in charge of providing veterinary care for the laboratory rats being used for experiments at the National Cancer Institute near Washington, DC. When she told me about it, she said she was keenly aware of the irony of switching from cats to mice. She even laughed about it. It was the only time I ever heard her laugh.

Chris Belden retired from the state wildlife commission and immediately took another government job. He became the panther coordinator for the US Fish and Wildlife Service in Vero Beach. Once again, he ran into problems. He discovered that all of his hard-won expertise didn't allow him to improve things for panthers because of the way the system was set up.

"It was a little disappointing," he told me. "People move around all the time—it's the only way they get a promotion. I went to a meeting about a year and a half ago and it was all new people there. They were all starting from scratch. I almost felt like my years there were wasted. Everybody I had talked to about panther biology had moved on."

Belden retired again, this time for good. He went back to the woods of North Florida, spending a lot of time outdoors, enjoying nature without having to write any reports about it. He's also learning to be a blacksmith, a hobby that rewards someone for being meticulous and patient while handling hot stuff.

Roy McBride passed his eightieth year on this earth and started thinking about the end of his long road. But he didn't want to let go of panther hunting entirely. Hunkered down at his trailer in rural Ochopee, he told me he was teaching his grandson what he needed to know to step in and take over.

I don't know if you could say the kid's a natural, but he *is* named Cougar. When I raised an eyebrow at that, McBride grimaced and said, "I didn't name him."

After Andy Eller cut his deal with the Fish and Wildlife Service, his case quickly faded from the headlines and the introvert reverted to his old ways. He wound up assigned to a job in another state, working on something completely unrelated to panthers, but he felt unsettled and unsatisfied. He eventually quit federal service anyway. He's now working as a wildlife photographer, which he says he finds much more satisfying. Larry Richardson, who retired from his job at the Florida Panther National Wildlife Refuge, has also taken up nature photography, although he still goes along on a panther capture now and then.

By now Deborah Jansen has put in enough years with the National Park Service that people keep asking her if she's thought about retirement. She has, and she doesn't like the sound of it. Early in her career she was married for five years. She never had kids, and after that divorce she never remarried. She says she's wedded to her work, period. Panther kittens are children enough for her.

But she has found a hobby she likes: competitive ballroom dancing. She's won a couple of trophies too.

"I've been taking lessons in Naples for six years," she told me. "I go from blue jeans and boots during the day to dresses, heels and lipstick at night. It is so good for balance, flexibility and toning. It is my second passion in life."

Darrell Land, now in his late fifties, still gets up three mornings a week and climbs into a plane to fly around checking radio signals from the dwindling number of collared panthers. He's thinking it may be time to wind that down after thirty-seven years—not his flying, but the "collar and foller" program. There are more humane ways to learn about panthers now.

"Why go molest the animals if you don't need to?" he said when I asked him about it. "They would probably prefer not to be chased up a tree by dogs, shot in the butt, go into a drug-induced coma, fall out of a tree and wake up with bling."

Instead, he said, he wants to try using more trap cameras. Planted in carefully selected spots wherever panther tracks turn up, the cameras are motion sensitive and can snap pictures whenever any animal gets near enough to trip the sensor. Carlton Ward was a big fan of the Cat Cams, planting them all over for his new project.

After all, how better to spy on the private life of an animal that tends to shy away from people?

★ ★ ★

By 2013, so many male panthers had forded the Caloosa-hatchee that the wildlife commission, for the first time ever, hired a biologist to work north of the river. Her name was Jennifer Korn but friends called her Jen. She had long, dark hair, a slender build, and the bright, buoyant smile of an up-and-coming country singer. She was in her late thirties, and had earned a Ph.D. studying ocelots and bobcats in her native Texas—not unlike Roy McBride. Quite a few of the new generation of panther biologists shared that geographic link, she said.

"Texans are infiltrating everywhere," she joked.

Her Texas studies proved to be the perfect preparation for dealing with Florida panthers, she told me: "You're dealing with private landowners, bad genetics and all the same politics too."

Part of Korn's new job was to meet with landowners north of the river—ranchers, mostly—and talk to them about panthers. She'd tell them that panthers were passing through their land more often and there were ways to adapt to their presence. She would also try to counteract any rumors going around about how finding panthers on your property would mean the government could dictate what you did with your land. She once faced an entire room full of ranchers who were convinced that the government was lying about how many panthers there were. The ranchers were happy to help Carlton Ward show the natural linkages in the landscape, but reluctant to admit that an endangered animal might be using those linkages to cross their land.

The other half of her job—the half that she found most interesting—was planting trap cameras in possible panther habitat across fourteen counties, from the Caloosahatchee to I-4, and then checking them for signs of panther activity.

Thanks to the cameras, she discovered that there were more than a few panthers crossing under I-4 overpasses and prowling around the edges of suburbs just like 62 had. She put out more cameras, including some she bought with her own money.

Those Cat Cams were anything but a sure bet for finding panthers. They might be pointed the wrong way to catch what she was looking for, or the panther might be facing away from the camera. Or the camera would catch just a single leg as the panther passed by. Or the flash of the camera would illuminate a panther but still be too dark to catch crucial details. Or, occasionally, some human would discover a camera and steal it or smash it, purely out of meanness.

But then, in 2015, she got the Cat Cam bingo that everyone had been waiting for: a photo of a female panther, north of the Caloosahatchee.

At least, that's what the picture appeared to show: a cat that was smaller than a male normally would be. But the details were fuzzy. Korn and the other panther biologists studied the photo closely, but they just couldn't be certain. This was an uncollared panther, which meant they had not been tracking this cat at all before it showed up on camera. There was no evidence on the ground to corroborate the find—including no size-small paw prints.

Korn's bosses decided to hold off announcing anything until they could get a better photo. Perhaps another, more definite image would pop up shortly.

"A year went by," Korn said.

They got another photo, but it still wasn't sharp enough. Then another six months passed.

On November 3, 2016, Korn and another biologist were in the field, pulling the images from cameras, when Korn spotted the possible female in one frame. The other biologist checked the area near the camera where the photo showed the panther. Sure enough, there was a petite panther track there, one that was just the right size for a female.

That was the verification everyone wanted. Korn's bosses at the wildlife commission trumpeted the discovery in the press.

They exulted in this rare bit of good news about an animal more often featured in stories about how many had been run over.

The place where the female had been spotted was an odd hybrid of preservation and development. The Babcock Ranch was originally started in the 1800s by a Montana gold-mining family, then taken over in 1914 by a Pittsburgh lumber magnate. The Pittsburgh magnate's heirs expanded the business beyond just cattle, adding rock mining, alligator farming, vegetable farming and swamp buggy eco-tours.

Then, in 2006, a retired NFL player named Syd Kitson bought the ranch and cut a deal with state and local government officials. He sold 73,000 acres to the state and to Lee County for preservation, one of the largest such deals in Florida history. On the remaining 18,000 acres he announced plans to build the Sunshine State's first solar-powered city, with 330,000 solar panels to support 19,500 homes plus all the commercial space too.

The preserved part of the property was unusual. State officials allowed the ranch to continue operating as if it were still private property. They let the eco-tours continue too. When tour buses drive through the ranch, the cows sometimes try to climb aboard.

The developed part was unusual too. Instead of building on undisturbed land, Kitson confined his construction to property that had been mines or old sod fields. Still, panthers were more likely to use a sod farm as habitat than a shopping center or office complex.

Babcock Ranch was about 16 miles north of the river, meaning the female had crossed that watery barrier and found a place to settle down. One interesting coincidence: The preserved part of Babcock Ranch includes Telegraph Swamp, where 62 once wandered. State biologists nicknamed the Babcock panther "Babs," short for Babcock.

Ward, sensing a good angle for his new panther photo project, wanted to stalk Babs with his trap cameras too. Korn helped him set them up, and soon he'd captured a photo that symbolized just how far the panther revival had come since 1995.

In January 2017, Ward got photos of Babs that appeared to show that she was lactating. The biologists searched for signs of kittens, but found none.

By March 2017, Korn was about to leave for a job with an environmental consulting firm. On her last week of working for the wildlife commission, as she was making her rounds checking the cameras, she saw something that made her smile:

A series of photos showing young Babs being trailed by a pair of kittens.

Korn's reaction: "Woo-hoo, this is crazy!"

While she was elated, Korn told me she was not all that surprised.

"I'd already been getting photos of a male at Babcock for a few years, so I knew she'd have a mate," she explained. Still, to catch a photo like this was exhilarating.

You could not have asked for better trap camera pictures. They were shot during the daytime and were in vivid color. Babs was strolling along the edge of a ranch road, every detail of her postpartum body sharply defined. She was very obviously lactating. As for the kittens, they were big enough that the dark spots they wore when they were born were fading but still visible.

Korn was pretty sure Babs's mate was a male panther she'd spotted on the Babcock cameras several times. His tail wasn't kinked, but it had enough of a curve to its end that Korn began calling him "Crooked Tail." After a while that morphed into "Crookshanks," in tribute to Hermione Granger's cat in the Harry Potter book series.

Korn's bosses publicized the electrifying discovery without mentioning the panthers' nicknames. One wildlife commission official spelled out the significance for reporters: "These pictures of a female with kittens indicate there are now panthers breeding *north* of the river."

★ ★ ★

About a week later, another biologist who had been running trap cameras on property a few miles east of Babcock Ranch showed Korn *his* big find. He had sixty pictures of a male and female panther exhibiting mating behavior—not actual mating, mind you, just the panther form of foreplay. Korn checked the area for tracks and verified that this was a second female panther—another one with no radio collar that had suddenly appeared north of the river.

The male in the photo was an unlikely Lothario. The biologists all recognized him because he'd been appearing in trap camera pictures since 2011. Because he had what Korn called "a roly-poly belly," some of them had nicknamed him "Fatty." Korn used the term for a while, then felt bad about its connotations and stopped.

As exciting as this discovery of a second female was, Korn's next questions concerned Babs and Crookshanks's little family. Would their kittens survive? Would they grow up? Would they produce enough kittens to start a second panther colony?

After the initial publicity about their sighting died down, the kittens disappeared. Korn's new employer had a contract to do consulting work for Kitson's development company, so she was allowed to keep checking the cameras on Babcock Ranch. She made her rounds hoping to see them again, to catch a glimpse of their growth or at least a sign of their continued existence. But there was nothing. Finally she had to admit the obvious truth.

"She lost the litter," Korn said.

That happens with a lot of first-time panther moms, Korn said. The kitten survival rate is 33 percent. Babs's kittens had apparently died—no one knows why. The wildlife commission chose not to publicize this disheartening turn of events.

Korn persisted. She kept checking the cameras for signs that Babs was still around. She compared notes with Ward and with other biologists who had trap cameras. She found nothing. She wondered if whatever had killed the kittens had killed Babs too.

Or perhaps the female had dropped out of sight because she was denning with new kittens—although that would seem like too great a miracle to ask for.

In September 2017, Hurricane Irma clobbered Florida. The Category 4 storm made its first landfall at Cudjoe Key in the lower Florida Keys, then roared up the state's west coast to make a second landfall around Marco Island and Everglades City. The area around Babcock Ranch took a serious pounding from wind and rain, particularly rain. Ward lost eight of his cameras to Irma's powerful punch. Korn fretted over what the storm might have done to the female panthers.

Two months later, in November 2017, Korn saw something she had dreamed about: in a black-and-white photo, a pair of grayish figures against a dark background, their kittenish form fading but still visible in the flash of the camera.

Babs and, most likely, Crookshanks had had a new family.

"She showed up with a second litter," Korn said, still seeming giddy about the discovery when she talked about it nearly a year later.

How did they survive the hurricane? Korn thinks Babs picked a good spot for her den that kept the little family protected from the elements: "She was probably on a little island of dry land in the midst of the swamp."

A Cat Cam shooting video caught the whole family in February 2018. The kittens appeared to be about eight months old. Mama Cat "looks in good shape," Korn said.

Korn is hoping this pair will live and grow and eventually breed with other panthers. She's hoping the second female, the one hanging out with the male with the big belly, will start producing kittens too. She's hopeful a third female will find her way across the river and follow suit, building up that second panther colony in a part of the state that's still got some wildness to it.

Deb Jansen is hopeful too, but she is well aware of how much can go wrong with the young ones.

"The next gauntlet the offspring have to overcome is all the roads in Central Florida," she told me. If they manage to survive to adulthood, they won't stay where they are. They will be heading out on their own, moving through that landscape that Ward and Guthrie explored.

"Where are they going to disperse to?" she asked. "Eventually they might get hit on the road."

On the other hand, she said, once they're grown, those two blurry images could make it up into North Florida, or maybe even Georgia. If they do that, if they survive the speeding cars and trucks, the nervous hunters, paranoid ranchers and all the other potential perils, then things could at last be different for the panther.

If that happens, then after nearly going extinct, after captive breeding failed and only a Hail Mary pass kept them going, after all the political shenanigans and junk science and habitat paved over, she said, "there's a good chance of repopulating the Southeast."

That, of course, would make *them* the most important panthers in Florida history—not FP3. It would mean all the hard work and personal sacrifices by Belden, McBride, Jansen, Roelke, Comiskey, Eller, Land and the rest has at last paid off.

As I sit here staring at the photo of Babs's babies, I know that what I am seeing is probably just a pair of scared kittens scampering for the woods because the camera startled them. But the more I look at it, the more I read into it. I see them leaping into the future, vaulting obstacles, racing to make their place in this wide world. They get taller, longer, faster, sleeker. Their teeth get sharper and their hunger grows. They're chasing prey and finding mates of their own. They're having kittens just like the two in this photo.

Here's hoping that Babs's kittens will keep pressing on, keep finding new habitat that can accommodate their growing numbers, and that never again does one end up as a cat under glass.

★ ★ ★ ★ ★

ACKNOWLEDGMENTS

This is a book that I've been waiting more than twenty years to write. But I could not have done it alone.

First, I need to thank all the people who have talked to me about Florida panthers, both while I was reporting stories for the *Tampa Bay Times* and while I was writing this book. That especially includes biologists Darrell Land and Dave Onorato of the Florida Fish and Wildlife Conservation Commission, who answered all manner of nitpicky questions with great patience. I should also thank Roy McBride, Melody Roelke, Chris Belden, Deborah Jansen, Andy Eller, Walt McCown, and Jane Comiskey, who showed a similar patience toward my repeated phone calls to ask them about one tiny detail or another.

A crucial part of every book I write, and many of my newspaper stories, is the research done by Caryn Baird. What makes it really enjoyable is the obvious glee with which she digs into each request.

I'd also like to thank Roy Leblanc, who edited my 2010 series on panthers called "Dead Cat Walking," which became the basis for this book.

Many thanks to biologist and planner Jim Beever, who read over everything I wrote to check it for accuracy. If I still got something wrong, that's my fault, not his. Also, thanks to all the folks who helped me track down the photos that help tell this story.

I'm grateful to my attorney, Alison Steele, for helping me navigate the various legal issues I stumbled across. Thanks, too, to my agent, Andrew Stuart, for finding a good home for this labor of love. I can't leave out my Hanover Square editor, Peter Joseph, who believed in this book when others did not and made some smart improvements in my manuscript.

Last but not least, I want to thank my wife, Sherry, forever my first reader. Despite having a million other things to do, she sat down and plowed through every page of the manuscript, suggesting numerous changes that improved it. She also tossed in a groan-inducing pun that I had completely missed. It now is included in the book for your eye-rolling amazement. That woman knows me *so* well.

A SELECT BIBLIOGRAPHY

Alvarez, Ken. *Twilight of the Panther: Biology, Bureaucracy and Failure in an Endangered Species Program*. Sarasota: Myakka River Press, 1993.

Bergman, Charles. *Wild Echoes: Encounters with the Most Endangered Animals in North America*. Champaign: University of Illinois Press, 2003.

Bolgiano, Chris, and Jerry Roberts, eds. *The Eastern Cougar: Historic Accounts, Scientific Investigations, and New Evidence*. Mechanicsburg, PA: Stackpole Books, 2005.

Fergus, Charles. *Swamp Screamer: At Large with the Florida Panther*. Gainesville: University Press of Florida, 1998.

Hornocker, Maurice, and Sharon Negri, eds. *Cougar: Ecology and Conservation*. Chicago: University of Chicago Press, 2009.

Maehr, David S. *The Florida Panther: Life and Death of a Vanishing Carnivore*. Washington, DC: Island Press, 1997.

Nelson, Barney, ed. *God's Country or Devil's Playground: The Best Nature Writing from the Big Bend of Texas*. Austin: University of Texas Press, 2002.

O'Brien, Stephen J. *Tears of the Cheetah: The Genetic Secrets of Our Animal Ancestors.* New York: Thomas Dunne Books, 2005.

O'Connor, M. R. *Resurrection Science: Conservation, De-Extinction and the Precarious Future of Wild Things.* New York: St. Martin's Press, 2015.

Roman, Joe. *Listed: Dispatches from America's Endangered Species Act.* Boston: Harvard University Press, 2011.

NOTES ON SOURCES

Prologue: Cat Under Glass

11 *The panther ran as...:* Reconstructed from state game commission reports on the death of Florida Panther 3 and interviews with Chris Belden and Deborah Jansen.

12 *You can find the...:* The person who first told me about the fate of FP3 was Candace McCaffery of the Florida Museum of Natural History. More about her and her work in Chapter Eight.

12 *The museum is low-key...:* I've visited the museum several times, as well as the Florida State Archives in the same building. Here's the museum website: http://www.museumoffloridahistory.com/; here's the one for the Florida State Archives: https://dos.myflorida.com/library-archives/about-us/about-the-state-archives-of-florida/.

13 *In different places in...:* Hornocker and Negri, vii.

13 *Two centuries ago, panthers...:* Hornocker and Negri, 27.

13 *When panthers are born....:* Bolgiano and Roberts, 20-21; Hornocker

and Negri, 18-19; Mountain Lion Foundation website: https://www.
mountainlion.org/CAL_ch4.asp.

14 *By being such fierce…:* Liza Gross, "Master Regulators: How Mountain Lions Boost Biodiversity," *Nature Now* (Feb. 26, 2019): http://
www.pbs.org/wnet/nature/blog/master-regulators-how-mountain-
lions-boost-biodiversity/.

14 *The modern descendants of…:* Jason Bittel, "Big Cats in Big Trouble," Natural Resources Defense Council, *onEarth* (Nov. 28, 2014):
https://www.nrdc.org/onearth/big-cats-big-trouble; Karen Brul-
liard, "America's Shockingly Huge Tiger Population Is Finally
Getting More Oversight," *Washington Post* (April 6, 2016): https://
www.washingtonpost.com/news/animalia/wp/2016/04/06/the-
government-just-made-it-harder-to-buy-a-tiger-in-america/?
utm_term=.9d9d340b2508.

15 *The big cats of…:* "Removing the Eastern Cougar from the Federal List of Endangered Species," Federal Register 80 FR 34595:
https://www.federalregister.gov/documents/2015/06/17/2015-14931/
endangered-and-threatened-wildlife-and-plants-removing-eastern-
puma-cougar-from-the-federal-list-of; "Genetic Management Strategies and Population Viability of the Florida Panther (*Felis concolor
coryi*)," Proceedings from Workshops, National Zoological Park,
Washington, DC (May 30-31, 1991), and White Oak Plantation
Conservation Center, Yulee, FL (Oct. 21-22, 1992).

15 *In 2019, two environmental groups…:* Mary Papenfuss, "Wildlife Groups
Seek Endangered Status for California Mountain Lions," *Huffington
Post*, June 28, 2019: https://www.huffpost.com/entry/mountain-
lion-endangered-species-petition_n_5d1581fde4b03d611639223a.

18 *I have read that…:* Nate Blakeslee, *American Wolf* (New York: Crown
Publishing Group, 2017), 40.

Chapter One: The Cat of God

20 *The hired man pushed…:* Jack E. Davis, *The Gulf: The Making of an
American Sea* (New York: Liveright Publishing, 2017), 32-33; Phyllis
E. Kolianos and Brent R. Weisman, eds., *The Florida Journals of Frank*

Hamilton Cushing (Gainesville: University Press of Florida, 2005), 60; Ryan J. Wheeler, "On the Trail of the Panther in Ancient Florida," *The Florida Anthropologist* 64, no. 3-4 (Sep.-Dec. 2011): 139-162; Ben Brotemarkle, "The Key Marco Cat," *Florida Frontiers* blog (Jan. 13, 2015): https://myfloridahistory.org/frontiers/article/51; Alina Bradford, "Pumas, Panthers & Cougars: Facts About America's Big Cats," *Live Science* (July 29, 2014): https://www.livescience.com/27267-pumas.html.

23 *Despite what happened to...*: Buckingham Smith, trans., *Narratives of the Career of Hernando de Soto in the Conquest of Florida: As Told by a Knight of Elvas and in a Relation by Luys Hernandez de Biedma, Factor of the Expedition* (New York: Allerton Book Company, 1922), 222; Wheeler, 139-162; "The Voyage Made By John M. Hawkins, Esq.," American Journeys Collection, Document AJ-030, 18, no. 128: http://www.americanjourneys.org/pdf/AJ-030.pdf; William Bartram, "Documenting the American South," *Travels,* electronic edition 46 (2001): https://docsouth.unc.edu/nc/bartram/bartram. html?links=false. The Mountain Lion Foundation says the first Spaniard to report seeing a "lion" in Florida was Alvar Núñez Cabeza de Vaca in 1513, but the man whose name means "Cowhead" didn't arrive in Florida until 1528.

24 *The white and black settlers...*: A lot of these stories, including the one about the gun stores, are collected in Jim Bob Tinsley, *The Florida Panther* (St. Petersburg: Great Outdoors Pub. Co, 1970); Gary Mormino, "Panther Attacks: Fact or Fiction?" *Tampa Tribune* (Nov. 30, 2008); "A Florida Panther Fight: Struggle of the Jenkinses with a Wild Beast in a Buggy at High Speed," *New York Times* (June 28, 1897): https://www.nytimes.com/1897/06/28/archives/a-florida-panther-fight-struggle-of-the-jenkinses-with-a-wild-beast.html.

26 *Not everyone found the...*: Davis, 243. To view the painting called *In the Jungle,* click on the Brooklyn Museum of Art's website: https:// www.brooklynmuseum.org/opencollection/objects/2751.

26 *But beauty could never...*: US Fish and Wildlife Service species report on the Florida Panther, part of the Multi-Species Recovery Plan for South Florida, 4-124: https://www.fws.gov/verobeach/MSRPPDFs/ FloridaPanther.pdf.

27 *The first time I...:* Stuart B. McIver, *Dreamers, Schemers, and Scalawags: The Florida Chronicles Vol. 1* (Sarasota: Pineapple Press, 1994): 240–244; Charles B. Cory, *The Florida Panther,* an excerpt from Cory's 1896 book *Hunting and Fishing in Florida,* reprinted as part of Tinsley's *The Florida Panther,* 50-58; Charles B. Cory, *"Felis concolor Floridana,"* species description reprinted as part of Tinsley's *The Florida Panther,* 60; Wilfred Osgood, "In Memoriam: Charles Barney Cory, Born January 30, 1857—Died July 31, 1921," *The Auk: A Quarterly Journal of Ornithology* XXXIX, no. 2 (April 1922): 151-165: https://archive.org/details/jstor-4073946/page/n12; Outram Bangs, "The Land Mammals of Peninsular Florida and the Coast Region of Georgia," *Proceedings of the Boston Society of Natural History* 28, no. 7 (1898): 235.

29 *Florida's hunters were very...:* William Hornaday, *Our Vanishing Wildlife: Its Extermination and Preservation* (New York: Charles Scribner's Sons, 1913), 277, accessed via Project Gutenberg: https://www.gutenberg.org/files/13249/13249-h/13249-h.htm.

29 *In 1935, a writer...:* David Newell, "Panther!" *Saturday Evening Post* 208 (July 13, 1935): 10-11, 70–72; Tinsley, 22-23.

30 *The panthers needed a...:* Florida Fish and Wildlife Conservation Commission website, history of deer hunting: https://myfwc.com/hunting/deer/history/; John E. George, "Wildlife as a Constraint to the Eradication of *Boophilus* Spp. (Acari Exodidae)," *Journal of Agricultural Entomology* 7, no. 2 (April 1990): 119-125.

31 *At that point, most...:* Aldo Leopold, "Threatened Species: A Proposal to the Wildlife Conference for an Inventory of the Needs of Near Extinct Birds and Animals," *American Forests* 42, no. 3 (March 1936): 116–119; Daniel B. Beard, Frederick C. Lincoln, Victor H. Cabalane, Hartley H.T. Jackson, Ben H. Thompson, *Fading Trails: The Story of Endangered American Wildlife* (New York: Macmillan, 1942), 113.

32 *Eight years later, the...:* US Fish and Wildlife Service species report on the Florida Panther, 4-124.

32 *Florida is a tourist-friendly...:* You can see some of the long-gone parks on the delightful website "Florida's Lost Tourist Attractions": http://www.lostparks.com; Jonathan Foerster, "The Biggest! The Best! Exit Now!" *Naples Daily News* (Aug. 12, 2008); Jeremy Cox,

"On the Edge: Florida Panthers Stand Close to Disappearing," *Naples Daily News* (Oct. 20, 2007): http://archive.naplesnews.com/news/on-the-edge-florida-panthers-stand-close-to-disappearing-ep-403313000-332818341.html.

33 *In the mid-1960s, a…:* Tim W. Clark, Richard P. Reading and Alice L. Clarke, eds., *Endangered Species Recovery: Finding the Lessons, Improving the Process* (Washington: Island Press, 1994), 19-25.

Chapter Two: Pantherland

34 *Let me tell you…:* I've driven through the Big Cypress lots of times on both Alligator Alley (aka Interstate 75) and the Tamiami Trail (aka US 41), and have ridden very noisy airboats through the swamp numerous times. My hike with Clyde Butcher was a Society of Environmental Journalists field trip in September 2011. I've also been through the Fakahatchee Strand, and while I didn't see any glass orchids there, I did see one at the neighboring Corkscrew Swamp Sanctuary.

36 *In 1968, the Dade…:* Nelson Manfred Blake, *Land into Water, Water into Land: A History of Water Management in Florida* (Gainesville: University Press of Florida, 1980), 216-222; Michael Grunwald, *The Swamp: The Everglades, Florida, and the Politics of Paradise* (New York: Simon and Schuster, 2006), 253-259; Charlotte Orr Gantz, *A Naturalist in Southern Florida* (Coral Gables: University of Miami Press, 1971), 137; interview with Nat Reed; Diane Roberts, "The Maverick of Hobe Sound," *St. Petersburg Times* (May 30, 2004); Christine Stapleton, "Tales of Nature and Power: Award Enough for Legendary Enviro Nat Reed," *Palm Beach Post* (Nov. 29, 2014): https://www.palmbeachpost.com/news/state--regional-govt--politics/tales-nature-and-power-award-enough-for-legendary-enviro-nat-reed/IGeJCG9mimBDuetearCDvN/; Reed oral history interview at University of Florida, http://ufdc.ufl.edu/UF00005486/00001/; Matt Schudel, "Claude R. Kirk, Colorful Ex-Governor of Florida, Dies at 85," *Washington Post* (Sep. 28, 2011): https://www.washingtonpost.com/local/obituaries/claude-r-kirk-jr-colorful-ex-governor-of-florida-dies-at-85/2011/09/28/

gIQAWEMo5K_story.html?utm_term=.715110e17f33. Reed, 84, died in July 2018, while I was writing this book.

41 *In the end, the...:* US Department of the Interior, "Environmental Impact of the Big Cypress Swamp Jetport" (September 1969), 99–104: https://sflwww.er.usgs.gov/publications/reports/jetportimpact/jetportimpact.pdf.

43 *But his most long-lasting...:* Interview with Reed; Richard Nixon statement on signing the Endangered Species Act: https://www.presidency.ucsb.edu/node/255904.

Chapter Three: The Hunter

44 *The first time I...:* Interviews with Roy McBride and Ron Nowak; M.R. O'Connor, "A Puma Hunter Is Enlisted to Track Down and Help Save Florida Panthers," *Smithsonian* (Sep. 25, 2015): https://www.scientificamerican.com/article/a-puma-hunter-is-enlisted-to-track-down-and-help-save-florida-panthers-excerpt/; M. R. O'Connor, "No Home for the Florida Panther," *The New Yorker* (Sep. 9, 2015): https://www.newyorker.com/tech/elements/no-home-for-the-florida-panther; Trish Choate, "West Texas Biologist Rounds Up Wild Cats," *San Angelo Standard-Times*, (Sep. 26, 2010): http://archive.gosanangelo.com/news/west-texas-biologist-rounds-up-wild-cats-ep-440398772-357111481.html/; Barney Nelson, ed., *God's Country or Devil's Playground: The Best Nature Writing from the Big Bend of Texas* (Austin: University of Texas Press, 2002), 166, 202–204.

49 *All in all, McBride...:* Rick Bass, *The Ninemile Wolves* (Livingston, MT: Clark City Press, 1992), 75–82; McBride interview.

50 *An amateur psychologist might...:* Interviews with McBride and Jane Comiskey; Donald G. Schueler, *Incident at Eagle Ranch: Predators as Prey in the American West* (Phoenix: University of Arizona Press, 1990), 176–182.

51 *On the other end...:* Interviews with Nowak and McBride; Nowak's reports to World Wildlife Fund 1973 and 1974; US Department of the Interior, *Environmental Impact of the Big Cypress Swamp Jetport* (September 1969), 99–104: https://sflwww.er.usgs.gov/publications/

reports/jetportimpact/jetportimpact.pdf; Roy McBride, "Three Decades of Searching South Florida for Panthers," from the *Proceedings of the Florida Panther Conference* (Florida Panther Interagency Committee, Nov. 1-3, 1994), Dennis B. Jordan, ed.

Chapter Four: The State Animal

57 *The first time I...:* Interview with Pritchard; Pritchard profile on Chelonian Institute website: http://chelonianri.org/about-peter/index.html, and on Turtle Conservancy website: https://www.turtleconservancy.org/contact/pritchard/.

58 *One biologist invited to...:* Alvarez, 62; Peter Pritchard, ed., *Proceedings of the Florida Panther Conference, March 17-18, 1976* (Florida Audubon Society, 1977), 3-4; Peter B. Gallagher, "Robert Baudy Survives by Obeying Nature's Law," *St. Petersburg Times* (July 8, 1979); Robert Sargent, Jr., and Jason Garcia, "550-Pound Cat Kills Trainer," *Orlando Sentinel* (Aug. 1, 2001): http://articles.orlandosentinel.com/2001-08-01/news/0108010263_1_baudy-tiger-savage-kingdom.

59 *Pritchard's assembled "experts" spent...:* Background on Orlando Unitarian Universalist Church from church website: https://www.orlandouu.org/about/history/.

60 *One by one, the...:* Pritchard interview; Peter Pritchard, "Endangered Species: Florida Panther," *The Florida Naturalist* (August 1976): 21-22; the *Proceedings of Florida Panther Conference* contains a dozen papers submitted by the speakers, and they all make their own arguments. Baudy's quote is from his paper, "Breeding Techniques for Felines Destined for Release in the Wild," 100. The quote from the Interior official is from Pritchard's *Florida Naturalist* story, 21.

61 *The most important person...:* Interview with Chris Belden; review of Belden's state personnel file.

62 *He concluded that only...:* While there are no black panthers, there are black leopards—but they are a genetic mutation, not a separate species.

64 *To figure out which...:* Interviews with Belden and McBride; Belden, "If You See A Panther," *Florida Wildlife* (Sep.-Oct. 1977): 33-34; Jeff Klinkenberg, "Team Works to Save the Florida Panther," *St. Petersburg Times* (March 20, 1979).

65 *Belden also wanted to...:* Interview with Belden; Hornocker and Negri, 22-23.

66 *But first Belden had...:* Interview with Belden; Peter Gallagher, "Panther Politics," *Floridian, St. Petersburg Times* (Aug. 9, 1981), 9-13.

66 *When Belden at last...:* Interviews with McBride, Belden and Jansen; Chris Belden, "It Was the Hunt of a Lifetime," *Florida Wildlife* (May-June 1981).

71 *First, let's talk about...:* "Florida State Animal": http://www.netstate.com/states/symb/animals/fl_panther.htm; Patti Breckinridge, "Panther Students' Favorite," *Tampa Tribune* (Dec. 19, 1981); *Tribune* wires, "They're Loyal to the Panther," *Tampa Tribune* (Feb. 18, 1982); Robert McKnight, "Quorum Call for House Speaker Ralph Turlington, D-Gainesville," *Tallahassee Democrat* (Aug. 13, 2013): http://blogs.tallahassee.com/community/2013/08/13/52-quorum-call-for-house-speaker-ralph-turlington-d-gainesville/; Pittman, "The State You're In: Florida Tries to Halt Monkey Business," *Tampa Bay Times* (Feb. 27, 2018): https://www.tampabay.com/news/The-State-You-re-In-Florida-tries-to-halt-monkey-business_165550184.

Chapter Five: Mouth to Mouth

73 *After Deb Jansen earned...:* Jansen interview; Jennifer Reed, "The Lady and the Panther," *Gulfshore Life* (July 2017): https://www.gulfshorelife.com/2017/07/06/the-lady-and-the-panther/.

74 *The first two panthers...:* Belden and Jansen interviews.

75 *Some biologists frown on...:* Bass, 98-99.

79 *Belden's glowing public image...:* Belden interview; Fergus, 32-33; Marjory Stoneman Douglas, with John Rothchild, *Voice of the River* (Sarasota: Pineapple Press, 1990), 21; Jack E. Davis, *An Everglades*

Providence: Marjory Stoneman Douglas and the American Environmental Century (Athens: University of Georgia Press, 2009), 579–580; Juanita Greene, "Big Cat Study: State Biologist Stalks Panthers to Learn How to Save Them," *Miami Herald* (April 4, 1983).

Chapter Six: The Turbo-Vet

82 *To replace the Tennessee…:* Interview with John Roboski; Roboski's game commission personnel file.

83 *By then, the team…:* Interviews with Roboski and Walt McCown.

84 *Her name was Melody…:* Interview with Melody Roelke and Roboski; Fergus, 110–119.

86 *The panther capture team…:* Interviews with Roboski, McCown and Roelke; Lori Rozsa, "The Little Town That Turned to Drugs," *Washington Post* (Dec. 23, 1990): https://www.washingtonpost.com/archive/lifestyle/1990/12/23/the-little-town-that-turned-to-drugs/7f3f3675-cfee-44cc-bd1e-958e6dbcca16/?utm_term=.1edc88e167da; Peter B. Gallagher, "High Times in Everglades City," *Gulfshore Life* (August 2010).

87 *If they did get any…:* Alvarez, 77–78; Roelke, Roboski and McCown interviews.

89 *They only chased the…:* Associated Press, "Efforts Launched to Save Florida Panther and Companion Rare Louse," *Los Angeles Times* (August 25, 1985): http://articles.latimes.com/1985-08-25/news/mn-24892_1_florida-cat.

90 *For the capture team…:* Interviews with Roboski and McCown; Bergman, 95.

91 *Amid all the pranks…:* Interview with Roelke. I looked for video of the broadcast online or for sale as a VHS or DVD, but could not find it.

92 *Let's talk about kinks…:* Interviews with Roelke, Roboski and Laurie Wilkins.

Chapter Seven: The New Mr. Panther

96 *The new capture team...:* Maehr's Florida personnel file; Jeff Klinkenberg, "Cat Fight!" *St. Petersburg Times* (March 21, 1993); interviews with McCown, Roelke, Jansen and McBride.

97 *Maehr's first trip out...:* Bergman, 92-105.

99 *Eleven years later, Maehr...:* Maehr, 1-2.

99 *Despite his outward confidence...:* Maehr, 5, 10; Maehr personnel file.

100 *But finally his bosses...:* Maehr, "Can the Florida Panther Provide Insight into Restoring the Eastern Cougar?" *Eastern Cougar,* 169; Maehr, *The Florida Panther,* xiv-xv.

100 *Maehr went out and...:* Interview with Darrell Land, following a plane trip with him over panther habitat.

101 *The capture team had...:* Maehr, 51-52.

102 *Maehr's promotional efforts slowly...:* Carl Hiaasen, "Remembering the Panther's Champion," *Tampa Tribune* (July 3, 2008); interviews with Jansen, Roelke and McBride; Maehr personnel file.

103 *About the time Maehr...:* Maehr, 14; "Electroejaculation—An Overview," *Science Direct* (2011): https://www.sciencedirect.com/topics/biochemistry-genetics-and-molecular-biology/electroejaculation.

103 *She used a field...:* Maehr, 14-15; Roelke interview.

Chapter Eight: Medicine Man

105 *In the late fall...:* Maehr, 168-171; interview with McBride and Roelke.

106 *Lester and Wilford "Bill" Piper...:* Jonathan Foerster, "The Biggest! The Best! Exit Now!" *Naples Daily News* (Aug. 12, 2008); Andrea Stetson, "End Near for Panther Line: Pipers' Last Hope for More Cats Too Old to Breed," *News-Press* (Fort Myers) (Aug. 26, 2006); Geoffrey Tomb, "Animal Attractions Labeled 'Freak Shows' List,"

Miami Herald (Jan. 29, 1986); interview with Roelke. I should note that the current incarnation of the Everglades Wonder Gardens has disposed of its captive animals, except for the alligators and birds, and it enjoys a better reputation.

109 *A lot of the...*: "Brief History of the Museum," Florida Museum of Natural History website: https://www.floridamuseum.ufl.edu/about/history/; interviews with Candace McCaffery and Laurie Wilkins; Laurie Wilkins, Julio M. Arias-Reveron, Bradley Stith, Melody Roelke, Robert C. Belden, "The Florida Panther, *Puma concolor coryi*: A Morphological Investigation of the Subspecies with a Comparison to Other North and South American Cougars," *Bulletin of the Florida Museum of Natural History* 40, no. 3 (1997): 230.

113 *In October 1984, a...*: Deborah Petit, "Guilty Plea Entered in Killing of Rare Panther," *Sun-Sentinel* (Fort Lauderdale) (March 19, 1985): http://articles.sun-sentinel.com/1985-03-19/news/8501100629_1_florida-panther-female-panther-biff-lampton.

114 *James Billie's true title...*: Peter B. Gallagher, "The Rise and Fall of Chief Jim Billie," *Gulfshore Life* (Sep. 2010); Philip Shabecoff, "Killing of a Panther: Indian Treaty Rights vs. Law on Wildlife," *New York Times* (April 15, 1987).

115 *The Seminoles have long...*: Interview with Bruce Rogow. For a full exploration of how the Seminoles became gambling kingpins, see the chapter called "You Bet Your Life" in my book *Oh, Florida: How America's Weirdest State Influences the Rest of the Country* (St. Martin's Press, 2016).

116 *Both cases went to...*: Interviews with Rogow and Wilkins; Brian Kaufman, "Law, Tribal Culture Clash in Panther-killing Case," *Sun-Sentinel* (Fort Lauderdale) (Aug. 14, 1987): http://articles.sun-sentinel.com/1987-08-14/news/8703070044_1_panther-claws-florida-panther-seminole-medicine; Lisanne Renner, "Billie Didn't Kill Panther, Jury Rules," *Orlando Sentinel* (Oct. 9, 1987): http://articles.orlandosentinel.com/1987-10-09/news/0150220024_1_florida-panther-seminole-tribe-billie.

118 *Not long after the...*: Gallagher, "The Rise and Fall of Chief Jim Billie."

118 *In 1988, just five...*: Interview with Roelke; Maehr personnel file.

Chapter Nine: Bottleneck

120 *That's true for all...:* "Wilderness" definition and etymology from https://www.merriam-webster.com/dictionary/wilderness.

121 *In November 1984, though...:* Alvarez, 84, 154, 160–161; interviews with Belden and Roelke.

123 *They were being cautious...:* "Critically Endangered Species Should Be Left to Breed in the Wild" (June 2015): https://phys.org/news/2015-06-critically-endangered-species-left-wild.html; Cass Peterson, "Goodbye, Dusky Seaside Sparrow," *Washington Post* (June 18, 1987): https://www.washingtonpost.com/archive/politics/1987/06/18/goodbye-dusky-seaside-sparrow/b8c8d618-54eb-4f17-a10c-3fbae9eb0672/?utm_term=.7bc86f2ab8b0; Maehr, 125; interview with Roelke. A cousin of the dusky, the Florida grasshopper sparrow, is now in such dire peril that beginning in 2013 the US Fish and Wildlife Service authorized the start of a captive breeding program. This time, the scientists got there in time to get birds of both genders.

124 *The place was about...:* Fergus, 99–103; Robert McClure, "Animal Farm," *Sun-Sentinel* (June 28, 1992): https://www.sun-sentinel.com/news/fl-xpm-1992-03-15-9201280429-story.html.

125 *There was only one...:* Jim Hady, "The Reluctant Panther: 'Big Guy' Shuns Overtures from Female Cougar," *Sun-Sentinel* (Jan. 20, 1987): http://articles.sun-sentinel.com/1987-01-20/news/8701050040_1_cougar-florida-panther-white-oak-plantation; Fergus, 169; Roelke interview.

126 *Big Guy would live...:* Booth Gunter, "Panther Used in Breeding Project Dies," *Tampa Tribune* (June 13, 1994); Roelke interview; O'Brien, 61–63.

Chapter Ten: "Extinction Is God's Plan"

128 *Chris Belden had been...:* Interview with Belden; Fergus, 185–196; every iteration of the panther recovery plan has included the three-colony requirement.

129 *Between the tiny town...:* Osceola National Forest history from US

Department of Agriculture website: https://www.fs.usda.gov/main/
osceola/learning/history-culture; Ocala National Forest history
from USDA website: https://www.fs.usda.gov/main/ocala/learning/
history-culture.

129 *But Belden didn't rush...:* Interview with Belden; Alvarez, 174-177;
Chris Belden, "Florida Panther Reintroduction Feasibility Study,"
Annual Performance Report 1 July 1993–30 June 1994; Belden,
"Florida Panther Reintroduction Feasibility Study," PowerPoint
slide presentation for Florida Panther Symposium, March 21, 1994.

130 *The cats were trucked...:* Ron Word, "Wildlife Officials Announce
Panther Reintroduction Plan," Associated Press (Feb. 26, 1988);
David Olinger, "Cats' Survival Is in the Mix," *St. Petersburg Times*
(June 21, 1994); Pittman, "Future of Florida Panther Beset with
Uncertainty, Controversy," *St. Petersburg Times* (Nov. 29, 1998);
Jeff Klinkenberg, "This Cat Has Run Out of Lives," *St. Petersburg
Times* (Aug. 5, 1990).

131 *In a report on...:* Robert C. Belden and B.W. Hagedorn, "Feasibility
of Translocating Panthers into Northern Florida," *Journal of Wildlife
Management* 57:388-397.

132 *Once again, Belden tried...:* Interview with McCown; Fergus, 185-196.

133 *Biologists had a hard time...:* Craig Quintana, "Commission Can't
Quite Catalog Mystery Cat," *Orlando Sentinel* (Jan. 18, 1996); Michael Browning, "Strange Saga of 'Waldo,'" *Miami Herald* (Feb. 18,
1996); Mark Hollis, "Political Fur to Fly Over 'Waldo Cat,'" *Sarasota Herald-Tribune* (June 1, 1996).

133 *T-39 was trying to...:* Interviews with Belden. McCown, Maehr,
and Michael and Colvin Carter; game commission records of mediation sessions. The records do not record who said what, only
what was said.

135 *Even the Waldo...:* Browning, "Strange Saga of 'Waldo.'"

Chapter Eleven: The Vortex

137 *Fifty. That's how many...:* Maehr, 129.

138 *This was the downside...:* Maehr, 124.

138 *Meanwhile, federal officials had…:* "About the Refuge," Florida Panther National Wildlife Refuge website: https://www.fws.gov/refuge/Florida_Panther/about.html.

138 *To visit, I had…:* Interviews with refuge manager Layne Hamilton and biologist Larry Richardson, who gave me a memorable tour of the place.

141 *Opening the refuge was…:* Ulysses Seal obituary: http://www.legacy.com/obituaries/twincities/obituary.aspx?n=ulysses-s-seal&pid=877324&fhid=4769; Alvarez, 356; interviews with Bob Lacy, Roelke, Belden and McBride; minutes of Florida Panther Viability Analysis and Survival Plan Workshop, Oct. 31–Nov. 2, 1989; Cyril T. Zaneski, "Raising a Stink," *Miami Herald* (Jan. 12, 1993); Andy Reid, "Beginning of Sugar Cane Harvest Reignites Field Burning Debate," *Sun-Sentinel* (Sep. 30, 2015): https://www.sun-sentinel.com/local/palm-beach/fl-cane-burning-resumes-20150930-story.html; interview with Jim Beever of the Southwest Florida Regional Planning Council.

144 *In this case, as…:* Chuck Fergus, "The Florida Panther Verges on Extinction," *Science* Vol. 251, Issue 4998: 1178-1180.

145 *Despite Maehr's continued…:* Maehr, 128-133; Ellen McGarrahan, "Florida Panthers to be Bred in Zoos to Prevent Extinction," *Miami Herald* (Jan. 10, 1990).

145 *With every capture, Roelke…:* Interviews with Roelke; O'Brien, 61-62.

146 *Her name was Holly Jensen…:* Interview with Holly Jensen.

147 *Jensen pulled in the…:* Fergus, 149-150.

148 *"What's the point of…":* Interview with attorney Eric Glitzenstein. For more on Glitzenstein, see my book *Manatee Insanity* (University Press of Florida, 2010). He represented a coalition of environmental groups that in 2000 successfully sued the state and federal government for failing to enforce the Endangered Species Act and the Marine Mammal Protection Act and allowing manatees to be killed by boaters.

148 *Negotiations ensued. In the…:* Interview with Jensen and Glitzenstein; Heather Dewar, "Panther Breeding Compromise OK'd, Program

Can Proceed As Animal Rights Activists Drop Suit," *Miami Herald* (Feb. 7, 1991); Peter B. Gallagher, "Florida Panthers Perish amid Endless Bickering," *St. Petersburg Times* (Sep. 25, 1991).

Chapter Twelve: The Captives

150 *Dave Maehr stood in...:* Maehr, 150-151; David M. Villano, "Cat-nappers with a Cause," *XS Magazine, South Florida Sun-Sentinel* (Sep. 16, 1992): 12-15. My thanks to David Villano for providing me with a copy of this story from the defunct magazine and sharing his memories of the reporting he did.

153 *The Florida Legislature had...:* Florida Department of Highway Safety and Motor Vehicles "Save the Panther" tag website: http://www.flhsmv.gov/dmv/specialtytags/environmental/panther.html.

153 *Meanwhile the Florida Department...:* Melissa F. Foster and Stephen R. Humphrey, "Use of Highway Underpasses by Florida Panthers and Other Wildlife," *Wildlife Society Bulletin* 23, no. 1 (Spring 1995): 95-100; Kathleen Kernicky, "Panthers, Other Animals Use Inter-state Crossings; Photos Disprove Claims of Underpass Critics," *Sun-Sentinel* (March 15, 1991): http://articles.sun-sentinel.com/1991-03-15/news/9101130770_1_panthers-crossings-underpasses. I heard the gorilla suit story from Jim Beever, a strong advocate of the underpasses who then worked for the state game commission.

154 *But as Roelke had...:* Interview with Roelke.

155 *The discovery of the...:* Interview with McCown

156 *Roelke and McCown weren't...:* Interviews with Roelke and Mc-Cown; William J. Donawick, "A Tribute to Carolyn M. Glass, VMD, 1961-1992," *Bellwether* 1, no. 34 (Spring/Summer 1993): https://repository.upenn.edu/cgi/viewcontent.cgi?article=1664&context=bellwether.

Chapter Thirteen: Hail Mary

158 *In 1975, the Dallas...:* Jarrett Bell, "Origins of 'Hail Mary': Cowboys Legend Roger Staubach Remembers How It Stuck," *USA*

Today (Jan. 13, 2017): https://www.usatoday.com/story/sports/nfl/columnist/bell/2017/01/13/dallas-cowboys-roger-staubach-hail-mary-green-bay-packers-aaron-rodgers/96570268/. Some sources trace the term back much further, to a 1922 game involving Notre Dame's famed "Four Horsemen," but it didn't catch on with the general public until Staubach's spiral.

159   *The panther experts gathered...:* Interviews with O'Brien, Roelke, McCown and Lacy; "Report of a Workshop: Genetic Management Strategies and Population Viability of the Florida Panther (Felis concolor coryi)" (Oct. 21-22, 1994); O'Brien, 57.

162   *Ulie Seal's rescue team...:* "Report of a Workshop: Genetic Management Considerations for Threatened Species with a Detailed Analysis of the Florida Panther," May 30-31, 1991.

163   *Even five years later, in...:* Maehr, 201-203.

164   *The US Fish and Wildlife...:* Interview with O'Brien; Mike Clary, "Florida Panthers Get Genetic Boost from Texas: Inbreeding Has Weakened the Everglades Natives. Cougars Have Been Imported to Halt Decline," *Los Angeles Times* (Nov. 23, 1995): http://articles.latimes.com/1995-11-23/news/mn-6431_1_florida-panther.

164   *In January 1995, all...:* Interviews with McBride and Jansen; David Olinger, "Texas Cougars Florida-Bound," *St. Petersburg Times* (Jan. 19, 1995); McBride, "Three Decades"; Tori Peglar, "1995 Reintroduction of Wolves in Yellowstone," Yellowstone National Park website (July 9, 2018): https://www.yellowstonepark.com/park/yellowstone-wolves-reintroduction.

169   *At the end of...:* David Olinger, "From Texas Comes Hope to Save Florida Panthers," *St. Petersburg Times* (March 31, 1995); Booth Gunter, "Cougars Last Hope for Florida Panthers," *Tampa Tribune* (March 31, 1995).

170   *Seven months passed like...:* "Cougar Released in the Wild Gives Birth," *St. Petersburg Times* (Oct. 13, 1995).

Chapter Fourteen: "Florida Will Be Developed"

172   *There was something about...:* Maehr personnel file; interviews with Jansen and Tom Logan, Maehr's former boss.

175 *On his last day...:* Maehr, *Florida Panther,* 198–201; Neil Santaniello and Robert McClure, "Florida Panther Researcher Resigns, Citing Poor Plans, Cutbacks," *Sun-Sentinel* (Feb. 4, 1994); interview with Logan.

176 *Two weeks later, though...:* US Army Corps of Engineers permitting records for The Habitat; Maehr, *Florida Panther,* 185–186.

177 *Before Maehr died, a...:* I am grateful to Nathan Gove for sharing with me the full transcript of his June 14, 2007, interview with Maehr and allowing me to quote excerpts.

178 *When Maehr was sitting...:* Interviews with Andy Eller and Jane Comiskey; Manuel Roig-Franza, "Panther Advocate Fights to Get Job Back," *Washington Post* (March 8, 2005): http://www.washingtonpost.com/wp-dyn/articles/A15056-2005Mar7.html.

180 *Eller's maps showed exactly...:* Joanie Stiers, "Florida Is First in Cattle," *Farm Flavor* (Sep. 3, 2014): https://www.farmflavor.com/florida/florida-ag-products/florida-first-cattle/; Florida Department of Agriculture and Consumer Services brochure titled "Florida's Cattle Industry," https://www.freshfromflorida.com/content/download/17161/272486/P-00044.pdf. To learn more about Florida's historic range wars, I recommend reading Canter Brown Jr.'s *Florida's Peace River Frontier* (Orlando: University of Central Florida Press, 1991).

180 *One of the ranchers...:* Ben Hill Griffin III background from the Florida Agricultural Hall of Fame: https://www.freshfromflorida.com/Divisions-Offices/Marketing-and-Development/Agriculture-Industry/Agricultural-Awards-and-Honors/Florida-Agricultural-Hall-of-Fame/Ben-Hill-Griffin-III.

181 *In the early 1990s, the...:* David Olinger, "Free University Site Could Carry Steep Ecological Price," *St. Petersburg Times* (Oct. 13, 1994); Olinger, "University Site Swims in Muck," *St. Petersburg Times* (Oct. 19, 1995); documents from FGCU permitting provided by Corps of Engineers and civic activist Ann Hauck, who filed numerous FOIA requests about the approval of developments in Southwest Florida; interviews with David and Linda Ferrell; Bob Graham biography from "About Bob Graham" section of the Bob Graham

Center web page: http://www.bobgrahamcenter.ufl.edu/about/ bob-graham; interview notes from talk with Griffin provided by my *Times* colleague Kris Hundley; Julio Ochoa, "From Wetlands Sprang a Campus: FGCU Came at an Environmental Cost," *Naples Daily News* (Aug. 13, 2007).

187 *Years later, in an...:* "Oral History of David Flemming, Interviewed by Sandy Tucker" (April 25, 2016): https://digitalmedia.fws.gov/ digital/collection/document/id/2160/.

188 *What happened with the...:* Interview with Craig Johnson.

188 *Maehr, in his interview...:* Gove interview.

Chapter Fifteen: Mr. Influential

190 *In October 1995, Maehr...:* Maehr and Gerard B. Craddock, "Demographics and Genetic Introgression in the Florida Panther," *Conservation Biology* 9, no. 5 (Oct. 1995): 1295-1298; Maehr and James Cox, "Landscape Features and Panthers in Florida," *Conservation Biology* 9, no. 5 (Oct. 1995): 1008-1019.

191 *To produce this paper...:* Interview with James A. Cox.

193 *In scientific circles, journals...:* Liza Gross, "Why Not the Best? How Science Failed the Florida Panther," *PLoS Biol* 3, no. 9: e333: doi:10.1371/journal.pbio.0030333; interviews with Cox and Noss.

195 *To Cox, the biggest...:* Cox interview; Gross, ibid.; Corps of Engineers and Fish and Wildlife Service reports on Daniels Parkway extension; Dawson & Associates reports to Lee County on the Daniels Parkway extension.

199 *Over and over, this...:* Gross, ibid.; interviews with Linda and David Ferrell, Jay Slack, Bob Graham, Andy Eller and Sam Hamilton; David Fleshler, "Judge Refuses Mining Permit," *Sun-Sentinel* (Aug. 21, 2004). For more on how congressional pressure from both parties pushed development permits in Florida, see the chapter titled "The Cussing Congressman" in *Paving Paradise: Florida's Vanishing*

Wetlands and the Failure of No Net Loss by Pittman and Matthew Waite (Gainesville: University Press of Florida, 2009).

Chapter Sixteen: The Showdown

202 *Roy McBride was in...:* Interview with Jane Comiskey.

203 *The Everglades was in...:* Michael Grunwald, "A Rescue Plan, Bold and Uncertain," *Washington Post* (June 23, 2002): https://www.washingtonpost.com/archive/politics/2002/06/23/a-rescue-plan-bold-and-uncertain/2d04efdd-69dc-4f85-802b-c0b493ddaacd/?utm_term=.659b88a4568c. As the environmental reporter for Florida's largest paper, I've covered the Everglades restoration project since it was unveiled by then–Vice President Al Gore in 2000.

205 *Comiskey recommended the next...:* Interviews with Comiskey, Kautz and Hoctor.

206 *In December 1999 the...:* This section came from records of the Panther MERIT Subteam, which I obtained via Freedom of Information Act request from the US Fish and Wildlife Service, McBride's May 2000 report, "Current Panther Distribution and Habitat Use: A Review of Field Fall 1999 to Winter 2000," and interviews with Comiskey, McBride, Jansen, Eller, Kautz and Hoctor. The description of the Vero Beach office of the Fish and Wildlife Service comes from my own observations during multiple visits.

214 *Southwest Florida was in...:* Pittman, "As Collier Builds, So Does Tension," *St. Petersburg Times* (June 14, 1999); Pittman, "Collier Growth Had Seamy Side," *St. Petersburg Times* (Nov. 4, 2001); Michael Grunwald, "Growing Pains in Southwest Florida," *Washington Post* (June 25, 2002): https://www.washingtonpost.com/archive/politics/2002/06/25/growing-pains-in-southwest-fla/38410089-b9ce-40a4-8715-a22a0ae201e3/?utm_term=.f36812ef90bc.

214 *Around the time the...:* National Wildlife Federation v. Louis Caldera, Acting Secretary of the US Army, US District Court, District of Columbia, Case No. CIV.A. 00-1031(JR); interview with Nancy Payton of the Florida Wildlife Federation; records of Pan-

ther MERIT Subteam; interviews with Comiskey, McBride, Jansen, Kautz and Hoctor; E. J. Comiskey, O. L. Bass, Jr., L. J. Gross, R. T. McBride, R. Salinas, "Panthers and Forests in South Florida: An Ecological Perspective," *Conservation Ecology* 6, no. 1 (2002): 18: http://www.consecol.org/vol6/iss1/art18/; Rebecca Meegan and David S. Maehr, "Landscape Conservation and Regional Planning for the Florida Panther," *Southeastern Naturalist* 1, no. 3 (2002): 217-232: https://doi.org/10.1656/1528-7092(2002)001[0217:LCARPF] 2.0.CO;2.

221 *Kautz and the other...:* Kautz et al., "How Much Is Enough? Landscape Scale Conservation of the Florida Panther," *Biological Conservation* 130, no. 1 (2006): 118-133; interview with Jay Slack.

Chapter Seventeen: The Verdict

223 *Andy Eller missed out...:* Interview with Eller; *Andrew Eller and Public Employees for Environmental Responsibility v. U.S. Fish and Wildlife Service*, Data Quality Act Challenge to US Fish & Wildlife Service Documents Pertaining to the Survival and Recovery of the Florida Panther (*Puma concolor coryi*); Michael Shnayerson, "Sale of the Wild," *Vanity Fair* (Sep. 2003): https://www.vanityfair.com/news/2003/09/environment200309.

224 *Except maybe he wasn't...:* Interview with Craig Manson.

224 *The regional director in...:* "Sam D. Hamilton Dead at 54; U.S. Fish and Wildlife Service Director," *Washington Post* (Feb. 22, 2010): http://www.washingtonpost.com/wp-dyn/content/article/2010/02/21/AR2010022104120.html; Bill Dawson, "Nature's Balance: In Warbler Case, Facts Fly in the Face of Perception," *Houston Chronicle* (November 20, 1994); Marla Williams, "The Endangered Species Act—Texas and Its Costly Songbird," *The Seattle Times* (July 18, 1995); interview with Hamilton.

227 *Unlike Eller, John Kasbohm...:* Interviews with Kasbohm and Comiskey.

228 *Kasbohm set about assembling...:* Interviews with Kasbohm and Mike Conroy. The other panelists were Paul Beier, professor of conserva-

tion biology at Northern Arizona University; Michael R. Vaughn, professor of fisheries and wildlife sciences at Virginia Tech; and Howard Quigley, executive director of Panthera's Jaguar Program and director of Panthera's Puma Program.

229 *The four doctors had…:* Interviews with Conroy and Beier; P. Beier, M. R. Vaughan, M. J. Conroy, H. Quigley. 2003. "An Analysis of Scientific Literature Related to the Florida Panther," Final Report. Florida Fish and Wildlife Conservation Commission, Tallahassee, Florida, USA.

229 *The SRT convened for…:* Beier, ibid.; interviews with Conroy and Beier.

230 *Their next step was…:* Interviews with Conroy, Beier and Comiskey; Beier et al. 2003. "Comments and Communications Received by the Scientific Review Team during a Review of Literature Related to the Florida Panther," Florida Fish and Wildlife Conservation Commission, Tallahassee, Florida, USA.

232 *Around the time the…:* Interview with Reed Noss.

232 *In 2003, the SRT…:* Beier et al. 2003. "An Analysis of Scientific Literature Related to the Florida Panther," Final Report. Florida Fish and Wildlife Conservation Commission, Tallahassee, Florida, USA; Pamela Smith Hayford, "Florida Panther Research Gets Snarling Review," *Fort Myers News-Press* (Aug. 16, 2003); interviews with McBride, Noss and Ivan Oransky. Anyone interested in science-related stories who isn't following Oransky's *Retraction Watch* is missing out.

235 *Maehr may have seemed…:* "Panther Habitat Model Said to Rely on 'Unsound' Conclusions," *Endangered Species & Wetlands Report* 9, no. 4 (January 2004): 16; memo from David S. Maehr to Florida Panther Recovery Team, Subject: Review of "An Analysis of Scientific Publications Related to the Florida Panther" (Jan. 21, 2004); L. Gross, "Why Not the Best? How Science Failed the Florida Panther," *PLoS Biol* 3, no. 9 (2005): e333: doi:10.1371/journal.pbio.0030333; Gove interview with Maehr.

Chapter Eighteen: The Whistleblower

238   *Nothing could stop the...:* For greater detail on the rampant development permitting that occurred leading up to the 2008 economic meltdown in Florida, see the 2009 book I cowrote with Matthew Waite, *Paving Paradise: Florida's Vanishing Wetlands and the Failure of No Net Loss.*

238   *Andy Eller's mistake was...:* Eller interview; Winding Cypress Corps of Engineers Section 404 Permit No. SAJ-1996–02945 (IP-MJD), August 20, 2003; US Fish and Wildlife Service Biological Opinion 2002-F-0003.

239   *The pressure to produce...:* Michael Grunwald, "Growing Pains in Southwest Florida," *Washington Post* (June 25, 2002); Warren Richey, "Developers Squeeze Florida Big Cat," *Christian Science Monitor* (Sep. 24, 2004).

240   *A month after serving...:* Eller interview; E. Jane Comiskey et al., "Evaluating Impacts to Florida Panther Habitat: How Porous Is the Umbrella?" *Southeastern Naturalist* 3, no. 1 (2004): 51–74; JSTOR, www.jstor.org/stable/3877941.

240   *Webb was a burly...:* Interviews with Allen Webb and Eller.

241   *Before his bosses could...:* Eller et al. vs. US Fish and Wildlife Service. May 4, 2004. "Data Quality Act Challenge to U.S. Fish & Wildlife Service Documents Pertaining to the Survival and Recovery of the Florida Panther (*Puma concolor coryi*)": Findlaw, "Federal Agencies Subject to the Data Quality Act": https://corporate.findlaw.com/law-library/federal-agencies-subject-to-data-quality-act.html; John Horgan, "'The Republican War on Science' by Chris C. Mooney" (book review), *New York Times* (Dec. 18, 2005): http://www.nytimes.com/2005/12/18/books/review/18horgan.html?ei=5088&en=e0fbba5ceaf2448f&ex=1292562000&partner=rssnyt&emc=rss&pagewanted=print; "About Us," Public Employees for Environmental Responsibility: https://www.peer.org/about-us/.

242   *PEER's involvement meant that...:* Eller interview; Manuel Roig-Franza, "Panther Advocate Fights to Get Job Back," *Washington Post* (March 8, 2005); "Distorting Scientific Knowledge on Flor-

ida Panthers," Union of Concerned Scientists: https://www.ucsusa.
org/center-for-science-and-democracy/scientific_integrity/abuses_
of_science/a-to-z/science-undermined-at-fws.html#panthers;
"Discrediting a Decade of Panther Science," National Wildlife Federation (Jan. 2004): https://www.nwf.org/~/media/PDFs/Wildlife/
DiscreditingaDecadeofPantherScience.ashx.

242 *Nothing makes a bureaucracy...*: Interview with Eller; Eller termina-
tion letter, Nov. 5, 2004, signed by Thomas E. Grahl, deputy field
supervisor; Roig-Franza, ibid.; Pamela Smith Hayford, "Adoption
of Panther Plan Delayed; Wildlife Service Fires 18-Year Employee,"
News-Press (Nov. 9, 2004).

243 *But that wasn't quite...*: Robert P. King, "Panther Biologist Now
Fights for His Job," *Palm Beach Post* (April 9, 2005).

244 *The Fish and Wildlife Service...*: David Fleshler, "Judge Refuses Mining Permit," *South Florida Sun-Sentinel* (Aug. 21, 2004): https://
www.sun-sentinel.com/news/fl-xpm-2004-08-21-0408210134-
story.html; Pittman, "Developers Help Write Wildlife Assessments,"
St. Petersburg Times (May 12, 2006).

244 *Two weeks after the...*: "U.S. Fish and Wildlife Service Will Correct Panther Information In Response to Information Quality Act
Challenge," US Fish and Wildlife Service press release (March 11,
2005): https://www.fws.gov/informationquality/topics/FY2004/
Florida%20Panther/3-21-2005-news.pdf.

245 *Eller had little time...*: Eller interview; "Joint Statement of Andrew
Eller and the U.S. Fish and Wildlife Service," Public Employees
for Environmental Responsibility press release (June 29, 2005).

245 *Jay Slack, who had...*: Interview with Jay Slack; "Highest Paid
Employees of the U.S. Fish and Wildlife Service": https://www.
federalpay.org/employees/us-fish-and-wildlife-service/top-100.

246 *The regional director who...*: "President Obama Announces More
Key Administration Posts," White House press release (June 9,
2009): https://www.presidency.ucsb.edu/documents/press-release-
president-obama-announces-more-key-administration-posts-199;
"Fish and Wildlife Service in Florida: Portrait of a Failed Agency,"

Public Employees for Environmental Responsibility press release (July 9, 2009): hhttps://www.peer.org/fish-wildlife-service-in-florida-portrait-of-a-failed-agency/; Steve Davies, "Hamilton Becomes New FWS Director," *Endangered Species & Wetlands Report* (Aug. 5, 2009). Steve Davies, the reporter who buttonholed Hamilton after the hearing, was kind enough to share with me the full audio recording of his interview with Hamilton. Sam Hamilton served less than a year as the agency director before dying of a heart attack.

Chapter Nineteen: The Skunk Ape's Scapegoat

248 *On the same day…:* US Fish and Wildlife Service biological opinion 4-1-04-PL-6866 on US Army Corps of Engineers Section 404 permit application SAJ-2003-09416 (NW-MAE).

248 *At least, that was…:* Domino's history from company website: https://www.dominos.com/en/about-pizza/pizza-restaurant/; "End of Domino's Pizza Delivery Guarantee," Snopes.com: https://www.snopes.com/fact-check/mush-vroom-pizza/.

249 *Monaghan had spent some…:* Kate Taylor, "The Domino's Pizza Founder Created a Catholic 'Paradise' Town with No Birth Control or Pornography," *Business Insider* (Jan. 11, 2016): https://www.businessinsider.com/dominos-founders-catholic-paradise-2016-1; Michael A. Miller, "Ave Maria University: A Catholic Project Gone Wrong," *Miami New Times* (Oct. 20, 2011): https://www.miaminewtimes.com/news/ave-maria-university-a-catholic-project-gone-wrong-6384870; interview with Deb Jansen.

252 *In 2001, a panther…:* M.A. Brown, M.W. Cunningham, A.L. Roca, J.L. Troyer, W.E. Johnson, S.J. O'Brien, "Genetic Characterization of Feline Leukemia Virus from Florida Panthers," *Emerging Infectious Diseases* 14, no. 2 (2008): 252-9; interview with Land.

252 *Then, in 2002, one…:* Greg Stanley, "From Scam to Plan: Golden Gate Estates to Get Collier County Update," *Naples Daily News* (April 16, 2016): http://archive.naplesnews.com/news/local/from-scam-to-plan-golden-gate-estates-growth-to-get-collier-county-update-3001ae82-0866-5197-e053-01-375956461.html/; Florida

Fish and Wildlife Conservation Commission records of panther depredations; US Fish and Wildlife Service and Florida Fish and Wildlife Conservation Commission, "Environmental Assessment for the Interagency Florida Panther Response Plan," March 2008; interviews with ornithologist Chris Frey, Darrell Land, Roberto Zambrano and Mark Poole. Thanks to my former *Tampa Bay Times* colleague Marilyn Garateix for serving as translator for my interview with Zambrano.

254 *What you may not…:* Geoff Dobson, "History City Memories: The Bardin Booger," *History City News*: http://historiccity.com/2009/staugustine/news/florida/historic-city-memories-the-bardin-booger-2002; Cathy Salustri, *Backroads of Paradise: A Journey to Rediscover Old Florida* (Gainesville: University Press of Florida, 2016), 35-36, 75-78; "Skunk Ape Research Headquarters," *Roadside America*: https://www.roadsideamerica.com/story/13341; Lucia Davis, "The Man Behind Florida's Favorite Cryptid, The Skunk Ape," *Atlas Obscura* (May 11, 2015); Joseph Stromberg, "On the Trail of Florida's Bigfoot—the Skunk Ape," *Smithsonian* (March 6, 2014): https://www.smithsonianmag.com/science-nature/trail-floridas-bigfoot-skunk-ape-180949981/.

256 *Thus, over a series…:* "Hungry Panther No Threat to Humans," *Fort Myers News-Press* (June 18, 2004); David Fleshler, "Panther Video Spurs Inquiry," *South Florida Sun-Sentinel* (June 24, 2004); Fleshler, "Panther Filmed in Attack at Petting Zoo Is Caught," *South Florida Sun-Sentinel* (June 30, 2004); Denes Husty, "Men Face Cruelty Charge Over 'Bait,'" *Fort Myers News-Press* (Oct. 15, 2004); Husty, "Third Man Charged in Panther Baiting Case; Animal Was Raiding Petting Zoo Livestock," *Fort Myers News-Press* (Dec. 22, 2004); Husty, "Man Gets 30 Days, Fine in Goat Trial; Judge Says Suspended Sentence a Warning," *Fort Myers News-Press* (April 26, 2005).

258 *Then, two years later…:* Abby Goodnough, "A Rare Predator Bounces Back (Now Get It out of Here)," *New York Times* (March 14, 2006): https://www.nytimes.com/2006/03/14/science/14pant.html; Jeff Klinkenberg, "The Uninvited Guest," *St. Petersburg Times* (April 22, 2007): http://www.floridapanther.com/articles/THE%20UNINVITED%20GUEST.htm; Jack H. Evans, "Lucifer, America's Oldest Hippo, Confronts His Age in Homosassa Springs," *Tampa Bay Times*

(Feb. 14, 2019): https://www.tampabay.com/hernando/lucifer-americas-oldest-hippo-confronts-his-age-in-homosassa-springs-20190214/.

259 *Take what happened with…:* Interviews with Jansen as well as with Laurie MacDonald and Elizabeth Fleming of Defenders of Wildlife; David Fleshler, "Florida Panther Dies after Relocation Requested by Miccosukees," *South Florida Sun-Sentinel* (March 3, 2005); Will Rothschild, "Rebounding into Danger: Growing Numbers Bring Growing Troubles," *Sarasota Herald-Tribune* (March 26, 2006).

261 *That story began spreading…:* People with this set of beliefs (who overlap with the groups who deny climate change exists and express a strong dislike of all federal agencies involved in natural resource protection) have shown up repeatedly at state wildlife commission meetings and other venues to argue these points. Some of them post on a Facebook group page called "The Panthers of South Florida," which is here: https://www.facebook.com/The-Panthers-of-South-Florida-776777469005575/. They don't like or trust Roy McBride, either, which is ironic because they tend to be on the same side as him on other political issues. Some of them bolster their argument by pointing to a 2000 study by a team of four scientists led by Melanie Culver of the US Geological Survey that said genetics show that all the pumas in North America are one species, period. Because pumas are fairly common, that would mean panthers might no longer be considered endangered. However, when I interviewed Culver, she said that panthers still belong on the endangered list—because they are geographically isolated. I should add that Florida panther biologists disagree with Culver's team.

262 *But things got worse…:* Pittman, "Federal Proposal Would Pay Landowners to Preserve Panthers," *Tampa Bay Times* (May 22, 2014): https://www.tampabay.com/news/environment/wildlife/federal-proposal-would-pay-landowners-to-preserve-florida-panther-habitat/2180998; Pittman, "Over Scientists' Objections, Rancher Pushes Panther Policy," *Tampa Bay Times* (July 11, 2015): https://www.tampabay.com/news/environment/wildlife/over-scientists-objections-rancher-pushes-panther-policy/2236943; Pittman, "Biggest Critic of Rancher Losses to Panthers Is First to Get Government Reimbursement," *Tampa Bay Times* (Nov. 17, 2016): https://www.

tampabay.com/news/environment/wildlife/biggest-critic-of-rancher-losses-to-florida-panthers-is-first-to-get/2303214.

263 *Amid all the wild…:* The source for this rundown is Fish and Wildlife Conservation Commission panther research records, although because these deaths are under investigation by the US Fish and Wildlife Service, even the state records are routinely redacted or undisclosed. I have strongly suggested to federal wildlife officials that they seek public help in solving these cases, the way most police agencies do when they're stumped, but so far that hasn't happened.

264 *From atop his tree…:* US Fish and Wildlife Service Office of Law Enforcement Report No. 2009405517 (the agency redacted big chunks of the investigative report, including the defendant's name—in spite of the fact that I specifically requested the documents using the defendant's name); US vs. Todd Benfield, US District Court, Middle District of Florida, Case No. 2:12-CR-60-FtM-99SPC; Pittman, "Hunter Pleads Guilty to Killing Endangered Florida Panther," *Tampa Bay Times* (May 18, 2012): https://www.tampabay.com/news/environment/wildlife/hunter-pleads-guilty-to-killing-endangered-florida-panther/1230915; Pittman, "Man Sentenced for Killing Florida Panther," *Tampa Bay Times* (July 26, 2012): https://www.tampabay.com/news/environment/wildlife/man-sentenced-for-killing-florida-panther/1242326.

Chapter Twenty: The Wanderers

266 *The panther crouched in…:* I recreated Florida Panther 62's journey through a review of the state's records, interviews with Darrell Land and Pat Mitchell, and site visits to the places where he'd been detected.

267 *Historically, the dwindling population…:* Chelie Koster Walton, "Along the River: The Caloosahatchee in Southwest Florida," Visit Florida: https://www.visitflorida.com/en-us/cities/sanibel-island/caloosahatchee-river.html; bridge description from National Bridge Inventory, found here: http://www.city-data.com/bridges/bridges-Fort-Myers-Florida.html.

267 *In April 1998, he…:* The Ortona campground is just one of the many locations I visited in retracing the steps (paw prints?) of FP 62.

270 *In 2009, a trio…:* Cindy A. Thatcher, Frank van Manen, Joseph D. Clark, "Identifying Suitable Sites for Florida Panther Reintroduction," *Journal of Mammalogy* 90, no. 4 (Aug. 14 2009): 918–925: https://doi.org/10.1644/08-MAMM-A-219.1; Jeremy Cox, "States Not Putting Out Welcome Mat for Florida Panther," *Naples Daily News* (May 26, 2006); Pittman, "Too Many Panthers, Too Little Habitat," *St. Petersburg Times* (Dec. 19, 2008).

270 *For months The Wanderer…:* State records of FP62 travels; interviews with Pat Mitchell and Darrell Land; Catfish Creek Preserve State Park website: https://floridadep.gov/parks/unit-management-plans/documents/catfish-creek-preserve-state-park.

273 *While 62 was the…:* Interview with Land, state records of panther travels; Kate Spinner, "What Follows a Panther? A Debate," *Sarasota Herald-Tribune* (Feb. 18, 2010): https://www.heraldtribune.com/news/20100218/what-follows-a-panther-a-debate.

274 *More and more panthers…:* Pittman, "Report Indicates Vehicle Killed Panther on Roadway," *St. Petersburg Times* (March 12, 2003); Dave Nicholson, "Slain Panther's Ga. Trip a Rarity, Officials Say," *Tampa Tribune* (Sep. 6, 2009); "Georgia Man Sentenced to 2 Years' Probation for Killing Panther," *Naples Daily News* (Aug. 24, 2011): http://archive.naplesnews.com/news/crime/georgia-man-sentenced-to-2-years-probation-for-killing-florida-panther-ep-391151033-342841152.html/.

274 *While The Wanderer and his…:* Pittman, "Panther Habitat Sought," *St. Petersburg Times* (April 10, 2009); Pittman, "Federal Critical Habitat Denied," *St. Petersburg Times* (Feb. 12, 2010); Pittman, "Judge Dismisses Panther Habitat Suit," *St. Petersburg Times* (April 7, 2011); interviews with Paul Souza of the Fish and Wildlife Service's Vero Beach office and Laurie Macdonald of Defenders of Wildlife. As of the end of 2018, the wildlife agency still had not approved the "Habitat Conservation Plan," that the landowners and some environmental groups negotiated, allowing development on 45,000 acres of land—20,000 acres of it in the Primary Zone—while preserving 107,000 acres. Some environmental groups continue to strongly

oppose the plan. For details, see Pittman, "Fate of Florida Panther Could Rest on This Collier County Housing Plan," *Tampa Bay Times* (Nov. 30, 2018): https://www.tampabay.com/environment/habitat-conservation-plan-would-wipe-out-20000-acres-of-prime-panther-habitat-20181130/.

Chapter Twenty-One: Cat Cam Bingo

278 *If you knew Carlton...:* Interview with Carlton Ward Jr.; Cathy Salustri, "Here, Kitty, Kitty, Kitty: Hope for Florida Panthers," *Creative Loafing* (April 20, 2017): https://www.cltampa.com/arts-entertainment/travel-leisure/article/20858328/here-kitty-kitty-kitty-hope-for-florida-panthers; Florida Wildlife Corridor website: http://floridawildlifecorridor.org/. I highly recommend the Florida Wildlife Corridor documentary, which you can see in its entirety on YouTube: https://www.youtube.com/watch?v=i-jv208rdlM.

281 *As everyone waited to...:* Interviews with Roelke, Belden, McBride, Eller, Richardson, Jansen and Land; Johnson et al., "Genetic Restoration of the Florida Panther," *Science* 329, no. 5999 (Sep. 24, 2010):1641-1645: doi: 10.1126/science.1192891.

284 *By 2013, so many...:* Interview with Jennifer Korn.

285 *That was the verification...:* Craig Pittman, "First Female Panther Spotted North of the Caloosahatchee River in 40 Years," *Tampa Bay Times* (Nov. 15, 2016); history of Babcock Ranch from Babcock Ranch website: https://www.babcockranch.com/the-history-of-babcock-ranch/; Casey Logan, "Babcock Ranch, the Solar Town, Ramps Up in 2018," *Fort Myers News Press* (Dec. 26, 2017): http://www.news-press.com/story/news/2017/12/26/babcock-ranch-solar-town-ramps-up-2018/968667001/; Robert Trigaux, "Bold Plan for Solar-Powered Babcock Ranch Development, Stalled by Recession, Hits Restart Button," *Tampa Bay Times* (April 22, 2016): https://www.tampabay.com/news/business/realestate/bold-plan-for-solar-driven-town-babcock-ranch-stalled-by-recession-hits/2274313.

286 *Ward, sensing a good...:* Interviews with Ward and Korn; Pittman, "Florida Panther Kittens Found North of Caloosahatchee River

CRAIG PITTMAN

for First Time in Decades," *Tampa Bay Times* (March 28, 2017): https://www.tampabay.com/news/environment/wildlife/florida-panther-kittens-found-north-of-caloosahatchee-river-for-first-time/2318043.

289 *In September 2017, Hurricane…:* John P. Cangialosi, Andrew S. Latto, Robbie Berg, "Hurricane Irma," AL112017, National Hurricane Center, June 30, 2018: https://www.nhc.noaa.gov/data/tcr/AL112017_Irma.pdf; interviews with Ward and Korn.

INDEX